STREET SMARTS

Mormon cult p29 para 5

STREET SMARTS

/////////////////

A Survival Guide to Personal Evangelism and the Law

Steve Levicoff

Baker Books

A Division of Baker Book House Co
Grand Rapids, Michigan 49516

© 1994 by Steve Levicoff

Published by Baker Books
a division of Baker Book House Company
P.O. Box 6287, Grand Rapids, MI 49516-6287

Printed in the United States of America

Library of Congress Cataloging-in-Publication Data

Levicoff, Steve.
    Street smarts : a survival guide to personal evangelism and the law / Steve Levicoff.
       p. cm.
    Includes bibliographical references.
    ISBN 0-8010-5688-8
    1. Freedom of religion—United States. 2. Church and state—United States. 3. Evangelists—Legal status, laws, etc.—United States. 4. Evangelistic work—United States. I. Title.
    KF4865.L48 1994
    342.73'0852—dc20
    [347.302852]   93-22721

The information contained herein is general in nature, and should not be construed as legal advice. It is sold with the understanding that neither the publisher nor the author are engaged in rendering legal or other professional service. If legal advice is required, the services of a competent attorney should be sought.

To William Durland and John Eidsmoe,

defenders of the First Amendment

/ *Contents* /

/ *Foreword* /

In a pluralistic society, which the United States of America unabashedly declares itself to be, Christians have been put on the defensive. Court case after court case is decided by an interpretation of the division of church and state principle and that has meant the Christian presence has been muted in the public schools and marketplace. Foundations routinely reject Christian requests for funding on the premise that they cannot support one religious denomination or religious group over another in a pluralistic society.

All religious and moral opinions are supposedly equally valid in a pluralistic society, and none is to be given favor over another. The net result is the moral unraveling of our nation, and Christians in bewilderment communicate their anguish among themselves, but feel they have been forced from the public arena. It's almost as if we have been driven onto reservations where we are free to vent our tribal praise or concern each Sunday but we have been threatened into silence once we leave the reservation and go out into the real world.

Steve Levicoff has a major contribution to make to the Christian's place in public life because he sets before us in *Street Smarts* the case by case court decisions that inform us of our legal standing as we endeavor to broadcast the gospel of Christ.

Street Smarts is written to inform the Christian community of where the law is on their side in the task of evangelism. It helps resolve many of the legal questions as to when, where, and how, in the now complicated business of public Christian witness, the Christian may proceed in confidence. And we do need to move aggressively and with confidence in the evangelism of our nation, for it is its only hope.

The significant by-product of *Street Smarts* is to highlight the persistent, often courageous, men, women, and young people who refuse to lie down and play dead or be isolated on the Christian reservations and are willing to go to court, pay the price, and see that the witness of Christ is not muted. Similarly, we become aware of the Christian legal agencies, which operate as nonprofit ministries, to support the Christian cause in the courts. The Rutherford Institute and similar groups deserve our acclaim and our financial support in the fight for the right to be a public Christian!

Pluralism is misunderstood and misrepresented, often deliberately, in what appears to be a concerted attack on our Judeo-Christian heritage as a nation. Genuine pluralism ought not mute or silence the presence of religious and moral convictions but, in reality, should encourage it. Genuine pluralism, rather than telling the Jew to keep his or her religion private, or telling the Christian he or she should not mention the name of Christ in prayer or conversation in public, should, in fact, stimulate us to appreciate freedom of expression for all points of view—Buddhist, New Age, and Islamic as well. Pluralism is not pretending I'm not a Christian in public for fear of offending someone, but rather, pluralism is gladly allowing everyone to be who they really are in public. Pluralism, in principle, should encourage the open declaration of any given religious or moral viewpoint.

Thank you, Steve Levicoff, for writing *Street Smarts* and giving the Christian community a legal reason to stand tall for Christ, the gospel, and a characterful nation that may one day welcome distinctiveness rather than cherishing a bland characterless public neutrality.

—John Guest

/ *Preface* /

A whole, wide world is out there waiting to hear the gospel of Jesus Christ. Whether the world is a jungle or a zoo is a matter of opinion. (I sometimes believe it's both, and that belief is occasionally determined by which side of the bed I wake up on each morning.)

One thing is certain: Evangelism can be a joy, but it's not always easy. *Street Smarts* will not provide you with ultimate solutions, but hopefully this book will be of assistance in affirming your right to share the gospel with those who need to hear it.

Before we enter the world of religion and law, however, a few words are in order.

First, after reading this book, you will very likely know more about the law's impact on evangelism than do most attorneys. Really. Even though you may be a layperson or nonlawyer, you will likely become a conduit of information for friends, church members, and others who want to know how the law affects their rights to engage in evangelism.

Second, because the law is a regulated profession in American society, it's important to have a perspective on how to avoid engaging in any activities that could be construed as the unauthorized practice of law. The best way to avoid such a predicament is to know what constitutes the practice of law.

Most states have statutes that regulate the practice of law, which is generally held to include three primary elements: (1) the representation of others before judicial or administrative bodies; (2) advising others on specific legal problems on a regular basis and for a fee; and (3) the drafting of legal instruments.[1] Only attorneys licensed by a state bar association may engage in these practices.

There are some exceptions to this rule, the most common of which is *appearance pro se*, that is, a person representing himself or herself in a court of law personally and without legal counsel. Other common exceptions, peculiar to individual states or jurisdictions, include representation by laypersons before particular courts (such as justice of the peace courts or small claims courts), a corporation attending to its own business, the recognition of nonresident attorneys (those who practice in jurisdictions other than where a case is being heard), and some representation of charitable and benevolent associations.[2]

You are free to discuss legal matters, including your knowledge of legal issues that affect evangelism, with anyone. However, you should be careful to ensure that you do not engage in the unauthorized practice of law as outlined above.

Another caveat is in order, the old expression that "the attorney who defends himself has a fool for a client." If you are confronted by a legal problem, whether it involves your right to engage in evangelism or in any other area, you should seek representation by a competent attorney. While there are exceptions, a little knowledge of the law can be worse than none at all if it results in a person being tempted to self-representation.

Lest I sound biased in favor of lawyers, I should make it clear that I am not an attorney (and am as cynical about the legal profession as the next person). My own credentials include a Ph.D. in religion and law with a specialization in church-state issues, but my background is academic in nature rather than geared toward legal practice. The reason I am able to write books like this one is that I have spent several years studying an area of the law to which most attorneys are not exposed in their law school education at all. However, keep in mind that this book addresses legal issues in a general context and should not be construed as legal advice. For specific legal problems, competent counsel should be retained.

I am indebted to several colleagues, mentors, and other persons who provided valuable feedback and commented on the draft of this book, especially Herbert Betz, adjunct professor of evangelism at Biblical Theological Seminary; Attorney Wm. Dennis Huber; Robert McCarthy, a lieutenant in the Philadelphia Police Department; Charles Ness, ministry director of Liberty Ministries; and Bob Dryer, Jr., John Henne, and Stephen Matthews, all of whom are active in street ministry and personal evangelism. Nonetheless, the subjective conclusions in this book are my own, and for them I take full responsibility.

/ 1 /

The Challenge in Personal Evangelism

Imagine the intersection of a busy thoroughfare located in the heart of any major city in America. A center for social activity during the evening, the street is traveled by everyone from rock music fans to high school and college students out after a long week of classes, yuppies who have parked their BMWs to take in the nightlife, prostitutes out to ply their trade, an audience that has just left a performance at a local theater, and a host of other people who make American cities a bustle of activity.

On each corner, members of different religious groups are also plying their trade—the seeking of souls. On one corner stands a group of Krishna devotees, playing finger cymbals and chanting the Hare Krishna mantra. Across the street is a Moonie selling roses and encouraging young people to attend a meeting of the Unification Church. On the third corner, a small group of Buddhists in robes stand in meditation as a silent witness to the teachings of the Buddha.

Electricity is in the air, the sights and sounds of a city alive at night. The police are on patrol, keeping watch over the assortment of humanity assembled along the street, when they come to the fourth corner, on which a few Christians are handing out tracts and presenting the gospel of Jesus Christ to passersby.

People are actually interested in learning more about the gospel and begin to congregate about the Christians. Then police approach the group and tell them to move along because they are "interfering with the flow of pedestrian traffic."

The Krishnas, Moonies, and Buddhists are left alone; only the Christians are asked to move. Sound farfetched? For better or worse, it happens every day.

This book contains some stories of Christians who have met legal resistance or interference in the course of their evangelistic activities. For example:

In Escondido, California, Herbert Savage was prevented by mall security guards from placing Christian tracts on cars at the Del Norte Shopping Center.

In Omaha, Nebraska, Bridget Mergens and several other students were prevented from starting a Bible study group that would meet on her high school campus, despite a federal law that says schools may not discriminate against speech because of its political, philosophical, or religious content.

Sharlyn Vanderlaan was fired from her job as a dental hygienist in Michigan because she witnessed to patients while cleaning their teeth, and Philip D'Amico, a respiratory therapist, was reprimanded after sharing the gospel with patients while he worked.

John Boomsma, a member of the Christian Reformed Church, was fired by his employer because of his refusal to work on Sundays based on his religious convictions.

Mitch Paulsen was detained by the police and had his religious literature confiscated by the police when he tried to distribute tracts at the Nassau County Coliseum in Long Island, New York.

Moishe Rosen, chairman of Jews for Jesus, was arrested while handing out tracts at an airport in Portland, Oregon.

When Rollen Stewart and Stephen Francis hung a banner reading JOHN 3:16 from the railings behind the twenty-yard line during a Washington Redskins game at RFK Stadium, their signs were ripped down by the stadium management.

In some of these cases, the courts upheld the curtailment of the Christians' activities as constitutional; in others, the courts found that the right of Christians to express their faith was protected, and that interfering with their evangelistic activities infringed on their constitutional rights under the law.

In some of the cases, these brothers and sisters in the Lord acted totally within the boundaries of the law; in others, they overstepped those boundaries in their zeal to spread the Word.

But how do we know what those boundaries are? And once we do know the law, how can we ensure our right to communicate the gospel in a free and open society?

The answer is simple. In addition to prayer, learning how to effectively present the gospel, and how the law can have an impact on our evangelistic activities, we have to develop a sense of street smarts. We have to learn to be, as Jesus taught the disciples, "shrewd as serpents, and innocent as doves" (Matt. 10:16). This book, hopefully, will help the reader to integrate a knowledge of the law into evangelistic activities.

The first step, then, is to understand how the law affects evangelism from a theoretical framework.

Schools of Thinking in Religion and Law

The intersection of religion and law comes under a general heading we call church-state issues. When it comes to the relationship between Christians and the government, there are three schools of thinking, or interpretation of the Constitution, that deal with the degree of freedom of Christians to spread the gospel: accommodationist, separationist, and benevolent neutrality.

The accommodationists believe that the United States was founded as a Christian nation and that religion should play a significant role in both society and the government. Accommodationists support organized prayer in the public schools, believe that the rights of the Christian majority should take precedence over the rights of non-Christian minority religions, and believe that the nation should openly acknowledge the lordship of Jesus Christ.

Separationists believe in the total separation of religion from government functions, to the extent that many people think the phrase *separation of church and state* appears in the United States Constitution. Even the Supreme Court has written, "The First Amendment has erected a wall between church and state. That wall must be kept high and impregnable. We could not approve the slightest breach."[1]

However, the church-state metaphor appears in neither the Constitution nor any of the nation's other founding documents, but was used by Thomas Jefferson in a letter he wrote in 1802 to the Danbury Baptist Association:

I contemplate with sovereign reverence that act of the whole American people which declared that their legislature should "make no law respecting an establishment of religion, or prohibiting the free exercise thereof," thus building a wall of separation between Church and State.[2]

While Jefferson was not an orthodox Christian he was not, by any means, hostile to the role of religion in society. Constitutional law scholar John Eidsmoe, who has done extensive research on the religious beliefs of the nation's founders, observed the following:

> Jefferson was a believer in "the Laws of Nature and Nature's God," and looked to the Creator and his laws as the source of all rights. Human rights are the gift of God, so their realization and enjoyment cannot be separated from God. Jefferson believed in religious liberty because religious liberty was part of the law of God. The words engraved on the Jefferson Memorial echo that belief: "The God who gave us life, gave us liberty at the same time. . . . Can the liberties of a nation be secure when we have removed their only firm basis, a conviction in the minds of the people that those liberties are the gift of God?"[3]

Nonetheless, Jefferson's letter to the Danbury Baptists and its varied interpretations point to the basic difference between accommodationists and separationists. Accommodationists believe that Jefferson's intent was to protect the church from the state, while many separationists believe it was to protect the state from the church.

Separationists are generally opposed to any intersection between religion and the government, including school prayer, invocations and benedictions at public ceremonies, financial aid to religious schools and colleges, and tuition tax credits for parents to use in choosing private schools for their children. They staunchly believe in the First Amendment rights to free speech, freedom of the press, freedom of assembly, and even free exercise of religion. However, they interpret the intent of the nation's founders differently than do the accommodationists.

Lest one think that separationists consist solely of heathens, communists, and others who are antagonistic toward Christianity, we should note that the separationist school of thought includes many committed Christians including Baptists, Mennonites, and Quakers. Many Christians believe in full religious freedom but question the role that government should play in religion.

There is, however, a third school of thought that combines elements of the other two: the theory of benevolent neutrality, which was articulated by former Chief Justice Warren Burger.

The general principle deducible from the First Amendment and all that has been said by the [United States Supreme] Court is this: that we will not tolerate either governmentally established religion or governmental interference with religion. Short of those expressly proscribed governmental acts there is room for play in the joints productive of a benevolent neutrality which will permit religious exercise to exist without sponsorship and without interference.[4]

Let's explore, for a moment, the different ways of looking at the relationship between religion and government in a more functional framework. There are two ways, for example, in which students have engaged in prayer in public schools. Until the early 1960s, prayers were led by teachers (usually along with the Pledge of Allegiance), often written by a school board or by the state, and conducted during class time. Since the mid-1980s, the law has allowed student-run Bible study or prayer clubs to meet in public schools during nonclass time under a principle known as equal access, which holds that students have as much right to engage in philosophical, political, or religious expression as they do in other forms of expression.[5]

The accommodationist would submit that both state-sponsored and student-initiated religious activities in public schools are constitutionally permissible. The separationist would hold that neither activity is permissible in public schools. Persons holding the benevolent neutrality position believe that while state-sponsored religious activities are unconstitutional because they are coercive in nature, voluntary student-initiated religious activities are permissible because they allow for freedom of religious expression without coercion or state sponsorship.

In matters of evangelism, as well as other areas in which religion and law intersect, the problems we run into are based on the human fallacy of extremism. Speaking in somewhat stereotypical terms, whether that extremism is expressed in favor of the right wing or the left wing, conservatives or liberals, Christians or non-Christians, Protestants or Catholics, majority or minority religious faiths (a term used here to imply numbers rather than race or ethnicity), and so on, depends on the ideological balance of justices sitting on the Supreme Court at any given time.

The Case of "Is" Versus "Ought"

Which school of thinking—accommodationist, separationist, or benevolent neutrality—is correct? Which method accurately represents the intent of the framers of the Constitution as to the relationship between church and state (or, in more generic terms, between religion and government)?

It doesn't matter. The fact is, you will find committed, Bible-believing Christians subscribing to all three positions. While it is important to have an understanding of why things are the way they are, however, there is a difference between discussing theoretical perspectives in church-state issues and exploring what the law actually says.

As we shall see in the next chapter, much of the law that determines religious rights in the United States is based on cases that have gone before the various courts in the nation.

There are two possible ways to approach the issues addressed in those cases: by the *is* and by the *ought*. We could spend the next hundred or so pages discussing what the law *ought* to be, but when the rubber meets the road, that will not do you much good in a court of law. Judges and other regulatory authorities ranging from police departments to the Equal Employment Opportunity Commission will, presumably, operate from the perspective, or at least their interpretation, of what *is*.

However, an even more important question to consider regarding personal evangelism is, once you find out what the law says about your rights, should you follow the law if it speaks against your commitment to express the gospel?

Crossing the Boundaries of the Law?

If you are in a situation in which the law says you do not have the right to witness—and there are such situations—you must consider whether to follow the law or whether the act of witnessing is important enough that you should disregard the law and communicate the gospel nonetheless.

What if you are spreading the gospel in a street ministry and the police tell you to move on? What if you are witnessing at work and threatened with the loss of your job if you continue? What should you do if you are passing out tracts at an airport and are confronted by security guards who don't like your activities?

You have three options: to refrain from witnessing or move to another environment and avoid the potential consequences of your activities; to continue witnessing in that environment and deal with any consequences; or to resist the interference and challenge the law yourself through legal options available to you. (These options are discussed more fully in chapter 13, "Getting Help When You're Hassled.")

I don't presume to advise you on which way is the best course of action; that decision must come through both prayer and consultation with professionals such as your pastor or an attorney. Nonetheless, it is important to note that there have been many instances of what we might call "evangelistic civil disobedience" in the Bible.

The story of Daniel in the lions' den provides a representative example of obeying God to the extent of disobeying the law. The commissioners came before King Darius and convinced him to "establish a statute and enforce an injunction that anyone who makes a petition to any god or man besides you, O king, for thirty days, shall be cast into the lions' den" (Dan. 6:7).

Despite the written law, Daniel continued to serve God over his earthly king:

> Now when Daniel knew that the document was signed, he entered his house (now in his roof chamber he had windows open toward Jerusalem); and he continued kneeling on his knees three times a day, praying and giving thanks before God, as he had been doing previously. Then these men came by agreement and found Daniel making petition and supplication before his God. . . .
> Then the king gave orders, and Daniel was brought in and cast into the lions' den. The king spoke and said to Daniel, "Your God whom you constantly serve will Himself deliver you" (Dan. 6:10–11, 16).

While the central point of this passage is Daniel's obedience to the Lord, consider the evangelistic effect of his action and how his prayer testified openly to the authority of God over the law of the state.

That kind of action is even more evident in the Book of Acts, which contains numerous examples of Christians engaging in evangelism despite the law. Shortly after Pentecost, for example, Peter and John were summoned by the captain of the temple guard and the Sadducees:

> And when they had summoned them, they commanded them not to speak or teach at all in the name of Jesus.
> But Peter and John answered and said to them, "Whether it is right

in the sight of God to give heed to you rather than to God, you be the judge; for we cannot stop speaking what we have seen and heard" (Acts 4:18–20).

While the temple guard and Sadducees were religious authorities (rather than civil authorities), history is replete with examples of governments interfering with the spread of the gospel. One need only look at some nations in the Middle East today, where the conversion of Moslems to Christianity is a crime punishable by death.

I cannot advise you what action to take if you run into legal resistance as you witness. Paraphrasing Peter and John, I can only tell you that you must judge for yourself whether it is right in the sight of God to give heed to a law that prevents you from spreading your religion rather than give heed to God.

There are certainly examples of people engaging in civil disobedience in God's name in contemporary American society, ranging from the pro-life activities of Operation Rescue to peace witnesses conducted by pacifist Christian churches. In fact, civil disobedience is a tradition we can ascribe to Jesus himself as he cleansed the temple of the money-changers' tables (Matt. 21:12–13; Mark 11:15–18; Luke 19:45–46; John 2:14–16). Nonetheless, as to your personal evangelism, the decision to obey or disobey the civil law is beyond the scope of this book. What is important is that you know what the law has to say.

The decisions you make are ultimately between you and the Lord (helped, hopefully, by counsel from other Christians). The important thing is that you consider in advance the laws that may have direct bearing on your evangelistic activities, and that you make an informed decision based on that.

Keeping the Law in Perspective

Despite my use of the Scriptures to support certain principles, it is also important to remember that this is not a book on theology or personal evangelism per se; it's primarily a book to make you aware of the law and evangelistic efforts and how you can develop the street smarts that will help ensure your right to spread the gospel. It is important, therefore, to place the law in perspective with regard to the success of your witnessing.

The law is a tool designed, for the most part, to protect the right to engage in a free and open dialogue with other persons on a myriad of issues, including the gospel of Jesus Christ. The freedoms of speech, press, assembly, and free exercise of religion outlined in the United States Constitution and in state constitutions, statutes, and court cases help ensure our right to "go into all the world and preach the gospel to all creation" (Mark 16:15).

It's important, though, that we don't place the law on a pedestal and place more emphasis on our legal rights than we do on our mandate from God. Our authority ultimately does not come from civil law but from our having been accepted by God through our faith in Jesus Christ (John 1:12). At the same time, even the apostle Paul used the law to his advantage when he claimed the protection of his Roman citizenship to avoid persecution (Acts 16:37–39; 22:25–29).

Success in our witnessing will not come about because we make effective presentations of the gospel using "three illustrative points of salvation" or "four spiritual laws," nor because we know what the civil law has to say about our right to evangelize; it will come about because of the power of the Holy Spirit (Acts 1:8).

Thus, the law is merely a tool. As you move through this book, keep in mind that your ultimate weapon is prayer. Remember that regardless of how the civil law protects you, the ultimate affirmation of your right to speak the gospel will come about not by your ability to quote statutes and legal precedents but because of the truths and protections Paul taught.

> Take up the full armor of God, that you may be able to resist in the evil day, and having done everything, to stand firm.
>
> Stand firm, therefore, having girded your loins with truth, and having put on the breastplate of righteousness, and having shod your feet with the preparation of the gospel of peace; in addition to all, taking up the shield of faith with which you will be able to extinguish all the flaming missiles of the evil one.
>
> And take the helmet of salvation, and the sword of the Spirit, which is the word of God. With all prayer and petition pray at all times (Eph. 6:13–18).

You can build a home with tools, but the tools will not be of much help unless you have a good instruction manual. You can ensure your right to evangelize by knowing the law, but the tool you call the law won't be of much assistance unless you have a good instruction manual on evangelization. The best manual for that purpose is God's Word. Even though the law may assist you to engage in the activities that will help build God's kingdom, you won't be able to get much accomplished without the help of the master builder.

Lest we set our priorities incorrectly, remember that the law, as valuable as it can be in our efforts, should not be placed on the throne of our lives. With Jesus on the throne, then, let's look at the relationship of the law to evangelism and how we can use it to our advantage.

/ 2 /

Some Law for
the Nonlawyer

To understand how the law affects religious rights in the United States today, we should examine the historic foundation of the relationship between Christianity and the government.

The first ten amendments to the United States Constitution, ratified in 1791, constitute the Bill of Rights. The foundational body of law as it pertains to religion is contained in the First Amendment to the Constitution:

> Congress shall make no law respecting an establishment of religion, or prohibiting the free exercise thereof; or abridging the freedom of speech, or of the press; or the right of the people peaceably to assemble, and to petition the Government for a redress of grievances.[1]

The first sixteen words of the First Amendment establish the entire foundation of federal law regarding religion. There have been thousands of court cases regarding religious issues over the two centuries since the Bill of Rights was ratified, but all of them have been based on these sixteen words.

Obviously, though, the First Amendment deals with more than freedom of religion. It also addresses freedom of speech, freedom of the press, and the right of persons to assemble in groups. As we shall see when we examine specific issues dealing with personal evangelism, many religious rights cases have been won not on the basis of freedom of religion but on one of the other freedoms set forth in the First Amendment.

The Religion Clauses

Known collectively as the religion clauses, the first sixteen words of the First Amendment break down further into two provisions, the Establishment Clause and the Free Exercise Clause.

The Establishment Clause

The Establishment Clause consists of these words: *Congress shall make no law respecting an establishment of religion.* This originally meant that the legislative branch of government could not establish a religion or a national church which, for example, might be called the Church of America.

The fact that we have no nationally established church makes the United States different from a country such as England, where the Anglican Church is the established religion. Officially called the Church of England, Queen Elizabeth II is the Anglican Church's titular head and is authorized to appoint the denomination's spiritual leader, the Archbishop of Canterbury.

The framers of the Constitution were not thinking about Christian evangelism when they determined that the United States should not, as a nation, have an established church. Their goal was far more realistic: to make sure that the religions that had been officially established in the individual states did not compete with each other on a national level. While the United States has never had a nationally established church, many of the original colonies did.

At the outbreak of the American Revolution in 1775, there were established churches in nine of the thirteen colonies. The Anglican Church had been established in Virginia in 1609, in New York's lower counties in 1693, in Maryland in 1702, in South Carolina in 1706, in North Carolina nominally in 1711, and in Georgia in 1758. The Congregational Church was established in Massachusetts, Connecticut, and New Hampshire. By the time that the Constitutional Convention assembled in Philadelphia in the summer of 1787, however, only Georgia, South Carolina, Connecticut, Massachusetts, and New Hampshire had retained their religious establishments. The Anglican Church had been disestablished in Virginia in 1786, and in New York, Maryland, and North Carolina during the Revolutionary War. The elimination of established churches in the several states continued after the ratification of the Federal Constitution in 1788 and culminated in the disestablishment of the Congregational Church in

Connecticut in 1818, in New Hampshire in 1819, and in Massachusetts in 1833.[2]

Only Delaware, New Jersey, Pennsylvania, and Rhode Island did not have established churches. All of the other states had established the Anglican or Congregational Church as official religions.

While evangelism may not have been on the minds of the Constitution's framers, however, their decision not to establish a national church resulted in people having the freedom to make their own decisions about what church to join. This has ultimately helped to make American Christianity much more dynamic than in countries where one denomination has been the officially established faith. John Warwick Montgomery has observed that Christianity in England, where the Anglican Church is established, tends to be more of a dead faith than it is in America, where there is open dialogue on religious issues and a smorgasbord of religions from which to choose. Montgomery writes:

> As such widely diverse writers as Cushing Strout, Martin Marty, and Justice William O. Douglas have observed, the establishment of Christianity in England and elsewhere has done Christianity irreparable harm, since people no longer come to regard Christianity as a matter of free decision but as a state obligation, and therefore run from it.[3]

Even though the individual states were allowed to establish official religions, and did so until Massachusetts disestablished the Congregational Church in 1833, states may no longer have established churches today. The reason for this is that the Establishment Clause was applicable only to the federal government, but not to individual states, until the early twentieth century.

The application of the First Amendment to both federal and state governments came about, indirectly, because of the outlawing of slavery in the United States. After the Civil War, Congress added three amendments to the Constitution designed to end the institution of slavery—the Thirteenth, Fourteenth, and Fifteenth Amendments. Ratified in 1868, the Fourteenth Amendment said, in part:

> No State shall make or enforce any law which shall abridge the privileges or immunities of citizens of the United States; nor shall any State deprive any person of life, liberty, or property, without due process of law; nor deny to any person within its jurisdiction of the equal protection of the laws.[4]

The Bill of Rights had been designed as a check on the national government, and as late as 1833 the United States Supreme Court held that the Bill of Rights was not applicable to individual states.[5] However, based on the due process clause of the Fourteenth Amendment, which prohibits the individual states as well as the federal government from interfering with a person's liberty, in 1925 the Supreme Court adopted a legal theory known as the Incorporation Doctrine, which required that the provisions in the Bill of Rights, which the Court considered to be fundamental, should be applied to the states as well as to the federal government.[6]

The result is that today the First Amendment applies to federal, state, and local legislative bodies, and "no law respecting an establishment of religion" can be passed at any level of government.

Yet the Establishment Clause means more than having no established church. According to the Supreme Court, it also means the following:

> Neither a state nor the Federal Government can set up a church. Neither can pass laws which aid one religion, aid all religions, or prefer one religion over another. Neither can force nor influence a person to go to or to remain away from church against his will or force him to profess a belief or disbelief in any religion. No person can be punished for entertaining or professing religious beliefs or disbeliefs, for church attendance or nonattendance. . . . Neither a state nor the Federal Government can, openly or secretly, participate in the affairs of any religious organizations or groups and *vice versa*.[7]

Before we move on to the Free Exercise Clause, let's place the Court's interpretation of the Establishment Clause in perspective.

Many conservative Christians believe that the United States was founded as a Christian nation and feel that its government should be run from a Christian perspective today. There is nothing intrinsically wrong with such a belief (notwithstanding the fact that Jews, Mormons, Buddhists, and a myriad of others might have a problem with it), provided Christians can agree on how their Christianity should be expressed.

To understand the full ramification of such a position, however, come with me on a hypothetical journey. Suppose, for example, that you are a Baptist. You belong to a church that has all of the right words on its outdoor sign, such as *premillennial, fundamental, independent,* and *evangelistic*.

Now suppose Congress mandates that the officially established church of the United States shall be the Assemblies of God, and that to serve in the federal or state legislature you have to prove that you are baptized in the Holy Spirit, the evidence of which, the denomination says, is speaking in tongues according to Acts 2:4.

Or, for the sake of argument, suppose you are a member of the Assemblies of God and Congress forbids you to run for public office because the officially established religion is the fundamental Baptist faith, which holds that speaking in tongues is no longer valid.

Regardless of which way the scenario goes, you can understand the reason that not only is the government prohibited from endorsing Christianity as the nation's official religion, it could not even decide what expression of Christianity would be valid. Remember, when nine of the original thirteen colonies had established religions, even they could not agree on what form of Christianity to establish. The result was that some colonies had established the Anglican Church while others had established the Congregational Church, both of which hold different doctrines and different systems of church government. Law professor Robert Davidow has observed the following:

> It would be virtually impossible to establish a form of Christianity that did not either offend one or more Christian churches, or express itself in such generalities as to constitute banalities unworthy of serious religion.[8]

Even when the Constitution was written, there were others besides Anglicans and Congregationalists in the United States. Pennsylvania had substantial Jewish and Quaker populations, Maryland had a large Roman Catholic population, and Rhode Island had been founded as a safe haven for persecuted Baptists in New England. According to church-state scholar Richard McMillan, there were "some thirty Christian sects and denominations present in colonial America, and none were able to generate an influence sufficiently widespread to allow establishment [on a national scale]."[9]

There are hundreds more Christian denominations in the United States today, not to mention a myriad of non-Christian religions, cults, and sects.[10] Doctrinal differences notwithstanding, the good news is that Christians are free to spread the gospel without being impeded by the official establishment of any one denomination over another or any other religion over Christianity.

The Free Exercise Clause

In addition to Congress making "no law respecting an establishment of religion," the First Amendment says that Congress shall make no law "prohibiting the free exercise thereof." Known as the Free Exercise Clause, these words ensure that not only do citizens have the right to believe what they choose to believe, they also have the right to exercise their beliefs. Again, let's look at the words of the Supreme Court that acknowledge the meaning of the First Amendment:

> Neither [the federal government nor a state government] can force nor influence a person to go to or to remain away from church against his will or force him to profess a belief or disbelief in any religion. No person can be punished for entertaining or professing religious beliefs or disbeliefs, for church attendance or non-attendance.[11]

Not only can the government not prevent you from believing what you choose to believe, it cannot determine whether what you believe is true or false. In 1944 the Supreme Court held the following:

> Men may believe what they cannot prove. They may not be put to the proof of their religious doctrines or beliefs. Religious experiences which are as real to life to some may be incomprehensible to others. Yet the fact that they may be beyond the ken of mortals does not mean that they can be made suspect before the law.[12]

For better or worse, however, the Court has established that there is a legitimate difference between believing something and acting on that belief. While the government cannot control what a person believes, it may place restrictions on a person's right to act on those beliefs.

For example, I may believe that I have a religious duty to repeat the Lord's Prayer for an hour each day while sitting naked in the lotus position at the top of the Empire State Building. (Sounds silly, but there may be somebody, somewhere, who believes just that. You'd be surprised at what some people claim to believe in the name of religion.) The law says that I have the right to believe that I have such a religious duty, but I don't have the right to act on that belief.

A more down-to-earth example may help place this belief-action doctrine in perspective. In 1879, the Supreme Court held in *Reynolds v. United States* that the Mormon practice of polygamy was unconstitutional.

George Reynolds was the private secretary to Brigham Young, the second president of the Mormon Church and governor of the territory of Utah from 1850 to 1854. In 1852 Young, who had twenty-seven wives himself, proclaimed that polygamy, or plural marriage, was an official tenet of the church.

Ten years later, the United States Congress passed the Morrill Act "to punish and prevent the practice of polygamy in the territories." George Reynolds was prosecuted and convicted under the act, and he contended, based on the Free Exercise Clause, that the act could not be constitutionally applied to Mormons who practiced polygamy in the belief that it was a religious duty.

In ruling against Reynolds, the Court held the following:

> Laws are made for the government of actions, and while they cannot interfere with mere religious belief and opinions, they may with practices. Suppose one believed that human sacrifices were a necessary part of religious worship, would it be seriously contended that the civil government under which he lived could not interfere to prevent a sacrifice? Or if a wife religiously believed it was her duty to burn herself upon the funeral pyre of her husband, would it be beyond the power of the civil government to prevent her carrying her belief into practice?[13]

The Court concluded: "To permit this [polygamy] would be to make the professed doctrines of religious belief superior to the law of the land, and in effect to permit every citizen to become a law unto himself. Government could exist only in name under such circumstances."[14] Ultimately, the Mormon Church forbade polygamy in 1890, though some renegade Mormons (those not affiliated with the official Mormon Church) continue the practice today.

A side note is appropriate here. The Mormon Church (known officially as the Church of Jesus Christ, Latter Day Saints) is a cult that believes, among other things, that Jesus was polygamously married to three women, that he and his wives had children, that he visited the American continent after his resurrection, and that Mormons in good standing will become gods themselves.[15]

The Free Exercise Clause means, among other things, that the Mormons have the right to spread their beliefs (even if they do not have the right to act on all of those beliefs), as do other non-Christian cults such as the Unification Church or Krishna Consciousness movement. The good news is that under the Free Exercise Clause, Christians have the right to openly express their disagreement with those beliefs and to spread the biblical gospel.

Such rulings affect not only cults but fringe groups within Christianity as well. In 1949, for example, the Supreme Court upheld the constitutionality of an ordinance against snake handling by rural churches that profess to be Christian and believe in a literal interpretation of Mark 16:18. Affirming a North Carolina law, the Court held that the safety of the public outweighed the Free Exercise Clause of the First Amendment.[16]

The bottom line is that the Free Exercise Clause protects your right to express your Christian faith and to present that faith to others, with limitations. Suppose, for example, that you are standing in the middle of a street preaching the gospel and an ambulance transporting a heart attack victim to the local hospital comes barreling down the road. Assuming the ambulance does not run over you and continue on its way, it is still reasonable to suppose that the law requires you to get out of the way and let the ambulance go about its business.

You may believe that you should stop the ambulance and preach to the poor guy who had the heart attack (just in case he dies before he hears the gospel), but a court would rule that the need to rush him to the hospital outweighs your rights under the Free Exercise Clause. That's the difference between your belief and your right to act on that belief.

The question, then, becomes, Who decides that what you do is within your right to act on your beliefs, and how did they get the authority to make those decisions?

The Ultimate Arbiter

Thinking back to your high school course in American history, you may remember that there are three branches of the United States government: legislative, executive, and judicial. The three-branch system of federal government was set up by the framers of the Constitution to provide a system of checks and balances that would ensure that no one branch of the government would exceed its authority. The legislative branch, consisting of the Senate and House of Representatives, would originate all laws and statutes and establish administrative entities to carry on the business of government. The executive branch, led by the president of the United States, would approve or veto the laws made by Congress, make treaties, administer foreign policy, and the president would serve as commander-in-chief of the armed forces. The judicial branch, consisting of the Supreme Court and the lower courts, would adjudicate cases and interpret the statutes that originated in Congress and were signed into law by the president.

No one branch had the sole authority to determine issues such as religious rights. At least that was the intention, until the Supreme Court took a step that neither Congress nor the president had anticipated. The framers of the Constitution intended that the Supreme Court would have "appellate jurisdiction"[17] in many issues, meaning that in most cases the Court would review the decisions of the lower courts for accuracy and proper judicial procedure. One thing the Court was not established to do was review the laws passed by Congress to determine whether they were constitutional.

In 1803, however, the Supreme Court held that it had the power to review the acts of Congress and declare them void if they were interpreted to be in conflict with the Constitution.[18] This doctrine of judicial review is not intrinsically bad, though it has had severe effects in some areas of the law.

For example, the Constitution has established that the United States Senate shall have two members from each state, regardless of the size or population of the state.[19] The House of Representatives, on the other hand, has a different number of representatives for each state, based on the population of the different states. Thus, New York has more representatives than Vermont since it is a more populous state. Suppose, for example, that one day the Senate gets together and says, "You know, we don't think it's fair that each state has two senators regardless of its size. Let's pass a law saying that since California, New York, and Texas are the most populous states, they can each have three senators."

In such a case, the Supreme Court would step in and, using the power of judicial review, declare the law to be unconstitutional. Such a decision would not be wrong, since it would be unconstitutional for some states to have three senators, for the Constitution specifies two senators per state. Unless the government amends the Constitution to make such a change (which it is empowered to do, though such amendments must be ratified by two-thirds of the individual states), it would be improper for Congress to pass a law that is in conflict with the Constitution.

The problem is that the power of judicial review has been abused to the extent that instead of merely interpreting laws, the Supreme Court has ended up making laws. The best-known example of this phenomenon is *Roe v. Wade*, in which the Court legalized the right to abortion in 1973.[20] Usurping the legislative process at both the federal and state levels, the Court's decision overturned the abortion laws of many states and created a controversy that remains one of the most prominent social issues today.

Additionally, even though federal or state legislatures may pass laws that affirm a person's right to act on his or her religious belief, such laws may go unheeded until the courts decide whether they are constitutional. In short, even though all three branches of government are supposed to have an equal voice in the process of running things, the courts—especially the Supreme Court—have become the ultimate referee of what is or is not a permissible religious activity.

The Rule of Case Law

The United States' system of law is based on a principle called *stare decisis* (literally translated "the decision stands"), also known as the principle of precedent. Most of the issues discussed in this book are documented by referring to court cases, and *stare decisis* is the reason.

Assume, for example, that Congress passes a statute that has an impact on religious rights. Sooner or later, that law will be challenged in court. It doesn't matter whether the statute is for or against religion; there will be people on either side who are willing to challenge it in court. If the law favors religion, it will likely be challenged by a secular group such as the American Civil Liberties Union or a state civil liberties union. If the law is antagonistic toward religion, it will likely be challenged by a Christian legal organization such as the Rutherford Institute, National Legal Foundation, or Western Center for Law and Religious Freedom.

The court in which the law is challenged will determine its constitutionality under the First Amendment and how the law is to be interpreted. The next time the law is challenged—and there will be a next time—the court will not necessarily look to the original law, but will look to the previous case that interpreted that law.

Cases that are adjudicated (decided) in different courts of law are binding on all geographic areas in which each court has jurisdiction. For example, a case decided by the Superior Court for the County of Los Angeles is binding only in Los Angeles, though other courts that hear similar cases may use it as a precedent to decide the issue in their geographic areas. Decisions issued by the California Supreme Court, however, are binding on the entire state.

At the federal level, cases decided by various courts are also binding on the areas in which each court has jurisdiction. Thus, a case decided by the Federal District Court for the Eastern District of Pennsylvania is binding on the Philadelphia area and surrounding counties in southeastern Pennsylvania that are under the authority of that district. If the case is appealed to the next higher court, the United States Court of Appeals for the Third Circuit, the appeals court's decision will then be binding on the entire area within the Third Circuit Court's jurisdiction, which includes Pennsylvania, New Jersey, Delaware, and the Virgin Islands. Again, the decision would be binding only in the third circuit, though courts in other geographical areas could use the decision as a precedent if they choose to do so.

Decisions issued by the United States Supreme Court are binding on the entire nation. However, the Supreme Court does not review all cases that are presented to it. In constitutional issues, persons involved in a case may appeal a decision to the Supreme Court, which then grants *certiorari* or denies *certiorari*. This means that the Court will, or will not, consent to review the lower court decision. If the Supreme Court grants *certiorari,* it will review the case and issue an opinion, which then becomes the final opinion in that case. If they deny *certiorari*, then the lower court decision is allowed to stand as the final decision.

However, the Supreme Court grants *certiorari* in only a fraction of the cases that are submitted for its review. The Court is more likely to review the case if lower courts have reached different conclusions on the same issue. For example, in January 1989 the United States Court of Appeals for the Ninth Circuit ruled that students in the state of Washington could not form Bible study clubs in public high schools.[21] The following month, the Eighth Circuit Court of Appeals held that students in Nebraska could form high school Bible study clubs.[22] The Supreme Court granted *certiorari* in the Nebraska case and in 1990 decided that such clubs are constitutional.[23] When other school districts challenge the constitutionality of high school Bible study clubs in various state or federal courts—and they will—the Supreme Court decision will be used as the primary precedent for deciding such challenges.

Unfortunately, the lower courts will not always reach decisions that are consistent with each other. Despite the Supreme Court's ruling in the Nebraska case, in the Washington State case a federal district court later determined that the federal and state constitutions conflicted with each other and that the more restrictive state constitution should take precedence. However, in 1993 the Ninth Circuit Court of Appeals, citing the Supreme Court precedent, reversed the district court and affirmed the students' right to meet at school for Bible study.[24]

That's how *stare decisis*, or the principle of case law, works. As you go about evangelizing, the primary protections you will have (other than prayer and the leading of the Holy Spirit) will be the myriad of cases heard in the local, state, and federal court systems and the rulings that have worked in favor of religious rights. In those cases where the freedom of religious expression was not victorious, you will at least be able to "calculate the cost" of going into the evangelistic battlefield (Luke 14:28).

Before we examine specific issues, and the cases and laws we have at our disposal, it may help to put some of the principles of personal evangelism into perspective in terms of the law.

/ 3 /

Equal Rights for Those Who Are Wrong

Welcome to the most open, yet the most exclusive, club in the world—the salvation club. Jesus invites members with these words: "Come to Me, all who are weary and heavy laden, and I will give you rest" (Matt. 11:28); and, "Behold, I stand at the door and knock; if any one hears my voice and opens the door, I will come in to him, and will dine with him, and he with Me" (Rev. 3:20).

Anyone can join the club and experience what salvation is about since, as Jesus said, "He who hears My word, and believes Him who sent Me, has eternal life, and does not come into judgment, but has passed out of death into life" (John 5:24).

At the same time the salvation club is open to anyone who wants to join, there is a condition for membership, namely, an acknowledgment that there is only one membership director, only one person who can stamp your admission card. Many counterfeit stamps are circulating outside the doors of the club, but only the genuine stamp will get you in.

How exclusive is it? Jesus made it clear when he said, "I am the way, the truth, and the life; no one comes to the Father, but through Me" (John 14:6). Luke affirmed the role of Jesus when he wrote, "There is salvation in no one else; for there is no other name under heaven that has been given among men, by which we must be saved" (Acts 4:12).

That message Christians have been given a mandate to spread: "Go therefore and make disciples of all the nations, baptizing them in the name of the Father and the Son and the Holy Spirit" (Matt. 28:19), to go out into the world to "preach the word; be ready in season and out of season; reprove, rebuke, exhort, with great patience and instruction" (2 Tim. 4:2).

There is a myriad of ways in any number of situations in which Christians can preach the Word to those who have not joined the salvation club. Every day presents an opportunity to share the gospel. While this book will not discuss how to present the gospel (there are lots of books on personal evangelism and witnessing that will help you do that), it will help you meet some of the obstacles you may encounter.

Before we confront the legal issues involved in witnessing, however, we should understand a basic difference between the good news about Jesus Christ and the legal system in the United States.

A Marketplace of Ideas

Some non-Christian cults and religions believe in multitudes of ways through which one can attain that ultimate reward we call salvation. The ultimate reward may go by another name, such as the Buddhist concept of *nirvana* or the Erhard Seminar Training concept of *it*, but the goal is still to achieve that ultimate reward. The Baha'i faith, for example, teaches that any number of the great religions of the world (of which, they say, Baha'i is the greatest) will lead to what we call salvation. Followers of Islam maintain that while Jesus was a prophet, so were Moses, Buddha, and Mohammed (who, they say, was God's greatest prophet). Unitarians believe that Jesus was a nice guy who may have been a prophet, but he was not God. The New Age Movement teaches that if you want to find God, you should not look outward to any source of religion; just look inside yourself and you will find God.

Christians disagree. We unequivocally proclaim that Jesus is God, the only begotten Son of the Father, the second person of the Trinity, and that salvation comes only through him. Christianity is set apart from every other religion in the world because it claims Jesus as the exclusive route to salvation.

From a legal point of view, however, Christianity is on par with other religions. The legal system neither acknowledges nor denies that Jesus is the way, the truth, and the life. Rather, the law declares that you live in a free and open marketplace of ideas, and that you are free to proclaim your own faith, whatever that faith is or however you wish to express it.

The choices people can make in terms of religion are too numerous to list here, and, as we know, people often make the wrong choices. Perhaps the apostle Paul foresaw a situation such as we confront in the United States when he wrote: "For the time will come when they will not endure sound doctrine; but wanting to have their ears tickled, they will accumulate for themselves teachers in accordance to their own desires; and will turn away their ears from the truth, and will turn aside to myths" (2 Tim. 4:3–4). The Living Bible puts it this way: "For there is going to come a time when people won't listen to the truth, but will go around looking for teachers who will tell them just what they want to hear. They won't listen to what the Bible says but will blithely follow their own misguided ideas."

There is no shortage of religious teachers or faith systems that provide just what people are looking for, even though what they provide is far from the truth proclaimed by Jesus Christ. And the fact that Jesus represents the only truth system cannot be acknowledged in an American court of law. Why? Because, for better or worse, "Congress shall make no law respecting an establishment of religion, or prohibiting the free exercise thereof." (Sound familiar? It's the First Amendment.)

To understand why the truth or falsehood of religious teachings cannot be adjudicated in court, it may help to look at a few key cases in which the Supreme Court has addressed this position.

The Support of No Dogma

The first major case the United States Supreme Court heard that dealt with a religious issue was *Watson v. Jones*. After the Civil War, a Presbyterian church in Kentucky became divided over the issue of slavery, and the congregation split into two factions. In the Court's 1872 determination of which side should have title to the church, its building, and its funds, Justice Samuel Miller wrote:

> In this country the full and free right to entertain any religious belief, to practice any religious principle, and to teach any religious doctrine which does not violate the laws of morality and property, and which does not infringe personal rights, is conceded to all. The law knows no heresy, and is committed to the support of no dogma, the establishment of no sect.[1]

The sentence, "The law knows no heresy, and is committed to the support of no dogma, the establishment of no sect," has been cited in numerous cases through today. Justice Miller's statement has become a foundational principle of the courts in the adjudication of religious disputes.

In the last chapter I quoted a doctrine from the 1944 case of *United States v. Ballard*, in which Justice William O. Douglas wrote:

> Men may believe what they cannot prove. They may not be put to the proof of their religious doctrines or beliefs. Religious experiences which are as real to life to some may be incomprehensible to others. Yet the fact that they may be beyond the ken of mortals does not mean that they can be made suspect before the law.[2]

The story of the Ballard case may be helpful in discerning how the courts act, or refuse to act, in religious matters.

Guy and Edna Ballard were the founders of the I Am Movement, a non-Christian cult founded in 1930 and similar in its teachings to the metaphysical Ascended Masters of the New Age Movement.[3] Guy Ballard went by many aliases, including Saint Germain, Jesus, George Washington, and Godfre Ray King, and believed that he, his wife Edna, and their son Donald had been selected as divine messengers. The Ballards claimed that they had the power to heal persons of ailments and diseases. Because they advertised their claims through the United States mail, they were indicted and convicted of twelve counts of mail fraud.

When the Ballards were tried in a federal district court, the trial judge instructed the jury that as they considered the fate of the Ballards, they should confine their deliberations to the "good faith of the respondents" and not the truth or falsehood of the Ballards' beliefs. The question to be addressed by the jury, then, was not whether the Ballards' claims were true but simply whether the Ballards believed their claims to be true. The jury concluded that the Ballards made their claims with intent to defraud and convicted them on all counts of the indictment. On appeal, the Circuit Court of Appeals held that the truth of the Ballards' representations should have been submitted to the jury. The case was appealed to the Supreme Court, which reversed the appeals court and upheld the district court's actions.

When the case went to the Supreme Court, the key question was whether the trial judge had given the jury proper instructions. The Court held that the jury was properly guided and established the precedent that, while a civil court could determine whether a person was sincere in proclaiming his or her religious beliefs, a court could not discern the truth or falsehood of the beliefs themselves. Justice Douglas wrote:

We do not agree that the truth or verity of respondents' religious doctrines or beliefs should have been submitted to the jury. Whatever this particular indictment may require, the First Amendment precludes such a course, as the United States seem to concede. "The law knows no heresy, and is committed to the support of no dogma, the establishment of no sect."[4]

The quotation in Justice Douglas' opinion comes from the 1872 case of *Watson v. Jones* and reaffirmed that the courts could neither support nor oppose a religious belief system.

In a sense, the Ballard case is amusing. It is highly unlikely that such a case would be heard in the courts today, since there are religious teachers and televangelists who make claims far more daring than those of the Ballards. Notwithstanding the teachings of cults and other non-Christian sects, professing Christian evangelists such as Oral Roberts and Robert Tilton claim, both through the mail and on television and radio, to effect miraculous healings. In short, not only would the Ballards not have been prosecuted for making their claims, they probably would not have been indicted in the first place in recent times. (Remember that the Ballard case was decided in 1944, before the age of television, and that media evangelism has greatly changed the religious fabric of society.)

Another factor to be considered in the Ballard case is that the Supreme Court affirmed that, while civil courts could not consider the truth or falsehood of a religious belief system, they could consider whether a person's professed beliefs were sincere or not. That remains true today, especially in cases involving persons who hold conscientious objection to military service.

The question, of course, is whether it is possible to determine a person's sincerity with accuracy. Assume, for example, that I buy a dog named Fido, place ads in local newspapers proclaiming that Fido can heal diseases and ailments, then charge people fifty dollars to pet Fido and absorb his healing power. (Okay, I'll say it. Kids, don't try this at home.)

As Christians, you and I know that my claim would be a false religious teaching. However, a court of law cannot make the same value judgment. Remember, the courts are precluded from determining whether a religious belief is true or false. Except for making a determination of whether I sincerely believe that Fido can heal diseases, the court cannot take action against me.

But how would the court know whether I am sincere or not? Well, I could gather a few of my friends and confess, "I've got a great scam going. It's baloney, but people are actually buying into this. Do I believe it? Of course not!" If my friends were to testify against me in court, there would be enough evidence to establish that I had acted with the intent to defraud people. On the other hand, if I were shrewd enough not to make such a confession, the result is obvious. There would be no proof whether I do or do not believe what I proclaim Fido can do.

The bottom line is that the Ballard scenario is a moot argument today, but the case provided a principle used by the courts to decide religious cases: that religious beliefs themselves, whether true or false, cannot be adjudicated in a court of law. That conclusion determined another factor that is important in issues regarding personal evangelism and witnessing: All groups, regardless of whether they are Christian or non-Christian, have an equal right to engage in evangelistic activities.

Neutral Principles of Law

In refusing to decide matters of doctrinal truth and error, the Supreme Court has also determined that it is inappropriate for civil courts to weigh matters of religious doctrine at all. Twenty-five years after the Ballard case, the Court reviewed another case that placed the role of the civil courts in perspective.

In the 1960s, the Presbyterian Church in the United States spoke out against the Vietnam War and began to debate the issue of the ordination of women. The denomination's positions touched a nerve in two local congregations in Savannah, Georgia, which decided to withdraw from the denomination and reorganize as independent Presbyterian churches.

The case that resulted presented issues similar to those that were presented in the 1872 case of *Watson v. Jones*: When a church is divided (whether the split is within the congregation or between a congregation and the denomination to which it belongs), who gets to keep the church (or, in an intracongregational schism, which side is the true congregation of that church)? Which faction gets to keep the building? Which side owns the church funds? You'd be amazed at how many such cases have involved church property disputes, providing an illustration of Paul's statement, "For there must also be factions among you, in order that those who are approved may have become evident among you" (1 Cor. 11:19).

The two congregations charged that the Presbyterian denomination had "departed from doctrine" by changing its position on theological and social issues. When the case went before a state trial court, the jury was instructed to determine whether the denomination's actions "amount to a fundamental or substantial abandonment of the original doctrines of the [general church], so that the new tenets and doctrines are utterly variant from the purposes for which the [general church] was founded."[5] The jury declared that the denomination had, in fact, departed from doctrine, awarded the church properties to the local congregations, and the Georgia Supreme Court affirmed the jury's decision.

In *Presbyterian Church in the United States v. Mary Elizabeth Blue Hull Memorial Presbyterian Church* (1969), the United States Supreme Court reversed the Georgia courts and declared the following:

> There are neutral principles of law, developed for use in all property disputes, which can be applied without "establishing" churches to which property is awarded. . . . If civil courts undertake to resolve such controversies [over religious doctrine and practice] in order to adjudicate the property dispute, the hazards are ever present of inhibiting the free development of religious doctrine and of implicating secular interests in matters of purely ecclesiastical concern. Because of these hazards, the First Amendment enjoins the employment of organs of government for essentially religious purposes.[6]

The Supreme Court concluded that the Georgia courts' departure-from-doctrine basis for deciding the case "requires the civil court to determine matters at the very core of a religion—the interpretation of particular church doctrines and the importance of those doctrines to the religion. Plainly, the First Amendment forbids civil courts from playing such a role."[7]

Ten years later, in another case dealing with a different Presbyterian congregation in Georgia, the Supreme Court elaborated on its concept of using the "neutral principles of law" to determine religious questions. In the case of property disputes, the court noted, matters of doctrine cannot be considered. However, civil courts can consider doctrine-neutral factors such as a church's deeds, the terms of the local church charter, state statutes governing the holding of church property, and the provisions of the denomination's constitutions concerning ownership and control of the property.[8] "In undertaking such an examination," wrote Justice Harry Blackmun in *Jones v. Wolf* (1979), "a civil court must take care to scrutinize the document in purely secular terms, and not to rely on religious precepts in determining whether the document indicates that the parties have intended to create a trust."[9]

What can we conclude from the cases we have looked at this far? In adjudicating matters dealing with religion, civil courts can discern neither the truth nor falsehood inherent in religious teachings, nor can courts even examine such teachings from a doctrinal perspective. When the courts do decide religious cases, they must use "neutral principles of law" that neither endorse nor condemn the religious teachings themselves.

Additionally, in adjudicating cases in which different rights collide, such as the First Amendment freedoms of religion and speech with the Fifth Amendment right to private property, the courts use a "balancing test" to determine which rights prevail.

Take the hypothetical case of John Doe, a zealous brother in the Lord who feels called to present the gospel to patients in a local hospital. John goes to the hospital, takes the elevator to a floor with patient rooms, and starts preaching the message of salvation in the hallway in as loud a voice as he can muster. A nurse calls the police, and two officers show up a few minutes later and cart John off to jail. (Okay, I'll say it. Kids, don't try this in a hospital.)

When John appears in court, he can be charged neither with preaching a false gospel nor with even preaching a gospel that may be true. Remember, courts cannot discern whether the content of his message is true or false. What the court can do is charge John with disturbing the peace, creating a public nuisance, and, depending upon the hospital rules, trespassing. All of these charges are neutral on religion, regardless of the content of the message John was preaching.

If some of the patients in the hospital die unsaved and go to hell in a proverbial hand basket, the court cannot acknowledge that John's reaching them with the gospel might have resulted in their salvation. Nor can the court say that it would not have brought them to the cross of Christ. All a secular court can do is apply the law in a neutral manner.

A word or two about evangelistic methods might be appropriate here. It's all too common that a Christian who is arrested for screaming the gospel from a hospital hallway accuses the hospital, or the state, of engaging in religious discrimination. Such a charge is nonsense, if our hypothetical brother or sister in Christ does use such witnessing tactics. This is not a matter of religious discrimination, but obnoxious evangelism. In some of the cases we shall look at later, it's easy to assume that the government was prosecuting Christians merely because they engaged in evangelistic activities. Sometimes that is true, and sometimes the state is guilty of religious discrimination. But there are cases where poor judgment on the part of people engaging in personal evangelism or witnessing results in neutral laws being broken, and the state is not guilty of religious discrimination at all.

Sharing Our Space

Because the law cannot discern the truth or falsehood of religious beliefs, persons from all religions have an equal right to engage in personal evangelism and witnessing. At a busy intersection in any major city in the United States, evangelism may be done by Christians on one corner, Krishna devotees on another corner, Moonies on the third corner, and Buddhists on the fourth. The law says that every one of them has an equal right to do these evangelistic activities.

There is good news and bad news in the concept of a free and open marketplace of ideas. The bad news is that unsaved people are being exposed to a myriad of false religious teachings. Christians have a lot of competition out in the world and hope that people will choose to hang out on their corner rather than one of the other three.

The good news is that Christians have as much of a right to compete with the other religions as the others have to compete with Christianity. A number of elements will determine whether unsaved people will, in fact, choose Christianity over a false religious system. Obviously, prayer and the leading of the Holy Spirit are necessary elements in the evangelistic process. Another element is Christians' ability to present the gospel in an intelligent manner and the ability to persuade people to come to the cross of Christ rather than the ashram of a false god. I do not discuss the content of your evangelism in this book; however, I will take a moment to recommend that you read a book or two (or three or four) on how to present the gospel.

The area of study called apologetics is defined as the rational defense of the Christian faith. The concept comes from the apostle Peter's admonition, "Sanctify Christ as Lord in your hearts, always being ready to make a defense to every one who asks you to give an account for the hope that is in you, yet with gentleness and reverence" (1 Peter 3:15). The term *apologetics* comes from the Greek word *apologia*, which is translated "defense" in Peter's statement.

In the course of evangelistic activities I have seen street evangelists who did not know how to answer the objections of Krishna devotees to the gospel, Christians who could not articulate the Bible's position on homosexuality as they witnessed outside gay bars, and well-meaning brothers and sisters turned into theological pretzels by humanists or New Age adherents who could twist a philosophical phrase.

You may think that I am trying to make a point here. I am. The message of the gospel is a simple and powerful one, "to those who are perishing foolishness, but to us who are being saved it is the power of God" (1 Cor. 1:18). It's easy to be saved, requiring only that you place your trust in Jesus and accept him as your personal Lord and Savior. It's not quite as easy to communicate that message to a hostile world that does not want to hear the gospel, especially when the gospel you preach is not the same gospel that other religious groups are preaching.

Am I saying that there is more than one gospel? In a way I am. Paul wrote to the Galatians: "I am amazed that you are so quickly deserting Him who called you by the grace of Christ, for a different gospel; which is really not another; only there are some who are disturbing you, and want to distort the gospel of Christ. But even though we, or an angel from heaven, should preach to you a gospel contrary to that which we have preached to you, let him be accursed" (Gal. 1:6–8).

The problem is that people who hear false gospels preached by members of the cults and other non-Christian sects can just as easily buy into the false gospels as they can accept the biblical gospel of Jesus Christ. Paul lamented to the Corinthians: "For if one comes and preaches another Jesus whom we have not preached, or you receive a different spirit which you have not received, or a different gospel which you have not accepted, you bear this beautifully" (2 Cor. 11:4). The Living Bible renders Paul's judgment, "You seem so gullible. . . . You swallow it all."

In short, there is no excuse to hit the streets, schools, malls, libraries, rock concerts, stadiums, or anywhere else you can proclaim your faith without being prepared to articulate what the Christian faith is all about. Standing on a street corner and handing out tracts is an honorable form of personal evangelism, but if someone asks you why he or she should become a Christian, you should be prepared to provide an answer. It's interesting that the King James version of the Bible renders 1 Peter 3:15 thus: "Be ready always to give an answer to every man that asketh you a reason of the hope that is in you."

You don't have to be a theological scholar to utilize apologetics, just a Christian who has done your homework and can speak of your faith in an intelligent manner. And as much as I appreciate your reading this book, before you do street witnessing or another form of personal evangelism, you should read at least one other book on personal evangelism or apologetics to ensure that you are prepared to respond to some of the questions or objections you will run into on the street.

Jehovah's Witnesses for Christ?

As difficult as evangelism can be in this age of cults and "isms," it may surprise you to find out that many of the court cases that have had a positive effect on Christian witnessing have involved the cults. The issue of religious rights has had an impact on many faiths other than Christianity. Some of the groups that have brought religious rights cases to the forefront of the legal system include the Jehovah's Witnesses, Krishna Consciousness Movement, Mormons, Church of Scientology, and the Unification Church, all of which are cults.[10]

The Jehovah's Witnesses, for example, deny many of the foundational truths of the Christian faith, including the deity of Jesus, his bodily resurrection and visible return, the Trinity, and the existence of hell. Known officially as the Watchtower Bible and Tract Society, the Witnesses reject blood transfusions, the celebration of birthdays or holidays, military service, and saluting the flag. They also reject human government, though they have often been the first to challenge restrictions on their religious rights in the civil court system.

The Witnesses are also extremely evangelical in a generic sense, producing more evangelistic literature than all Christian denominations in the United States combined. They have more door-to-door and street-corner missionaries than any Christian denomination and zealously spread their teachings through magazines such as *The Watchtower* and *Awake!* Like many other religions, they also believe that only members of their own faith will be saved.

In 1940, the United States Supreme Court decided *Cantwell v. Connecticut*,[11] the first major case involving the right to engage in street ministry. Newton Cantwell and his sons Jesse and Russell, practicing Jehovah's Witnesses, were arrested while going door to door on Cassius Street in New Haven, Connecticut, then a predominantly Roman Catholic neighborhood. They played a phonograph record called "Enemies," which attacked the Catholic faith, to those who would listen. (Remember phonograph records? They were a novel item in those days.) Jesse Cantwell played the record for two men on the street who were Roman Catholic, angering them both to the point that they threatened to strike him unless he went away, after which he left their presence. Charged with inciting a breach of the peace, the Cantwells appealed their case to the Supreme Court, which ruled that the Connecticut statute regulating door-to-door solicitation was overbroad (too vague to be interpreted fairly and accurately) and gave the local government too much discretionary authority to regulate religious speech.

The case is notable for two reasons. For the first time, the Supreme Court articulated the incorporation doctrine (discussed in the last chapter) in a religious matter:

> We hold that the [solicitation] statute, as construed and applied to the appellants, deprives them of their liberty without due process of law in contravention of the Fourteenth Amendment. . . . The First Amendment declares that Congress shall make no law respecting an establishment of religion or prohibiting the free exercise thereof. The Fourteenth Amendment has rendered the legislatures of the states as incompetent as Congress to enact such laws.[12]

Second, the case provided a precedent that could apply not only to the Jehovah's Witnesses but also to Christians who wanted to engage in street ministry. You may have noticed that I have titled this part of the chapter "Jehovah's Witnesses for Christ?" Obviously, the Witnesses impede the gospel a lot more than they spread it, but there is a subtle point to make here: Even though it was not the Witnesses' intention to help Christians who want to carry on street ministry or door-to-door witness, the *Cantwell* case and other Jehovah's Witnesses cases have also helped affirm the right of Christians to engage in these activities.

In another Jehovah's Witness case three years later, the Supreme Court held that it was unconstitutional for the city of Jeannette, Pennsylvania, to charge a tax to persons doing door-to-door religious solicitation. In *Murdock v. Pennsylvania* (1943), Justice William O. Douglas powerfully described the evangelism process, especially the handing out of tracts, as a preferred right under the First Amendment, when he wrote:

> The hand distribution of religious tracts is an age-old form of missionary evangelism—as old as the history of printing presses. It has been a potent force in various religious movements down through the years. This form of evangelism is utilized today on a large scale by various religious sects whose [adherents] carry the Gospel to thousands upon thousands of homes and seek through personal visitations to win adherents to their faith. It is more than preaching; it is more than distribution of religious

literature. It is a combination of both. Its purpose is as evangelical as the revival meeting. This form of religious activity occupies the same high estate under the First Amendment as do worship in the churches and preaching from the pulpits. It has the same claim to protection as the more orthodox and conventional exercises of religion. It also has the same claim as the others to the guarantees of freedom of speech and freedom of the press.[13]

As you see some of the cases that have affected personal evangelism and witnessing, you will notice that many have involved non-Christian cults. Hopefully, the good-news-bad-news qualities of the cult cases are obvious. The bad news is that the cults are out there evangelizing people, much to our detriment and often more effectively than people are evangelized by Christians. The good news is that because the cults have won many court cases affirming their right to engage in evangelism, the same principles apply to Christians and affirm Christians' right to evangelize.

As much as it might be tempting to get the cults off the streets, let's hypothetically assume that the laws were different and that religious speech could be regulated based on its content. In 1988, Christians were morally outraged over Martin Scorcese's film *The Last Temptation of Christ*, which presented a distorted view of the Gospels. In addition to picketing Universal Studios, many Christians began to lobby for the passage of an antiblasphemy law to prevent future films from treating the Christian message in a blasphemous manner.

Fortunately, such a statute could not be passed, since an antiblasphemy law would require civil courts to determine what constitutes blasphemy. Under the Establishment Clause the courts are not allowed to do this, since to delineate between what is or is not blasphemous would require the courts to interpret religious doctrine, prohibited by several cases we examined earlier.

Lest you think I am a heretic for saying that the absence of an antiblasphemy law is fortunate, consider the ultimate consequences of such a statute. Since all religions are treated equally under the law, to declare blasphemy illegal would not only result in non-Christians losing their right to criticize Christianity, it would also result in Christians losing the right to criticize non-Christian religious beliefs. In fact, I could be prosecuted for exposing the beliefs of the Mormons, Jehovah's Witnesses, and other groups as false teachings in this book. The bottom line is that the sword cuts both ways.

There is another factor to be considered in terms of how the law deals with cults. Look at how Marc Galanter, a professor of psychiatry at the New York University School of Medicine, described a religious meeting in his book *Cults: Faith, Healing, and Coercion*:

> Neophytes would report their experiences of religious revival, often revealing that this had followed their involvement in the drug subculture. States of altered consciousness were called "gifts of the Holy Spirit" and were expected to lead members to a spiritual rebirth. These experiences included glossolalia, involuntary motor activities, and trances.[14]

What dastardly religious cult could Professor Galanter be exposing? What perverted teachings could such an ominous gathering represent? Galanter was writing about a charismatic prayer meeting.

The point is simple: To many people in the secular world, some expressions of Christianity are perceived to be as certainly cultic as are those of the Krishna Consciousness Movement or the Unification Church. Sociologist Stuart Wright makes the following comment:

> The term "cult" has been applied indiscriminately to such groups as Catholic Charismatics, Jews for Jesus, Maranatha Campus Ministries, and the Moral Majority. Jews for Jesus, a Hebrew-Christian missionary organization, has been the object of growing anti-cult activity among some traditional Jewish leaders and organizations, despite the lack of empirical evidence for brainwashing. . . . One recent "cult" targeted by deprogrammers appears to be the Assemblies of God denomination.[15]

Christians are engaged in spiritual warfare against, among others, the cults and must "put on the full armor of God, that you may be able to stand firm against the schemes of the devil. For our struggle is not against flesh and blood, but against the rulers, against the powers, against the world-forces of this darkness, against the spiritual forces of wickedness in the heavenly places" (Eph. 6:11–12). From the theological perspective, it's the old scenario of "us against them," and the prize consists of the souls of non-Christians who seek the ultimate answers to the questions in their lives. For the non-Christian who comes to the cross through Christian evangelistic efforts, the prize is eternal life itself.

In terms of civil law, however, Christians and cultists are in the same boat. What would sink cultists' right to evangelize would also sink Christians' right to evangelize. It is important, therefore, for Christians to keep the cults in perspective vis-à-vis personal evangelism and witnessing. Christians can support the legal rights of Jehovah's Witnesses, Mormons, and other cultists to engage in their evangelism, knowing that their doing so affirms the legal rights to engage in Christian witnessing. And Christians can do so without supporting the cults themselves or endorsing their false belief systems.

When a case goes before the Supreme Court, parties who are not involved in the case often file *amici curae*, or friend-of-the-court briefs. These legal papers are designed to inform the Court of the opinion of people who are not involved in the actual case but have an interest in its outcome. It is interesting to note that in many of the religious rights cases heard by the Supreme Court over the past twenty years that have involved cults, many of the *amici curae* that have been filed were written by evangelical Christian churches and denominations.[16] We do not endorse the cults and should continue to teach against the errors of their doctrines in our own churches, yet we know that if they lose the right to evangelize, so do we. Even if losing that right were to mean that thousands of people would not be exposed to the cults' false teachings, it is likely that they might not be exposed to the truth of biblical Christianity, either.

So, fellow soldiers, it's an open market out there, and there's a healthy competition going on that will help us either win or lose the cause for Christ. Assuming we want to win the battle, come with me on a trip through that marketplace, tripping over occasional pitfalls along the way, and letting the Lord—and the law—lift us back up to continue the battle.

/ 4 /

Taking the Word
to the Streets

O kay, campers, this is it. You've prayed about witnessing, and now you're about to go out onto the streets of your city to do personal evangelism. You may not feel comfortable yet about engaging people in dialogue about the gospel, so you've decided to get your feet wet by simply standing on a sidewalk and handing out tracts to passersby.

But which corner? Where do you stand? In the middle of the sidewalk or up against a building? Do you have to get a permit from the city or the police department to hand out tracts?

What about people who take a tract and then throw it away? Are you responsible for picking up the litter? What if a merchant walks out of his store and tells you that he doesn't want you distributing religious literature outside his store? What if you run into a Moonie who is selling roses? Can you stand in the same place and distribute Christian tracts?

What if a police officer walks up to you and tells you to move on? What if the officer says that you can't discuss religion with people who are willing to have a dialogue with you? Can you stand in one place while you hand out tracts, or do you have to keep moving so you won't be charged with loitering?

Are the people who may hassle you—others on the street, merchants, or the police—really out to get you because you are a Christian? Are they really antireligious, do they represent the Antichrist, or are they well-meaning citizens who don't know that you have rights, too?

Finally, once you get your feet wet and want to talk openly about the gospel with people, whether you approach them one-on-one or preach to a group of people on the street, can you do so legally?

Whew! You probably didn't realize there are so many legal questions about something as simple as handing out tracts. But there are, and most of those questions have been answered by the courts in favor of Christians.

To understand how firm are Christians' rights to distribute religious literature and use other means to proclaim their faith on the streets, it might help to define the word *street* in terms of the law.

A Forum Is More Than a Theater

Streets and parks have traditionally been considered by the court to be public forums, defined as public property that has as a principal purpose the free exchange of ideas. In *Hague v. Committee for Industrial Organization* (1939), Justice Owen J. Roberts recognized the role that public streets and parks had come to play in the dissemination of ideas when he wrote:

> Wherever the title of streets and parks may rest, they have immemorially been held in trust for the use of the public and, time out of mind, have been used for purposes of assembly, communicating thoughts between citizens, and discussing public questions. Such use of the streets and public places has, from ancient times, been a part of the privileges, immunities, rights, and liberties of citizens. The privilege of a citizen of the United States to use the streets and parks for communication of views on national questions may be regulated in the interest of all; it is not absolute, but relative, and must be exercised in subordination to the general comfort and convenience, and in consonance with peace and good order; but it must not, in the guise of regulation, be abridged or denied.[1]

Many evangelistic meetings have taken place on streets and in parks over the centuries, but perhaps the best-known meeting of this type is the one described by Luke in Acts chapter 17:

> [Paul] was reasoning in the synagogue with the Jews and God-fearing Gentiles, and in the market place every day with those who happened to be present. And also some of the Epicurean and Stoic philosophers were conversing with him. And some were saying, "What would this idle babbler wish to say?" Others, "He seems to be a proclaimer of strange deities"—because he was preaching Jesus and the resurrection. (Acts 17:17–18.)

The term *marketplace* comes from the Greek word *agora*. It was the center of civic life where philosophers debated and presented their views. The Epicurean and Stoic philosophers could be likened, respectively, to today's secularists and New Age adherents:

The Epicureans, who followed Epicurus (341–270 B.C.) said the chief end of man was pleasure and happiness. This pleasure, they believed, is attained by avoiding excesses and the fear of death, by seeking tranquillity from pain, and by loving mankind. They believed that if gods exist they do not become involved in human events.[2]

The Stoics, founded by Zeno (c. 300 B.C.), believed that God was the world's soul which indwelt all things, and that the happy life was lived in accordance with nature. Since God was in all men, all men were brothers.[3]

Because the Christian gospel was different from what the Epicureans and Stoics were used to, they brought Paul to the Council of the Areopagus, which met on the Hill of Ares (also known as Mars Hill) west of the Acropolis. The council had charge of religious and educational matters in Athens, a society noted for its curiosity, and Paul preached the gospel to them in the open-air gathering.

While Paul's sermon did not result in as many converts as other sermons he had preached, his message is notable for another reason. In his discourse, Paul referred to several aspects of the Athenian society. He said, "For while I was passing through and examining the objects of your worship, I also found an altar with this inscription, 'TO AN UNKNOWN GOD.' What therefore you worship in ignorance, I proclaim to you" (Acts 17:23). He later quoted the Cretan poet Epimenides and words that had been written in both Cleanthes's *Hymn to Zeus* and Cilician poet Aratus's *Phainomena*, "For in Him we live and move and exist, as even some of your own poets have said, 'For we also are His offspring'" (Acts 17:28). In other parts of the New Testament, Paul would quote Epimenides (Titus 1:12) and *Thais*, a comedy by the Greek poet Meander (1 Cor. 15:33).

Now, wait a second. Paul was trained as a rabbi, a persecutor of Christians who himself became a Christian and one of the most effective evangelists in history. How would he have been able to quote the writings of Greek poets to those he evangelized? The answer is simple. In the last chapter, we discussed the need to learn how to evangelize the unsaved. Paul had done his research well and was able to intelligently present the gospel in terms that the Gentiles would understand.

However, for our purposes, the main point is that Paul's discourse took place in the open marketplace (streets) and on a hill on which the chief counsel of Athens met (a park)—areas that we would call a public forum in the United States today.

Looking back to the description of streets and parks written by Justice Owen J. Roberts, however, we see that the use of a public forum is not without restriction:

> The privilege of a citizen of the United States to use the streets and parks for communication of views on national questions may be regulated in the interest of all; it is not absolute, but relative, and must be exercised in subordination to the general comfort and convenience, and in consonance with peace and good order.[4]

Under the law, the government may reasonably regulate the use of the streets in three ways: time, place, and manner. Any restrictions in these three areas must be narrowly tailored to meet a compelling state interest (such as the peace and good order of society), construed by the courts in favor of free speech whenever possible, and objectively worded so they do not leave subjective discretionary authority to an individual. They must leave open ample alternative channels of communication, and must be neutrally applied without regard to the content of the message (meaning that the government cannot restrict speech merely because its content is religious, political, or philosophical).

To Everything a Time, Place, and Manner

In the last chapter I presented a scenario in which John Doe, a hypothetical but overzealous evangelist, was arrested for loudly preaching the gospel in the hallway of a hospital where there were patient rooms.

Since a hospital does not constitute a public forum, let's change the scenario a bit and have our zealous brother in Christ preaching on the sidewalk outside the hospital. John is waving a ninety-pound Scofield Reference Bible, loudly preaching that the world, including the patients inside the hospital, needs to be saved. Everything John says is doctrinally correct, but there is one problem: He is making a racket.

If the city in which the hospital is located has a statute saying that preaching the gospel outside a hospital is prohibited, it is likely that such a statute would be declared unconstitutional: It restricts speech based on the *content* of the message. If, on the other hand, the city has a law saying that no loud speeches can be delivered on the sidewalk outside a hospital, the statute would be considered reasonable, neutral in content, and not intended to discriminate against religion. In *Grayned v. Rockford* (1972), for example, the Supreme Court upheld the enforcement of an antinoise ordinance outside a school because loud speech interrupted the central purpose of the school. Holding that the nature and pattern of normal activities of an institution or organization dictate appropriate noise levels immediately outside the premises, the Court held the ordinance to be a reasonable time, place, and manner restriction.[5] John's noisy evangelism on the hospital sidewalk could likewise be constitutionally prohibited, assuming that such an antinoise statute were not directed exclusively at religious speech.

Now, let's move our friend John Doe away from the hospital and put him on the corner of any secular nighttime gathering spot in any major city—42nd Street in New York City, Hollywood Boulevard in Los Angeles, or South Street in Philadelphia, for example. Obviously, John will have a lot more freedom to wave his ninety-pound Scofield and preach to his heart's content.

Or would he? Let's assume that John is such a dynamic preacher that he begins to attract a crowd. A big crowd. Let's say a really big crowd. At that point, reasonable time, place, and manner restrictions are likely to come into play. Such neutrally written restrictions that might be used to prevent John from preaching could include the following:

A disruption of the free flow of pedestrian traffic along the sidewalk, causing people to have to move into the streets to get around the crowd that has gathered to hear John preach.

The spreading of the crowd out into the street, disrupting the free flow of vehicular traffic.

Interference with ingress or egress, meaning that people are blocked from entering a place of business or other building because of the crowd gathered on the sidewalk outside the doors.

Interference with activities going on inside a building. If John's preaching carried into a theater while a ballet was in process and interfered with the audience's ability to enjoy the performance, prohibiting his preaching would be a reasonable time, place, and manner restriction (again, as long as the prohibition was generically directed at obtrusive noise and not against the religious content of his speech).

The use of "fighting words," or other speech that would cause a "clear and present danger." For example, if John is challenging people in such a manner that an altercation, fight, or even a riot is likely (or if the crowd is violently challenging John), then the police may constitutionally prevent him from continuing based on the legal doctrine of a clear and present danger. The mere fact that the crowd may disagree with John, or that the content of his speech is unpopular, is not enough to restrict his freedom of speech; the threat of civil disturbance or violence has to be of an immediate or imminent nature.

So what is John's solution? Simple: Move to a spot where traffic will not be impeded, an audience will not be disturbed, people are not blocked from getting into or out of a building, and the crowd is not sufficiently agitated to start physical violence. At that point the law says that John has every right to do his street preaching.

The bottom line is that the right to spread the gospel in a public forum is absolute but may be subject to reasonable time, place, and manner restrictions. The following cases serve as examples:

In *Eanes v. State* (1990), the Supreme Court of Maryland held that a statute which makes it a crime to disturb neighborhoods with "loud and unseemly noises" does not violate the First Amendment. Eanes had been arrested for preaching the gospel in a loud voice in front of an abortion clinic in a residential/business neighborhood, without a sound system but loud enough to be heard above the traffic. The court held that the statute was constitutional because it was content neutral (that is, not directly addressed to religious speech).[6]

In *City of Lakewood v. Elsass* (1989), the Ohio Court of Appeals held that a person's conviction for unlawful congregation while proclaiming his religious views and refusal to move when ordered by the police was not unconstitutional. Why? Because he and two other persons were standing in front of a driveway at the time, an example of "blocking ingress and egress."[7]

In *Ohio v. Livingston* (1986), the Ohio Court of Appeals upheld the conviction of a Baptist minister for violating a noise ordinance during an outdoor crusade, after neighbors complained. He challenged the trial court's decision on the basis of freedom of speech, but in rejecting his challenge the court noted that it was the volume of his speech, not its content, that was the basis for his conviction.[8]

In *Heffron v. International Society for Krishna Consciousness* (1981), the Minnesota Agricultural Society restricted the distribution of literature, exhibition of materials, and sale of goods at the Minnesota state fair to booths rented from the agricultural society. The United States Supreme Court upheld the agricultural society's rule, holding that it was neutrally applied without discrimination and that the state's interest in the orderly movement of crowds and avoidance of congestion justified the rule.[9]

In *Chaplinsky v. New Hampshire* (1942), the Supreme Court held that the conviction of a Jehovah's Witness for being verbally abusive toward a police marshal while distributing religious literature was constitutional, and that his freedom of religion was not violated, because he was using "fighting words," which are not protected speech.[10]

Meanwhile, our friend John Doe has been preaching so long and loudly that at this point we will assume he has a touch of laryngitis. Therefore, John decides merely to hand out tracts to people as they pass by and to engage in dialogue on a one-on-one basis with individuals who might be interested in learning more about the Christian faith.

Can John hand out religious literature without restriction? Absolutely, provided he is not standing in one place in the middle of a narrow sidewalk and causing people to divert around him. He might stand up against a building or next to a permanent fixture such as a lamppost or traffic signal pole. At that point, he can distribute tracts without restriction.

There is just one problem: Out of every hundred tracts John hands out, the recipients toss fifty of them into the street or onto the sidewalk. In theory, John is creating a lot of litter.

Or is he? Believe it or not, John cannot be arrested for littering, in our scenario, provided he is not the one doing the littering. Even if 100 percent of the tracts he distributes are tossed away by the people to whom he gives them, and the city is stuck with the cost of picking them up, John is neither responsible nor liable. In *Schneider v. State* (1939), the United States Supreme Court held that municipalities may not prevent the distribution of literature based upon the cost of cleaning up the litter.

We are of [the] opinion that the purpose [of keeping] the street clean and of good appearance is insufficient to justify an ordinance which prohibits a person rightfully on a public street from handing literature to one willing to receive it. Any burden imposed upon the city authorities in cleaning and caring for the streets as an indirect consequence of such distribution results from the constitutional protection of freedom of speech and press. This constitutional protection does not deprive a city of all power to prevent street littering. There are obvious methods of preventing littering. Amongst these is the punishment of those who actually throw the papers on the streets.[11]

One final question should be addressed: Does John need a permit to distribute literature or engage in street preaching? Generally, the answer is no, because the requirement of a permit to engage in protected First Amendment activities is legally considered a "prior restraint" (the unconstitutional restraint of speech before it is spoken) and, except in the case of parades or large demonstrations (including large religious services), most ordinances requiring a permit for individual evangelistic activities are unconstitutional. Permits are not necessary for literature distribution, one-on-one discussions, or even small group gatherings (keeping in mind that the definition of small is subjective and can be mandated in a neutrally written statute).

In *Kunz v. City of New York* (1951), a Baptist preacher was convicted of holding a religious meeting on a street without a permit after his application for a permit had been denied. The Supreme Court held that the permit requirement was too vague to be fairly interpreted and that the requirement violated both the First and Fourteenth Amendments.[12]

More recently, a federal district court ruled that a city ordinance in Swansea, South Carolina, requiring those wishing to speak in public to procure a permit was an unconstitutional prior restraint on the First Amendment freedoms of speech and assembly. The court held that the ordinance was overbroad and did not provide objective standards to guide the licensing authority, resulting in too much discretionary power given to individuals to deny such permits.[13]

Before the Parade Passes By

In cases involving parades, large demonstrations, or religious services, permits are normally required to ensure that enough police protection is on hand to maintain civil order. Again, providing that such requirements are content neutral and applied without religious discrimination, they will generally be found to be constitutional.

Discerning the difference between a small group and a large gathering can sometimes be subjective. However, ordinances or statutes that require permits cannot be written in such a manner that they leave the subjective decision to an individual who can use a religiously discriminatory standard.

In *Cox v. New Hampshire* (1941), another Jehovah's Witnesses case, the Supreme Court held that to require a permit for a parade or procession is both constitutional and consistent with the goal of public safety.

> Civil liberties, as guaranteed by the Constitution, imply the existence of an organized society maintaining public order without which liberty itself would be lost in the excesses of unrestrained abuses. The authority of a municipality to impose regulations in order to assure the safety and convenience of the people in the use of public highways has never been regarded as inconsistent with civil liberties but rather as one of the means of safeguarding the good order upon which they ultimately depend.[14]

The Philadelphia, Pennsylvania, police department has a policy that provides a good, neutrally written example of the standards used to govern the religious activities of both individuals and of large groups. Philadelphia Police Department Directive 94A states the following:

> Under our constitution, every citizen is free to make a speech on any lawful subject to a public gathering. Normally, such speeches are called "Street Corner Meetings."
>
> Such speeches when made on sidewalks, public squares, or parks and other similar areas do not require a Permit. Displaying or carrying of banners with a political, social, or religious message is free speech and therefore permissible. Persons carrying banners are not required to move about, provided they are not impeding the movement of pedestrian or vehicular traffic. They are exercising their right of free speech by the use of and display of the printed word or picture.
>
> As long as these assemblies are conducted in a lawful and peaceable manner, police personnel have no authority to interfere.
>
> However, unusually large crowds may require the services and protection of police. For instance, spectators should not be permitted to occupy the street risking their own safety and creating a traffic hazard. Pass-

ing pedestrians should have free access to the sidewalk and not have to walk around the crowd and into the street.

The Philadelphia Traffic Code requires that a Permit be secured from the Department of Licenses and Inspections before any parade, procession or assemblages shall occupy, march or proceed along any street. Approval or disapproval is limited to consideration of traffic control.

It is the duty and responsibility of police personnel to protect the basic right of free speech and lawful assembly, to protect the rights and safety of the public, and to prevent any acts of violence.[15]

Note that the Philadelphia regulations are neutrally written and not solely directed to religious speech. The directive provides an example of the fact that all free speech is protected including that which is political, philosophical, social, and religious.

Literature Distribution versus Solicitation

All of the principles presented thus far assume that you are distributing religious literature (which may include tracts, pamphlets, New Testaments, or any other type of literature) free of charge, or that you are engaging in other activities such as street preaching without charge. The law, however, may say something different about the sale of such literature for a price or the solicitation of financial contributions.

Local or state governments can, for example, regulate the solicitation of funds, provided they do so in a neutral manner that does not discriminate against religious groups and that is narrowly tailored to meet a compelling state interest. For example, in *International Society for Krishna Consciousness v. City of Baton Rouge* (1989), the Federal Court of Appeals for the Fifth Circuit held that a city ordinance prohibiting the solicitation of employment, business, or charitable contributions from the occupants of vehicles driving on the street did not violate the Krishna devotees' constitutional rights. While the court acknowledged that the streets constituted a public forum, it found that the ordinance was content neutral and designed to assure the free movement of vehicles.[16]

On the other hand, in *Gaudiya Vaishnava Society v. City and County of San Francisco* (1990), the Ninth Circuit Court of Appeals affirmed a lower court injunction against a city ordinance that prohibited the sale of "expressive merchandise" without a license. Expressive merchandise may include Bibles, books, or other religious items and, in the case of cults, it may include items such as roses or incense. The court noted that charitable solicitation is "characteristically intertwined with informative and perhaps persuasive speech" and prohibited the city from enforcing the ordinance against nonprofit organizations with regard to the sale of merchandise "inextricably intertwined with a statement carrying a religious, philosophical, or ideological message."[17] Note, however, that the court's opinion is limited to nonprofit organizations (which would include churches) and does not necessarily apply to individuals who are not selling expressive merchandise through a church or religious organization.

In *City of Angeles Mission Church v. City of Houston, Texas* (1989), a federal district court declared a city ordinance making it illegal to solicit funds on city streets to be unconstitutional. Holding that access to public streets is an essential element of the freedoms of speech and the press, the court ruled that the ordinance was unreasonably broad and also violated the church members' rights under the equal protection clause of the Fourteenth Amendment.[18]

If a solicitation ordinance is neutrally written and narrowly tailored to meet a compelling state interest, however, it will likely be found to be constitutional. In addition to the compelling state interests we have reviewed thus far, such as keeping the peace, ensuring the free flow of pedestrian and vehicular traffic, and maintaining ingress into and egress from buildings, other compelling state interests include the protection of citizens from fraud. In *International Society for Krishna Consciousness of Houston, Inc. v. City of Houston* (1982), a federal appeals court upheld a city solicitation ordinance requiring persons who wish to do charitable solicitation to register with the city, holding that the city had a compelling interest in protecting its citizens from fraud and harassment.[19] Unlike other cases, this is one where the cults have had a negative impact on Christians who do solicitation (the Unification Church's doctrine of "divine deception" comes to mind), though such a statute helps ensure that fraudulent solicitation will not be carried out in the name of Christianity. (This has occurred in cases of fake priests soliciting funds in airports in California. You'd be surprised at how easy it is for anyone to buy a clerical shirt or nun's habit. One friend of mine was even approached at an airport by a Krishna devotee in a Santa Claus suit who greeted him, "Merry Krishna!")

Finally, if you sell expressive merchandise for a fixed price (rather than for a charitable contribution to be determined by the person making the donation), you may be responsible for collecting sales taxes. In *Jimmy Swaggart Ministries v. Board of Equalization of the State of California* (1990), the Supreme Court determined that states have the right to impose a sales tax upon items sold by religious organizations.[20] The imposition of sales taxes is determined on a state-by-state basis, so you should consult an attorney or accountant to determine whether you would be liable for this if you sell religious items in the course of your ministry.

So What's the Upshot?

Despite the fact that some street activities can be restricted by the state, the streets remain one of the most open places in which to do personal evangelism. Obviously, certain techniques will help ensure your right to freely witness without being harassed or arrested, such as the following:

Walk while you distribute tracts or literature, or stand along a fixed structure such as a building, light post, or traffic signal pole. Above all, don't place yourself in a position in which you block pedestrian or vehicular traffic.

If a person refuses to take a tract, don't force it on him or her. There are lots of opportunities to distribute your tracts; just offer it to the next person.

If someone stops and wants to engage in dialogue with you, don't do it in the middle of the sidewalk. Again, move to the edge of the sidewalk or up against a fixed structure so you will not impede the flow of traffic.

If you feel called to preach out loud, do so in a location where a gathering of people will not interfere with the flow of traffic on the sidewalk or in the street, or where your preaching will not interfere with other nearby activities.

If you engage in open street preaching, be careful not to incite a "clear-and-present danger" situation that could result in your arrest. Remember, your goal is to bring people to the cross of Christ, not to cause a confrontation.

If you and a group of other Christians engage in an activity such as street theater, singing, or the use of props such as an easel board, conduct your activities where there is enough space to allow interested people to gather without blocking traffic.

Meanwhile, you have planned your evangelism strategy and have followed the law to ensure that your witness or literature distribution will not interfere with the normal flow of activities on the street. What if you are hassled by a police officer or merchant despite the care you have taken to make sure your activities are within the law?

The most important thing to realize here is that if you are acting within the law, there are two possible reasons you will be hassled. The first is that the person who tries to prevent you from witnessing is anti-Christian or antireligious and simply does not want the gospel message spread on the street. Yes, it may even be the Antichrist! Or, as Dana Carvey might ask in his role as the Church Lady on "Saturday Night Live," "Could this be . . . Saaataan?"

The second reason may be that the person who interferes with your activities simply does not know that the law is in your favor, that free speech (including the content of that speech) is protected under the law, and that to interfere with your activities constitutes an infringement of your constitutional rights under the First Amendment and, possibly, religious discrimination.

It's easy to assume that interference with evangelistic activities is based on the first reason. We Christians sometimes think that the entire world is "out to get us" then indiscriminately quote Scripture verses about how Satan wants to destroy the church.

Sometimes that's true. But more often than not, we deal with an innocent ignorance of the law by well-meaning people who don't know what the Constitution and the courts have to say about the right to engage in public discourse.

In such cases, you have several weapons at your disposal. Prayer is obviously the most important one, but another is tact. An old expression is "You can catch more flies with honey than with vinegar." Therefore, here are a few suggestions on how to deal with harassment when you do personal evangelism on the street:

Consider moving to another location. If you can accomplish as much down the street as you can where you are being hassled, weigh your options and move on. Remember that in the time you spend discussing your right to witness, you could be witnessing instead.

Get to know the legal precedents in this book that work in your favor. Try to remember the names of appropriate cases and the years in which they were decided (you don't have to remember the actual legal citations). Be prepared to refer these cases to people who object to your right to witness. That will indicate that, like the apostle Paul, you have done your research, that you may know more about the law than the person with whom you speak, and that you are on firm legal ground.

If the person challenging you is a police officer, weigh your actions carefully. In any given city or town, the police may or may not have been trained in laws regarding street witnessing (you cannot make a presumption either way). Also, the police often assume that persons on a street discoursing with strangers are involved in drug dealing or prostitution. It may be helpful for you to approach an officer on patrol before you begin to witness or distribute literature so he or she knows why you are on the street.

Remember that those who cause trouble on the street usually are doing something illegal—prostitution, dealing drugs, committing vandalism, etc. The police, merchants, and neighborhood residents assume that anyone engaging in activities out of the ordinary may be doing something illegal. Be sure to make your purpose and the nature of your activities known up front so people don't think your activities are illegal. If you are in a high-crime area or an area where activities such as prostitution or drug dealing take place, it may help to mention that your goal is the same as those of citizens in the neighborhood—to stop these activities. You just do it in a different way: by trying to lead people to Christ.

When possible, work in a team. For example, witness in a two-person team or at least close enough to another person geographically so that if you are harassed you will have another Christian close by to back you up and to confirm the nature of your activities. It's no secret that some of the best evangelism takes place when Christians go out into the world two-by-two.

Be especially careful about evangelizing in potentially compromising or dangerous situations. Single women should not witness alone in a prostitution district, and single males should not witness alone outside a gay bar or in an area known for sexual cruising or hustling (male prostitution). In areas where drug dealing takes place, remember that there is safety in numbers. Your presence in some environments may give non-Christians the wrong impression or may be a stumbling block for Christians with whom you engage in evangelism. That does not mean that you should not witness in these situations, just that you should use caution and consider any negative ramifications. Above all, you should witness in a way "that you may prove yourselves to be blameless and innocent, children of God above reproach in the midst of a crooked and perverse generation, among whom you appear as lights in the world" (Phil. 2:15).

If you witness in an area where compromising or illegal activities take place (such as prostitution, hustling, drug use, or homosexual cruising), be careful about being caught up in a police "sweep." Very often, police departments round up persons in these areas and arrest all those they perceive to be involved in such activities. Depending on where the arrests take place, people are held for a few hours and issued a citation or bench warrant (requiring them to voluntarily show up in court at a later date), or, in some offenses, they may also be arraigned in court and required to post bail. There are two considerations in deciding how you might deal with a sweep. The first is that your presence in a questionable location may be misconstrued, even if you are there for a legitimate purpose. This may be a stumbling block for other Christians or have a negative effect on your own testimony as a Christian. On the other hand, if you allow yourself to be included in a sweep, you potentially have several hours to present the gospel to a captive audience (literally) that isn't going to walk out on you. Even prostitutes (and their customers), homosexuals, drug users, and others who are arrested are likely to be upset, and they may be open to counsel and receive the gospel. However, before including yourself in a police roundup you should carefully weigh the ramifications of your decision.

If you engage in street ministry as part of an organized program or evangelism class through your church, Bible college, or seminary, you should consider asking your pastor or evangelism professor for a letter that will confirm who you are, describe the program or ministry in which you are involved, and outline the activities in which you will engage. Remember that as far as the police are concerned, if you are found with a group of persons engaging in illegal activities it's most likely you are involved in those activities yourself. If you don't want to be arrested in a sweep, it will be helpful if you are able to produce documentation that will attest to your legitimate purpose in such an environment.

If you are going to witness in a popular or crowded gathering area of a major city or an area where questionable activities take place (especially on a regular basis), it will also be helpful for you to call or stop in the local police station and introduce yourself to the police chief, commanding officer, or shift commander. Remember, the police are generally not hostile to street ministry activities; they just like to know what's going on in their district or patrol area.

Above all, remember that Jesus did his work on the cross for everyone, including people who may hassle you. If you are hostile to them in return, you may lose the chance to lead them to Christ.

If you feel there is a possibility that you may be arrested for engaging in protected First Amendment activities and you are willing to take that risk (something about which you've hopefully prayed in advance), make sure you carry the name and phone number of a lawyer who is familiar with First Amendment issues. You should identify such a lawyer in your area before the possibility of an arrest presents itself. (See chapter 13, "Getting Help When You're Hassled," for assistance in this area.)

If you see someone else being arrested, whether or not the arrest appears legitimate, do not interfere with the arrest or step between a police officer and a suspect. Do your observing from the sidelines so you won't be charged with interfering with a police officer. Likewise, if you are being arrested, do not resist (or you might be charged with resisting arrest). Go peaceably, and call a lawyer from the police station.

/ 5 /

Taking the Word
to the Malls

Over the past twenty-five years the living patterns of the American public have changed significantly. What was in the 1930s to 1950s a move from rural culture to urban centers has turned into a move from urban centers to sprawling suburbs that surround most large cities in the nation. As the suburbs have developed into prime living centers, so has another institution of American culture: the shopping mall. In 1992, there were over 38,000 malls in the United States, ranging in style from outdoor shopping centers to enclosed megaplexes that offer every type of store, restaurant, and entertainment you could ever want.[1]

Additionally, the malls represent an expression of American buying patterns today. Even in the case of young people, the days are gone when kids received a five-dollar-a-week allowance to use for a movie, some popcorn, and a soda. Notwithstanding the fact that five bucks would not pay for most movies today, more and more high school and junior high students work at part-time jobs to earn their own money and wouldn't think twice about spending a hundred dollars or more on a pair of Nikes or Reeboks.

Yet malls have become more than places to shop. Suburban culture is more and more prominent in the United States, and the malls have turned into primary social gathering places appealing to all ages from the very young to the very old. And why not? They have everything to offer: movies, places to eat, monolithic department stores, clothing stores for all sizes and shapes, video arcades, and even mall-walker clubs in which senior citizens can get indoor exercise in all types of weather. They have benches, greeneries, and atriums at which one can simply sit and watch other people pass by, and they often provide medical and preventive health services ranging from Weight Watchers meetings to free blood pressure screenings performed by local hospitals. Some even have churches, so people can shop, eat, and pray under the same roof.

Malls have not only supplemented urban and downtown shopping districts, in many cities and towns malls have replaced them. In some cities, underground malls share their space with stores located along the street, but in many suburbs the mall is virtually the only place one can find a comprehensive shopping or entertainment experience.

In short, the mall has become America's favorite hangout. You don't have anything better to do today, tonight, or over the weekend? No problem; let's go to the mall!

Now, perhaps you're already thinking what I'm thinking—that the mall presents one of the best opportunities for personal evangelism available today. High school kids, college students, singles, senior citizens, and others hanging out with nothing better to do. People just waiting to hear those magic words, "Say, do you know that God loves you and has a wonderful plan for your life?" Let's face it, in many areas the mall has replaced the street as the place to witness.

Unfortunately, life isn't that simple. While streets, parks, and other areas offer an unlimited opportunity to present the gospel, witnessing at the malls is treated differently under the law, and the news is often discouraging.

A Forum Is Still More Than a Theater

In the last chapter we saw how streets and parks are legally considered public forums, places in which free speech has absolute protection, subject to reasonable time, place, and manner restrictions. The Supreme Court has defined the following types of forums, each of which is subject to various degrees of regulation in regard to First Amendment freedoms:

Public forums, such as streets and parks, defined as those places that "have immemorially been held in trust for the use of the public and, time out of mind, have been used for purposes of assembly, communicating thoughts between citizens, and discussing public questions."[2]

Designated public forums, consisting of "public property which the State has opened for use by the public as a place for expressive activity."[3] Examples include university meeting facilities, school-board meetings, and municipally owned theaters. A state is not required to indefinitely retain the open character of a facility, but as long as it does so it is bound by the same standards that apply to a traditional public forum.[4]

Limited open forums. This term came into vogue with the Equal Access Act of 1984 (see the next chapter, "Taking the Word to School") and is often used with regard to public schools and libraries that have opened themselves to noncurriculum-related activities or outside community use.

Nonpublic forums, consisting of government or municipally owned property that is not by tradition or designation a forum for public communication.[5] Such properties may be reserved for their intended purposes and would include post offices, military bases, hospitals, transportation centers (including airports), and schools and libraries that have not opened themselves as limited public forums.

Note that all types of forums mentioned above have one thing in common: The properties are all public in nature and owned by a government (federal, state, or local). If a shopping mall is owned by the government, for example, its forum classification would be determined by the extent to which the government has opened it to First Amendment communications. It could be a nonpublic forum (intended to be used solely for the purpose for which it was designed) or a designated public forum (meaning that while the government does not have to open it for First Amendment purposes, it may choose to do so).

Now the bad news: Shopping malls that are not owned by the government, which includes most of the malls in the United States, are private property and do not have to be opened for expressive activities of any kind. The reason for this is that the courts weigh the First Amendment freedoms of religion, speech, and assembly against the Fifth Amendment freedom of private property rights.

Most people are familiar with the Fifth Amendment in the context of criminal trials and self-incrimination; hence the old expression "taking the Fifth." The entire amendment reads:

No person shall be held to answer for a capital, or otherwise infamous crime, unless on a presentment or indictment of a Grand Jury, except in cases arising in the land or naval forces, or in the Militia, when in actual service in time of War or public danger; nor shall any person be subject for the same offence to be twice put in jeopardy of life or limb; nor shall be compelled in any criminal case to be a witness against himself, nor be deprived of life, liberty, or property, without due process of law; *nor shall private property be taken for public use without just compensation.*[6]

Federal law says that if I build a mall and choose to prevent you from spreading the gospel in my mall, I can do so. Why? Because it's my mall. As we shall see shortly, there are a number of reasons that this could change in the future, but at this point the law is on the side of the mall owner. However, some states have interpreted their own constitutions to allow more First Amendment privileges to their citizens, and their laws may take precedence over the federal law.

The fact that most courts have determined that malls are private property that do not have to be opened to expressive speech does not mean that the malls are necessarily off-limits to personal evangelism. In addition to looking at some of the legal precedents, we shall also look at some methods that may be helpful to someone who wants to engage in personal evangelism in the malls.

I Owe My Soul to the Company Store

It may sound like a strange subchapter heading, but "I owe my soul to the company store" comes from "Sixteen Tons," a song popularized in the 1950s by the late Christian country singer Tennessee Ernie Ford. Ford described a phenomenon known as company towns. Companies had built large factories or developed mines in rural areas and constructed entire towns for their workers, usually in the southern United States. There are few company towns left today, but one case involving a company town had a significant impact on religious rights.

Chickasaw, Alabama, was built and wholly owned by the Gulf Shipbuilding Company. In a First Amendment dispute in the early 1940s, a Jehovah's Witness attempted to distribute religious literature on a sidewalk near the town post office and was arrested on a trespassing charge. Finding that his rights under the First Amendment and Fourteenth Amendment were infringed, the Supreme Court declared, in *Marsh v. Alabama* (1946), that despite the entire town's ownership by a private corporation, the town itself was a public forum because it was, in fact, a town:

Except for ownership [by a private corporation] it has all the characteristics of any other American town. The property consists of residential buildings, streets, a system of sewers, a sewage disposal plant, and a "business block" on which business places are situated. A deputy of the Mobile County Sheriff, paid by the company, serves as the town's policeman. Merchants and service establishments have rented the stores and business places on the business block and the United States post office uses one of the places as a post office from which six carriers deliver mail to the people of Chickasaw and the adjacent area. The town and the surrounding neighborhood, which can not be distinguished from the Gulf property by anyone not familiar with the property lines, are thickly settled, and according to all indications the residents use the business block as their regular shopping center. To do so, they now, as they have for many years, make use of a company-owned paved street and sidewalk located alongside the store fronts in order to enter and leave the stores and the post office. Intersecting company-owned roads at each end of the business block lead into a four-lane public highway which runs parallel to a business block, at a distance of thirty feet. There is nothing to stop highway traffic from coming on the business block, and upon arrival a traveler may make free use of the facilities available there. In short, the town and its shopping district are accessible to and freely used by the public in general and there is nothing to distinguish them from any other town and shopping center except the fact that the title to the property belongs to a private corporation.[7]

Discussing the rationale behind its decision, the Court wrote: "Many people in the United States live in company-owned towns. These people, just as residents of municipalities, are free citizens of their State and country. Just as all other citizens they must make decisions which affect the welfare of community and nation. To act as good citizens they must be informed."[8]

The *Marsh* decision has been cited by plaintiffs in cases that attempt to affirm the right to engage in First Amendment activities in shopping malls today, but thus far the courts have held that the malls retain their private property characteristics. However, as the malls continue to become prevalent places in which social interaction takes place in the suburbs, and new planned communities are built by private real estate developers, it is possible that future mall cases will be decided in favor of First Amendment rights.

The Supreme Court and the Malls

In 1968, the Supreme Court decided one of its first cases dealing with shopping centers. The Logan Valley Plaza, located near Altoona, Pennsylvania, refused to allow peaceful picketing at Weis Markets, a supermarket chain that had opened a store at the mall and employed a nonunion staff. The union picketed in the parcel pickup area adjacent to the store and on the mall parking lot, and the store obtained a court injunction against the picketing. The Supreme Court granted review, and in *Amalgamated Food Employees Union v. Logan Valley Plaza* held that because the pickets addressed the specific way the store was operated, the right of the union to picket was firm and the state could not interfere with the exercise of First Amendment rights "on the premises in a manner and for a purpose generally consonant with the use to which the property is actually put."[9]

However, in the following paragraph the Court limited the scope of the decision, which did not extend to a blanket ruling that would have made the Logan Valley Plaza open to expressive activities:

> The picketing carried on by [the union] was directed specifically at patrons of the Weis Market located within the shopping center and the message sought to be conveyed to the public *concerned the manner in which that particular market was being operated.* We are, therefore, not called upon to consider whether [the shopping center's] property rights could, consistently with the First Amendment, justify a ban on picketing which was not thus directly related in its purpose to the use to which the shopping center property was being put.[10]

Though the Court's decision did not open the shopping center to First Amendment activity in general, it could be used to justify Christian activities that are directed against a mall tenant as a form of protest. For example, if a movie theater at a mall were to show a religiously offensive film such as Martin Scorcese's *The Last Temptation of Christ,* and local Christians wanted to protest the film's showing, such a protest would concern the manner in which the movie theater was being operated and could be legal under the principles enumerated in *Logan Valley*. However, *Logan Valley* does not endorse personal evangelism activities that are not addressed to the specific way a facility at the mall is operated.

In 1968, a peace education group called the Resistance Community was ejected from the Lloyd Center, an enclosed mall in Portland, Oregon, when it attempted to distribute literature protesting the Vietnam War. The Federal District Court issued an injunction prohibiting the mall from interfering with the Resistance Community, and the Court of Appeals for the Ninth Circuit affirmed the ruling. Both courts based their decisions on the Supreme Court rulings in *Marsh v. Alabama* and *Amalgamated Food Employees Union v. Logan Valley Plaza* and held that the Lloyd Center was open to the public and functioned as the equivalent of a public business district; thus its prohibition of the distribution of handbills violated First Amendment rights.[11]

The Supreme Court accepted the case for review and for the first time addressed the general distribution of literature in a typical enclosed mall of today. The Lloyd Center covered some fifty acres, including twenty acres devoted to parking that could accommodate over one thousand automobiles. The mall covered an area of almost one and one-half miles, directly bounded by four public streets. There were sixty commercial tenants, including small shops and several major department stores, some of which opened directly on the outside public sidewalks but most of which opened on the privately owned interior mall area. The interior space of the mall included ten-foot sidewalks and a thirty-foot wide center strip containing plants, statues, fountains, benches, and other amenities. An architect described the mall by observing, "Here the shopper is isolated from the noise, fumes, confusion and distraction which he normally finds along city streets, and a controlled, carefree environment is provided."[12]

The mall had a blanket policy against the distribution of handbills within the building complex, neutrally applied, since literature distribution "was considered likely to annoy customers, to create litter, potentially to create disorders, and generally to be incompatible with the purpose of the Center and the atmosphere sought to be preserved."[13] Despite the prohibition on distributing handbills, the mall had nonetheless opened itself to the use of its auditorium and charitable solicitation by community organizations including the Cancer Society, Boy and Girl Scouts, American Legion, Salvation Army, and Volunteers of America. Other groups could rent the auditorium for a fee, and though the mall also had a prohibition against political use it did allow presidential candidates from both parties to speak in the auditorium.[14]

Despite the *Marsh* precedent that had opened company towns to First Amendment activities as well as the previous *Logan Valley* decision, which held that picketing related to the activities of the property was constitutional, the Supreme Court overturned the lower court rulings against the Lloyd Center and ruled that there is no constitutional right to distribute literature in a privately owned shopping mall. In reaching its decision in *Lloyd Corporation v. Tanner* (1972), the Court quoted a dissenting opinion by Justice Byron White in *Logan Valley* and noted that the mall was designed for a specific purpose:

> In no sense are any parts of the shopping center dedicated to the public for general purposes. . . . The public is invited to the premises but only in order to do business with those who maintain establishments there. The invitation is to shop for the products which are sold. There is no general invitation to use the parking lot, the pickup zone, or the sidewalk except as an adjunct to shopping.[15]

Regardless of the fact that the Lloyd Center's facilities were used for meetings and promotional activities, the obvious purpose of a shopping mall, the Court observed, was for members of the public "to come to the Center to do business with the tenants . . . to bring potential shoppers to the Center, to create a favorable impression, and to generate goodwill."[16]

The Resistance Community contended that the mall was open to the public, served the same purposes as the "business district" of a municipality, and therefore had been dedicated to certain types of public use that would include First Amendment rights. Rejecting their argument, the Court held that property does not "lose its private character merely because the public is generally invited to use it for designated purposes. . . . The essentially private character of a store and its privately owned abutting property does not change by virtue of being large or clustered with other stores in a modern shopping center."[17]

Yet in the *Lloyd* case, there was a mitigating factor. In contrast to the Logan Valley Plaza, the Lloyd Center was surrounded directly on all four sides by public streets, and the Resistance Community had an alternative at its disposal.

> The situation at Lloyd Center was notably different. The central building complex was surrounded by public sidewalks, totaling 66 linear blocks. All persons who enter or leave the private areas within the complex must cross public streets and sidewalks, either on foot or in automobiles. . . . Indeed, respondents moved to these public areas and continued distribution of their handbills after being requested to leave the interior malls. It would be an unwarranted infringement of property rights to require

[the mall owners] to yield to the exercise of First Amendment rights under circumstances where adequate alternative avenues of communication exist.[18]

And, since the mall was in the city itself, the Court commented that the members of the Resistance Community "could have distributed these handbills on any public street, on any public sidewalk, in any public park, or in any public building in the city of Portland."[19]

The problem with the Court's decision, of course, is obvious. Most malls are located not in cities but in suburbs. And, unlike urban shopping centers, most malls are not located directly next to public streets. Suburban malls tend to be located in the middle of large parcels of land and surrounded by parking lots, and the sidewalks surrounding the mall buildings are located on private, not public, property.

Thus far, however, the Supreme Court has sidestepped the issue of whether the more typical suburban malls can be restricted to First Amendment activities, and *Lloyd* continues to be the primary precedent in this area.

Federal versus State Constitutional Rights

Despite the fact that the Supreme Court did not recognize a First Amendment right to distribute literature in the malls, it has held that persons who want to engage in expressive activities in malls may have more rights under their state constitutions than under the federal Constitution.

A few years after the *Lloyd* decision a group of high school students went to the PruneYard, a shopping center in Campbell, California, and sought signatures on a petition that expressed opposition to a United Nations resolution against Zionism. After being ejected by security guards they filed suit in the California Superior Court of Santa Clara County, which held that the students were not entitled under either the federal or California Constitution to exercise their asserted rights on the shopping center's property. The decision was affirmed by the California Court of Appeals.

On further appeal, the California Supreme Court reversed the lower courts, holding that the California Constitution protects "speech and petitioning, reasonably exercised, in shopping centers even when the centers are privately owned."[20] Commenting on the role the mall played in society, the court wrote the following:

It bears repeated emphasis that we do not have under consideration the property or privacy rights of an individual homeowner or the proprietor of a modest retail establishment. As a result of advertising and the lure of a congenial environment, 25,000 persons are induced to congregate daily to take advantage of the numerous amenities offered by the [shopping center there]. A handful of additional orderly persons soliciting signatures and distributing handbills in connection therewith, under reasonable regulations adopted by [the shopping center] to assure that these activities do not interfere with normal business operations would not markedly dilute defendant's property rights.[21]

Unlike the United States Supreme Court, which held in *Lloyd* that the Fifth Amendment right to private property took precedence over the First Amendment right to free speech under the federal Constitution, the California Supreme Court held that under the state constitution free speech was the more prominent right in the case of large shopping malls that were popular gathering places.

The owners of the PruneYard appealed the state supreme court's decision to the United States Supreme Court, which, in *PruneYard Shopping Center v. Robins* (1980), ruled that individual states had the option of adopting a wider interpretation of free speech rights than the Supreme Court had found under the First Amendment:

Our reasoning in *Lloyd* does not . . . limit the authority of the State to exercise its police power or its sovereign right to adopt in its own Constitution individual liberties more expansive than those conferred by the Federal Constitution.[22]

The Court also held that the exercise of free speech rights in the mall did not violate the principles of "taking of property" in the Fifth Amendment nor the "deprivation of property without due process of law" under the Fourteenth Amendment, and that the mall did not have to agree with the state's decision that the facility could be used as a forum for free speech by others:

Most important, the shopping center by choice of its owner is not limited to the personal use of [the owner]. It is instead a business establishment that is open to the public to come and go as they please. The views expressed by members of the public in passing out pamphlets or seeking signatures for a petition will not likely be identified with those of the owner. . . . As far as appears here [the owner] can expressly disavow any connection with the message by simply posting signs in the area where the speakers or handbillers stand. Such signs, for example, could disclaim any sponsorship of the message and could explain that the persons are communicating their own messages by virtue of state law.[23]

With the Supreme Court's affirmation of the California case, it was established that individual states have the option of interpreting their own constitutions more expansively than the federal Constitution.

At the same time, however, California courts have held that evangelistic activities in malls are subject to reasonable time, place, and manner restrictions. In 1989, Herbert Savage was prevented by a mall security guard from placing Christian tracts on cars at the Del Norte Plaza Shopping Center in Escondido, California. The shopping center owner had a neutrally applied parking lot policy that prohibited the distribution of literature on cars and testified that the prohibition was "because of the litter which inevitably results when hundreds of flyers are distributed by one or more groups. . . . The distribution of such handbills within our parking lot may unduly hamper ingress and egress patterns within the parking facility."[24]

Herbert Savage's petition for an injunction against the shopping center owner was denied by both the Superior Court of San Diego County and the California Court of Appeal, which found that the parking lot ban was "content neutral, narrowly drawn to protect the center's legitimate interests [in controlling litter and traffic], and provides an adequate alternative forum for expression."[25] The ban was especially appropriate, said the court, in light of the fact that the shopping center does not prevent leafletting on its sidewalks. Thus, said the court, "Savage and other leafletters are not prevented from reaching the center's patrons; rather, they are merely required to hand their leaflets out in person as opposed to placing them on cars."[26]

There are two significant side notes to the case. First, while the parking lot ban was content neutral, the shopping center had a separate policy restricting the dissemination of information to political speech, and the owners asserted that "because Savage was advancing his religious beliefs . . . they had the right to completely prohibit his activities at the shopping center." The California court rejected this logic, ruling that the owners could not discriminate against religious speech while allowing political speech.[27]

Second, Savage had petitioned for a rehearing of the case at the superior court level, because the judge who originally heard the case was a Roman Catholic, "and therefore biased against [Savage] and his efforts to spread the gospel."[28] The court of appeal also rejected this notion, quoting a California law that stated, "It shall not be grounds for disqualification that the judge is or is not a member of a racial, ethnic, religious, sexual or similar group and the proceeding involves the rights of such a group."[29] Thus, the court concluded, the judge "had no power to disqualify himself on the basis of his membership in the Roman Catholic Church; accordingly he did not err in denying Savage's motion for rehearing."[30] Savage's charge was questionable, of course, since civil court judges are charged with the responsibility to decide cases without religious prejudice, either in favor of their own faith or against a faith system with which they may disagree.

The bottom line, then, is that some states read their own constitutions more expansively than the federal Constitution, though expanded free speech rights are still subject to reasonable time, place, and manner restrictions. However, not all states have similar rights. The state of New York, for example, rejected free speech rights in a shopping center based on its own constitution, holding that while the drafters of the state's "free speech clause may not have envisioned shopping malls, there can be no question that they intended the State Constitution to govern the rights of citizens with respect to their government and not the rights of private individuals against private individuals."[31]

Therefore, you should check with a local attorney to see whether or not the laws of your own state take precedence over federal law.

The Future of the Malls

Two primary federal precedents govern personal evangelism in malls and shopping centers. The United States Supreme Court's 1972 *Lloyd* case determined that the malls constitute private property and that the First Amendment does not protect expressive activities on these properties. The *Lloyd* case dealt with a large mall in an urban area that was directly next to public streets; thus there was an alternative available for First Amendment activities.

In the 1980 *PruneYard* case the Court stated that free speech rights under individual state constitutions may be more expansive than under the First Amendment of the Federal Constitution. This, however, is a matter for state courts to decide.

Thus far the Court has not addressed First Amendment rights in terms of malls located in suburban areas without central business districts or of malls located on large parcels of property that are not directly located next to public streets. Likewise, there may be a question about malls that are built with tax dollars or in which the owners have received significant tax breaks. Do these malls constitute private property to the same degree as those built without government funding or tax credits? The Court has stated that the First Amendment would protect free speech "if the shopping center premises were not privately owned but instead constituted the business of a municipality,"[32] indicating that Christian evangelism can take place in malls that are not privately owned. Unfortunately, this affects only a minority of shopping malls.

In *Lloyd* the dissenting opinion written by Justice Thurgood Marshall provides insight into why First Amendment rights at privately owned malls may eventually be affirmed by the Supreme Court:

> The Lloyd Center is an integral part of the Portland community. From its inception, the city viewed it as a "business district" of the city and depended on it to supply much-needed employment opportunities. To insure the success of the Center, the city carefully integrated it into the pattern of streets already established and planned future development of streets around the Center. It is plain, therefore, that Lloyd Center is the equivalent of a public business district within the meaning of *Marsh* and *Logan Valley.* . . .
>
> The District Court found that Lloyd Center has deliberately chosen to open its private property to a broad range of expression and that having done so it could not constitutionally exclude respondents, and the Court of Appeals affirmed this finding.
>
> If the property of Lloyd Center is generally open to First Amendment activity, respondents cannot be excluded. . . . I perceive no basis for depriving respondents of the opportunity to distribute leaflets inviting patrons of the Center to attend a meeting in which different points of view would be expressed from those held by the organizations and persons privileged to use Lloyd Center as a forum for parading their ideas and symbols.[33]

Justice Marshall concluded with a vision for society that is equally applicable to increasingly growing suburban areas as it is to cities:

> It would not be surprising in the future to see cities rely more and more on private businesses to perform functions once performed by governmental agencies. . . . As governments rely on private enterprise, public property decreases in favor of privately owned property. It becomes hard-

er and harder for citizens to find means to communicate with other citizens. Only the wealthy may find effective communication possible unless we adhere to *Marsh v. Alabama* and continue to hold that "the more an owner, for his advantage, opens up his property for use by the public in general, the more do his rights become circumscribed by the statutory and constitutional rights of those who use it."

When there are no effective means of communication free speech is a mere shibboleth. I believe that the First Amendment requires it to be a reality.[34]

Justice Marshall's view is shared by David Rudovsky, a civil rights lawyer and professor at the University of Pennsylvania School of Law, who emphasizes the social trend toward a more suburbanized society.

While shopping malls are, in essence, the Main Streets of the suburban areas they serve, political soapboxes can be prohibited. The result of this geographical and social discrimination is to limit the presentation of unorthodox views in a manner that is effective as outright censorship.

Forty years ago, the downtown public square offered protesters and dissenters access to large numbers of people. The streets of our cities resonated with debate and discussion of important public issues: Civil rights demonstrators, ban-the-bomb advocates and labor organizers filled the city squares. Today, with the great migration from city to suburb and with the growth of the mall and industrial park, public speech on the city street reaches fewer people. . . .

The court's near-total deference to notions of private property and governmental regulation fails to come to terms with the dramatic demographic changes and private land developments that have swept across the country. The court's approach may render essential First Amendment rights obsolete.[35]

While Professor Rudovsky addresses secular speech, the same principles apply to Christian evangelism. The audience has moved, but the courts have prevented evangelism from moving with it.

Maintaining a Mall Witness

The law is clear: There is no First Amendment right to evangelize in privately owned shopping malls, though individual states may choose to expand free speech rights based on their own constitutions.

However, that does not mean that the malls are necessarily closed off to evangelism. Following are some suggestions that may help you witness in the malls:

As in the case of street evangelism, it is a good idea to contact the mall owners or managers before you start to witness at the mall. Like the police, shopping center owners may not be anti-Christian; they may just want to know what is happening in the mall. Remember one thing about all of the cases we have looked at: The people who were ejected from the malls did not contact the owners before they went in. You may be surprised to find out what a little diplomacy can do and how cooperative some mall owners are. (Yes, some mall owners are even born-again Christians.) Try to deal with the owner or manager directly, not with a secretary in the management office who may not know the mall's policy or cannot make a discretionary decision in your favor. Also, it may help to make it clear that your witnessing activities will not include financial solicitation.

If you cannot reach management or are turned down, get to know one or more of the mall's security guards. Again, if people know what you are doing before you do it, they tend to tolerate it a little more.

If you seek permission to hand out tracts at the mall, consider offering to pick up any tracts that other people throw away. The city has the responsibility to clean up litter, but private mall owners do not. If you offer to pick up your own tracts, it may help influence the owners to let you distribute them in the first place. (And you can always reuse them, which may save you some of the money you would have to spend on more tracts.)

Be careful about using questionnaires or surveys such as those in *Evangelism Explosion*[36] or Campus Crusade for Christ's *Lay Institute for Evangelism*[37] program. Many malls rent space to commercial firms that conduct consumer surveys, and they may view the use of evangelistic questionnaires as conflicting with those firms' activities. However, the techniques used in "questionnaire evangelism" may be helpful in opening a dialogue with people in a less formal structure. In malls, it's best to commit some pertinent questions to memory rather than to use a form on a clipboard that makes you appear to be doing a survey.

Even if you cannot pass out literature, do not rule out one-on-one dialogue with people who are hanging out at the mall. Remember that mall owners can prevent literature distribution, loud preaching, or singing, but they cannot interfere with the content of a private conversation.

Many malls sponsor mall-walker clubs, in which senior citizens and others get together for exercise-style walking, especially during colder weather. Some malls even open early so mall walkers can enter the mall and walk before regular business hours. Mall-walker clubs are very social and provide an excellent opportunity to present the gospel in the course of informal dialogue.

If you cannot approach people directly in a mall, be subtle. Wear a T-shirt with a Christian logo and carry a ninety-pound Bible, then let people approach you. Many of them will be Christian already, but you'd be surprised at how curious non-Christians can sometimes be. One suggestion: If it looks new, it wouldn't hurt to have your name engraved in gold foil on your Bible's front cover so the security guards won't think you stole it from a store in the mall. Many Christian bookstores have a machine that will personalize Bibles, and the cost is only a few dollars.

If the mall tries to evict you based on a loitering regulation, buy a hot dog or a soda. Remember, malls are in business to sell things, and once you make a purchase you are a customer. Larger shopping malls have food courts consisting of several restaurants around a central seating area that provide a natural setting in which to engage people in conversation. If you solely engage in one-on-one dialogue, and the mall evicts you but not other people who are just hanging out, they may be guilty of religious discrimination. Check with a lawyer.

Above all, remember the admonition of Jesus: "Behold, I send you out as sheep in the midst of wolves; therefore be shrewd as serpents, and innocent as doves" (Matt. 10:16). In large malls, each guard is usually responsible for a specific part of the mall, not the entire property. If you are stopped from witnessing, leave, go to the other end of the mall, come back in, and pick up where you left off. You may be recognized sooner or later, but you might reach a few souls in the meantime.

Check with a lawyer or a Christian legal organization to see if the free speech provision of your state's constitution has been interpreted as more expansive than the First Amendment. If so, your right to witness at the mall is more firm, subject to reasonable time, place, and manner restrictions. If that right has not been established, you may be able to challenge the mall in a state court.

Meanwhile, lest the laws regarding your right to evangelize in malls sound too discouraging, let's examine another area in which the courts have firmly established the right to engage in religious expression: public schools and colleges.

/ 6 /

Taking the Word
to School

One of the least influential institutions in the nation when it comes to religion is often the United States Congress. As we have already seen, the Supreme Court is the ultimate arbiter of whether we can openly spread our faith in areas such as the streets, parks, and shopping malls—the final authority in determining how far our First Amendment freedoms extend.

In this chapter, though, we have to give credit where credit is due—to the men and women in the Senate and House of Representatives who, in their own way, helped open another avenue of evangelism to Christians: the public schools. In fact, many people consider the Supreme Court the bad guys when it comes to public education. Back in 1962 and 1963, the Court declared school prayer and Bible reading unconstitutional, causing many conservative Christians to charge that the justices had "thrown God out of the schools."

Had they really done that? Not quite, but to demonstrate why public schools and colleges provide one of the most fruitful fields for Christian harvest today, it may help to review the relationship between religion and public education.

Before the Current Generation

A popular misconception in the Christian community today is that Christianity has always been a part of public education, ever since the beginning of the United States. After all, the reasoning goes, the nation's founders intended that we should be able to pray, read the Bible, and acknowledge our Christian heritage in the public schools.

That is not true historically, since public education did not exist at the time of the nation's founding. The first public school system was not founded until the 1830s in Massachusetts, by which time the last "established" church had been disestablished (also, coincidentally, in Massachusetts).

The Supreme Court did not even begin to address the issue of Christianity in the public schools until 1947, when the issue was neither prayer nor Bible reading but a program called released time. The Court's actions would set the stage for its declaration of prayer and Bible reading as unconstitutional some fifteen years later.

Released time was inaugurated in Gary, Indiana, in 1914 to alleviate a concern on the part of many parents that American children were becoming religiously illiterate. Under the program, students were released from school with the consent of their parents to attend churches or synagogues for an hour or so each week, receive instruction in their own faith, and return to school at the end of the religion classes to resume their normal schoolwork.

In 1940, a released-time plan was inaugurated in Champaign, Illinois, but it contained a significant difference from the Gary model. Rather than have the school release students to attend religion classes elsewhere, religious teachers from the interfaith Champaign Council on Religious Education came into the classrooms to teach. The Champaign released-time plan was challenged in court by Mrs. Vashti McCollum, whose son James was a nonparticipant in the program. She claimed that the plan was a violation of the Establishment Clause, and in 1948 the Supreme Court agreed. In *McCollum v. Board of Education* (1948), the Court held that the plan allowed religious groups to spread their teachings through improper use of the public school system. Writing for the majority, Justice Hugo Black observed that Illinois's compulsory school attendance laws provided a captive audience for the religious teachers:

> Here not only are the state's tax-supported public school buildings used for the dissemination of religious doctrines. The State also affords sectarian groups an invaluable aid in that it helps to provide pupils for their religious classes through use of the State's compulsory public school machinery. This is not separation of Church and State.[1]

Four years later, the Court considered another released time case, *Zorach v. Clauson* (1952).[2] Under a New York law that was closer to the original Gary, Indiana, released-time plan, students were released from classes to attend religious instruction away from school. Acknowledging that the facts were different from those presented in the *McCollum* case, the Court upheld the constitutionality of the New York plan. Church-state scholars Robert Miller and Ronald Flowers make the following comment:

> Calling attention to the fact that religion has always played a huge role in the life of the American people, Justice Douglas argued that by allowing children to be released for religious instruction the public schools were doing nothing more than adjusting their schedules to the religious interests of their constituents. Far from being a violation of the Establishment Clause, such a plan was following the best of our national traditions. To do any less would show government hostility to religion, which would be unconstitutional.[3]

In the released-time cases, the Supreme Court was actually setting up the pattern that would be with us today. To accommodate religion in public education was constitutional, as long as that accommodation was not sponsored by the state, as it was in the Champaign released-time program.

Despite the Court's rulings on released time, prayer and Bible reading were allowed to continue in the schools for another fifteen years. In the 1950s, the State Board of Regents of New York, which had broad powers over the New York public school system, published a "Statement on Moral and Spiritual Training in the Schools," which included the following twenty-two-word, nondenominational prayer that was recommended, though not required, for reading by teachers and students in the New York public schools at the beginning of each day:

> Almighty God, we acknowledge our dependence upon Thee, and we beg Thy blessings upon us, our parents, our teachers, and our country.[4]

Five parents in the school district of New Hyde Park, Long Island, which had adopted the regents' recommendation in 1958, sued on the ground that the use of the state-composed prayer violated both the separation of church and state and their freedom of religion. Finding in favor of the parents and ruling the prayer unconstitutional in *Engel v. Vitale* (1962), the Court held the following:

> We think that by using its public school system to encourage recitation of the Regents' prayer, the State of New York has adopted a practice

wholly inconsistent with the Establishment Clause. . . . The constitutional prohibition against laws respecting an establishment of religion must at least mean that in this country it is no part of the business of government to compose official prayers for any group of the American people to recite as part of a religious program carried on by government.[5]

Following the *Engel* decision an uproar ensued, with pro-prayer Christians charging that the Court had taken God out of the classroom and secularized the public schools; some even suggested that the schools had been made open prey to communism.[6] The following year the Court added oil to the fire by hearing two additional religion cases that would result in its ban on Bible reading as well.

The first case involved a Pennsylvania law that required the reading of at least ten verses from the King James Bible, without comment and from which students could request to be excused, at the beginning of each school day. The second case involved a Maryland law that required the reading of a chapter of the Bible and/or recitation of the Lord's Prayer each morning in all public schools. The two cases were heard under one name, *Abington Township School District v. Schempp* (1963), and resulted in a five-opinion compendium in which the Court declared that both the required recitation of the Lord's Prayer (or any other prayer) and the devotional reading of the Bible were violations of the Establishment Clause. Justice Tom Clark, a devout Presbyterian, wrote his opinion based on the theory of government neutrality:

> The place of religion in our society is an exalted one, achieved through a long tradition of reliance on the home, the church and the inviolable citadel of the individual heart and mind. We have come to recognize through bitter experience that it is not within the power of government to invade that citadel, whether its purpose or effect be to aid or oppose, to advance or retard. In the relationship between man and religion, the state is firmly committed to a position of neutrality.[7]

The *Engel* and *Schempp* decisions effectively removed most religious expression from the public schools and set the precedent for future legislative attempts at religious activities in public education to be found unconstitutional. Over the next two decades, other activities declared unconstitutional by the Court would include the posting of the Ten Commandments,[8] moment-of-silence laws,[9] and the mandatory teaching of creation science.[10]

There was one factor that many Christians did not acknowledge: The Court did not ban all religious activities in the schools but merely those that were sponsored or mandated by the state. It was not until the 1980s that Christians finally figured out how to express their religion in public schools in ways that would be not only constitutional but far more evangelistic.

The Beginnings of Equal Access

In 1968, Cornerstone, a group of Christian students, began to hold Bible studies at the University of Missouri in Kansas City. They were allowed to meet on campus with the permission of university authorities until 1972, when the board of curators of the university adopted a resolution forbidding the use of campus facilities "for purposes of religious worship or teaching by either student or nonstudent groups."[11] The board based its action on the mistaken notion that the resolution was mandated by the Establishment Clauses of both the United States and Missouri Constitutions.

Eleven members of Cornerstone filed suit. A federal district court ruled in favor of the university, but the Court of Appeals for the Eighth Circuit reversed and found in favor of the students, holding that the Establishment Clause does not bar a policy of "equal access," in which facilities open to groups and speakers of all kinds does not violate the Establishment Clause.[12]

The university appealed to the Supreme Court, which ruled in *Widmar v. Vincent* (1981) that, since the university had opened itself up to other student groups, it could not discriminate against religious groups.[13] The Court based its findings, in part, on a test it developed in the 1971 case of *Lemon v. Kurtzman*, which had addressed the issue of financial aid to religious schools. In determining the relationship between government and religion when it comes to legislative statutes, the Court held, the following three conditions must exist:

> Every analysis in this area must begin with consideration of the cumulative criteria developed by the Court over many years. Three such tests may be gleaned from our cases. First, the statute must have a secular legislative purpose; second, its principal or primary effect must be one that neither advances nor inhibits religion; finally, the statute must not foster an "excessive government entanglement with religion."[14]

These three conditions—purpose, effect, and entanglement—are also used to determine the constitutionality of policies and procedures implemented by the government. Since the University of Missouri is a public institution, it was subject to what has become known as the *Lemon* test. If any of the three conditions is violated, the statute or policy is unconstitutional. In the case of Cornerstone, the Court held that allowing students to meet on campus for religious purposes met all three conditions. Justice Lewis Powell wrote in *Widmar*:

> An open forum in a public university does not confer any imprimatur of State approval on religious sects or practices. . . . Such a policy would no more commit the University to religious groups than it is now committed to the goals of the Students for a Democratic Society, the Young Socialist Alliance, or any other group eligible to use its facilities.[15]

For the first time the Court extended the theory of content neutrality to religious expression in public education. Justice Powell held the following:

> Having created a forum generally open to student groups, the University seeks to enforce a content-based exclusion of religious speech. Its exclusionary policy violates the fundamental principle that a state regulation of speech should be content-neutral, and the University is unable to justify this violation under applicable constitutional standards.[16]

For the college level, then, the Court established a policy that would become known as equal access. If a public college or university opened its facilities to any noncurriculum related or outside group, which could include everything from student antiwar organizations to gay and lesbian rights groups, it could not exclude student religious groups.

What may not be obvious is an intrinsic difference between the religious activities that were declared unconstitutional by the Court in the public schools and those that were allowed in *Widmar v. Vincent*: sponsorship. School prayer, Bible reading, the posting of the Ten Commandments, and moment-of-silence statutes had all been mandated by the state. Cornerstone, however, was a student-sponsored, student-led group. Religion was not being forced on the students; they sought to express their faith on their own.

The result of the *Widmar* case is essentially this: If you are a student at a public college or university, or even at a private secular college or university, and if your school allows groups to meet that are noncurriculum related and not sponsored by the school, they cannot discriminate against a student-sponsored religious group. The only exception to this rule is that pervasively religious colleges and universities do not have to allow religious groups to meet if those groups are not in doctrinal agreement with the individual school.

What about church-sponsored colleges and universities that are not pervasively religious? The law says that they must be open to religious student groups in the same manner as any secular school. For example, a few years ago Georgetown University refused to recognize a student group called Gay People of Georgetown University. The students filed suit, and after their initial victory at the trial court level, the District of Columbia Court of Appeals held that the university did not have to recognize the group.[17] The Washington, D.C., city council then passed a bill prohibiting discrimination based on sexual orientation, after which the United States Congress passed a bill holding that the city council could not apply the bill to religious institutions. The city council then filed suit against Congress, and the Federal District Court for the District of Columbia declared, affirmed by the Court of Appeals for the District of Columbia Circuit, that the religious exemption was unconstitutional because it infringed on the council members' right of free speech.[18] Meanwhile, the university and the student gay groups reached an out-of-court settlement in which, while Georgetown would not officially recognize the groups, it would provide space for the groups to meet.

What makes the case notable is that Georgetown is a church-sponsored university, run by the Jesuit order of the Roman Catholic Church. However, it has no doctrinal test for admission, and most of the students at Georgetown major in secular fields of study. In the same way that Georgetown could not discriminate against a gay student group, neither could it discriminate against a Christian student group. To legally discriminate on the basis of religion the school must be pervasively religious. Bob Jones University, for example, is a pervasively fundamentalist school that requires a doctrinal test for all students and could not be forced to sponsor a Pentecostal or Buddhist student group. On the other hand, purely secular colleges and universities have the least discretion. In 1988, the Eighth Circuit Court of Appeals ordered the University of Arkansas to provide funding for the Gay and Lesbian Student Association at the university, holding that the school could not deny funding based on its disagreement with the group's message.[19]

Obviously, then, there is good news and bad news about the court rulings that have dealt with the equal access issue at the college level. The bad news is that there are a lot of very strange groups out there, all of which have the right to meet on college campuses. The good news is that Christian students, even at secular colleges and universities (whether state or private institutions), have the same right to meet on campus.

Equal Access at the High School Level

Despite the Supreme Court's ruling in *Widmar*, the lower courts continued to rule that student-led religious groups could not meet in public high schools.[20] Finally, the United States Congress stepped in and passed the Equal Access Act of 1984, which makes it illegal for many public secondary schools with noncurriculum-related clubs to deny access to student religious groups. The Act says, in relevant part, the following:

> It shall be unlawful for any public secondary school which receives Federal financial assistance and which has a limited open forum to deny equal access or a fair opportunity to, or discriminate against, any students who wish to conduct a meeting within that limited open forum on the basis of the religious, political, philosophical, or other content of that speech.
>
> A public secondary school has a limited open forum whenever such school grants an offering to or opportunity for one or more noncurriculum related student groups to meet on school premises during non-instructional time.
>
> Schools shall be deemed to offer a fair opportunity to students who wish to conduct a meeting within its limited open forum if such school uniformly provides that the meeting is voluntary and student-initiated; there is no sponsorship of the meeting by the school, the government, its agents or employees; employees or agents of the school or government are present at religious meetings only in a nonparticipatory capacity; the meeting does not materially and substantially interfere with the orderly conduct of educational activities within the school; and nonschool persons may not direct, conduct, control, or regularly attend activities of student groups.[21]

The act stipulates that if a school receives federal funding and allows "noncurriculum related student groups" to meet (which includes most public schools), it cannot discriminate against a student-initiated group that wants to focus on religion. Noncurriculum related groups are defined as those that do not relate directly to the school's actual curriculum. For example, many schools have a chess club, photography club, astrology club, Young Democrats or Young Republicans, Future Farmers of America, and other student clubs that meet during nonclass time. If a school has any of these clubs, it has created a "limited open forum" and must allow a student-initiated Bible study club, Christian fellowship club, or any other type of religious club to meet.

Unlike many statutes dealing with religious issues, the Equal Access Act received wide support, both conservative and liberal. Representative Barney Frank, a liberal Democrat and one of only two openly gay members of Congress, declared the following:

> In some ways, this is the best empowerment of teenagers that's come along. People should understand what this means, which is that fifteen-year-olds have some decisions that adults cannot interfere with. It means the young Trotskyites can meet, it means the gay rights activists can meet. I think it's wonderful, but I'm surprised at some of my allies.[22]

Supporting the act from the other side was Jerry Falwell, who stated, "We knew we couldn't win on school prayer [in Congress], but equal access got us what we wanted all along."[23]

Both Barney Frank and Jerry Falwell were right about the act. In theory, any student-initiated group could organize in a school, including unpopular groups such as student Ku Klux Klan chapters or student Nazi or skinhead groups. Fortunately, the act contained provisions that could be used to prevent potentially dangerous meetings:

> Nothing [in the Act] shall be construed to authorize the United States . . . to sanction meetings that are otherwise unlawful. . . .
>
> Nothing [in the Act] shall be construed to limit the authority of the school, its agents or employees, to maintain order and discipline on school premises, to protect the well-being of students and faculty, and to assure that attendance of students at meetings is voluntary.[24]

In short, both a student Bible study club and a student Ku Klux Klan club could apply to the school to meet on campus. If either one created a potential "clear and present danger" situation, the school could refuse the request. Fortunately, Bible study clubs have a much better track record of not creating that type of situation.

Despite the mandate of Congress, many schools continued to refuse to allow student-initiated religious groups to meet. In 1981, a group of students at the Williamsport Area High School in Pennsylvania organized Petros, a club they said would "promote spiritual growth and positive attitudes in the lives of its members."[25] Other groups at the school had included Future Homemakers of America, an ecology club, Future Nurses and Future Teachers, photography club, and ski club. After consulting with the school district's legal counsel, the principal and superintendent denied their request to meet on campus during the school's activity period to read Scripture, discuss religious matters, and pray.

Before permission for the club was denied, the school's principal had allowed Petros to hold an organizational meeting that was attended by forty-five students, comprising about two percent of the student body. In June 1982, ten of the students filed suit in federal court, which ruled in their favor and held that not to allow them to meet on the same basis as other student groups impermissibly infringed upon their right to free speech.[26]

The Williamsport School District accepted the judgment of the district court and did not appeal. However, John Youngman, then a member of the board, appealed the case as an individual, and the Federal Court of Appeals for the Third Circuit, which, concluding that the activities of Petros were unconstitutional, reversed the district court.

The students then appealed to the United States Supreme Court, which in *Bender v. Williamsport Area School District* (1986) vacated the judgment of the Court of Appeals, because John Youngman did not have "standing to sue," a legal term used to describe a plaintiff's direct interest in the outcome of a case. For the first time, the Supreme Court allowed a student religious group to meet in a public high school, but its ruling was based on a point of legal procedure rather than the merits of the issue itself. In a close decision, however, four dissenting justices held that the Court should have decided the case on the merits of equal access and that the *Widmar* precedent should be affirmed at the high school level.

The Court finally agreed to address the actual issue of equal access four years later. Students in two different school districts applied to their schools to allow Bible study clubs, and both schools denied their requests. The students filed suits, and the cases went up to the federal courts of appeals, which reached conflicting conclusions. In January 1989, the Court of Appeals for the Ninth Circuit held that students in

Renton, Washington, could not form a Christian club, because it was unconstitutional.[27] The following month, the Court of Appeals for the Eighth Circuit held that such clubs in schools were constitutional and that the Westside High School in Omaha, Nebraska, could not prevent the students from meeting.[28]

Both cases were appealed to the Supreme Court, which accepted the Nebraska case and, in an eight-to-one decision in *Board of Education of the Westside Community Schools v. Mergens* (1990)[29], held that the Equal Access Act was constitutional and that schools which had a limited open forum could not discriminate against religious groups. Extending their previous decision regarding equal access at the college level, Justice Sandra Day O'Connor wrote, "We think the logic of *Widmar* applies with force to the Equal Access Act."[30]

Federal law, then, is firm. If your school has any clubs that can be construed as "noncurriculum related," you have the right to organize a religiously based club for Bible study or Christian fellowship.

Unfortunately, the equal access issue still was not settled. After the *Mergens* decision, the students in Renton, Washington, attempted to organize a Christian club but were again rebuffed by the school district. They filed another suit, and a federal district court held that the Washington State Constitution was more restrictive than the First Amendment of the federal Constitution.[31]

You may remember from our discussion of shopping malls that the United States Supreme Court has ruled that state constitutions may provide more rights under the principles of freedom of speech than the federal Constitution. The district court determined that the Washington State Constitution provides fewer rights than the federal Constitution under the same principle, and that a student religious club would be in violation of the state constitution. On the other hand, a federal district court in Idaho ruled that students at the Robert Stuart Junior High School could not be prevented from forming a Christian club, even though the Equal Access Act violated the Idaho State Constitution. Viewing the conflict, the court held that the supremacy clause of the federal Constitution controlled the case.[32]

Finally, in 1993 the United States Court of Appeals for the Ninth Circuit reversed the district court and ruled in favor of the students, holding that when federal and state law conflict, the federal law prevails.[33] Thus the right of students to meet in schools that have established a limited open forum is firm.

Giving the Word to Others

Equal access itself is not a religious rights issue but a free speech issue. In *Mergens* the Supreme Court ruled that schools could not discriminate on the content of speech and affirmed the Equal Access Act, which comprehensively protects speech that is political, philosophical, or religious.

In addition to the right of students to gather for religious meetings in public schools, another question has presented itself to the courts: whether students can communicate their faith to other students by distributing religious publications on school property. This brings in another First Amendment right: freedom of the press.

The degree to which students enjoy this right depends, like religious meetings, on the sponsorship of the publication. If a school-sponsored publication is involved, the rights of religious students are not absolute. At the Hazelwood East High School in St. Louis County, Missouri, principal Robert Reynolds refused permission for students to publish articles in the *Spectrum*, the school newspaper, that dealt with pregnant students at the school. The newspaper was written and edited by a journalism class and paid for by funds allocated by the board of education. Reynolds was concerned that the pregnant students could be identified from the text of the articles and that references to sexual activities and birth control in the articles were inappropriate for some of the younger students at the school. In *Hazelwood School District v. Kuhlmeier* (1988), the Supreme Court held that school officials may exercise such editorial control over a school newspaper.[34]

Later that year, the Federal Court of Appeals for the Ninth Circuit reversed a district court that had prohibited students from distributing a four-page newsletter that criticized school administrative policies at Lindberg High School in Renton, Washington. Basing its opinion on the *Hazelwood* case the appeals court held in *Burch v. Barker* (1988) that the administration could not prevent the distribution of a nonschool-sponsored, unauthorized, student-written paper unless it could prove that the publication would result in substantial disruption.[35]

Combining the principles of *Hazelwood* and *Burch*, it is legal for students to distribute nonschool-sponsored publications in public high schools provided they are neither obscene nor designed to cause disruption in the schools. Unlike the Equal Access Act, which affects only public high schools, elementary and middle school students may also distribute publications in their schools.

In *Thompson v. Waynesboro Area School District* (1987), a federal district court held that junior high school students have a free speech right to distribute *Issues and Answers*, a Christian newspaper, in the school building. Relying on the Supreme Court's opinion in *Widmar v. Vincent* and the federal district court opinion in *Bender v. Williamsport Area School District*, the court held that the prohibition of the paper's distribution violated the students' free speech rights.[36]

Issues and Answers is a popular Christian publication for young people, and numerous courts have affirmed the right of students to distribute the paper in public schools. However, the distribution of religious literature is subject to reasonable time, place, and manner restrictions, providing such restrictions are not directed against the religious content of the literature.[37]

Looking from the Outside In

Even if you are not a high school student, school facilities may be available to you. While you cannot engage in religious activities on campus during the school day, there is another possibility: renting school facilities for a religious function such as a worship service, lecture, or film showing. Even though the Equal Access Act and literature distribution are limited to students, outside groups can often rent school facilities for religious purposes. The key factor in determining whether your group has the right to use a school facility is whether the school has created a limited public forum by renting its facilities to other groups. In theory, if it has rented space to other outsiders it cannot discriminate against religious groups.

In 1983, a federal district court in Kansas ruled that an elementary school that had rented space to other community groups could not engage in content-based discrimination against a church that did not own its own facility.[38] In 1990, the Federal Court of Appeals for the Third Circuit affirmed a lower court ruling that the William Tennent High School in Bucks County, Pennsylvania, had established a public forum by renting its auditorium to a wide range of community groups and could not prevent Student Venture, a subsidiary of Campus Crusade for Christ, from renting the school facilities for a program of entertainment and testimony by magician Andre Cole.[39] Also in 1990, a federal court in New York held that Birthright of Owego, New York, could not be prevented from renting the auditorium at the Owego-Appalachian Middle School for a benefit performance by Toby Travis, a professional magician and evangelist with Youth for Christ, since the school had established the auditorium as a limited public forum. The ruling was affirmed in 1991 by the Court of Appeals.[40] Also in 1991, the Federal Court of Appeals for the First Circuit affirmed a lower court decision granting a permanent injunction against a Maine school district that had refused to allow a church to use the Rockland High School cafeteria for a Christmas dinner, because the school had been established as a public forum through previous rentals to other groups.[41]

The track record of religious groups winning cases against school districts was a good one until 1992, when the Second Circuit Court of Appeals upheld a federal district court decision holding that school districts in New York could discriminate against religious groups. That decision resulted in the issue of school use by outside groups being addressed by the United States Supreme Court in a 1993 case that determined whether the principle of equal access applies to outside groups as it does to students.[42]

In 1988, Pastor John Steigerwald of the Lamb's Chapel, an evangelical church in Center Moriches, New York, applied to the Center Moriches Union Free School District for permission to rent the local high school to show *Turn Your Heart Towards Home*, a film series by Dr. James Dobson. Steigerwald had also sought the use of rooms in the high school for Sunday morning services and Sunday school, but his application had been turned down. The school district also turned down the church's application for space to show the film series, and subsequent follow-up applications were continuously denied over a two-year period. The district's denial was based on a portion of the New York Education Law prohibiting use of public school facilities "if such meetings, entertainments, and occasions are under the exclusive control, and the said proceeds are to be applied for the benefit of a society, association or organization of a religious sect or denomination, or of a fraternal, secret or exclusive society or organization other than organizations of the military, naval, and marine service of the United States and organizations of volunteer firefighters or volunteer ambulance workers."[43]

The Center Moriches High School had rented space to other outside groups in 1987 and 1988 that included The Mind Center (a New Age religious group), the Southern Harmonizer Gospel Singers, the Salvation Army Youth Band, a concert by jazz artist Billy Taylor sponsored by the Hampton Council of Churches, a performance of *Amahl and the Night Visitors*, and several functions sponsored by secular groups. The district also rented space for a lecture series titled "Psychology and the Unknown," which was sponsored by the Center Moriches Public Library and dealt with parapsychology, transpersonal psychology, eastern mysticism, and metaphysics.

The Lamb's Chapel filed suit, and in 1990 the Federal District Court for the Eastern District of New York held that, based on the New York education law, the school district could engage in content-based discrimination against the church. On appeal, the church relied upon three prior uses of the school facility to argue that the school district had demonstrated a prior practice of opening the public schools to outside religious uses: the Salvation Army Band benefit concert (in which the high school's own band participated), the gospel music concert, and the lecture series that dealt with parapsychology and metaphysics.

Despite the blatant religious nature of the activities, the Second Circuit Court of Appeals held that religion was incidental to all three functions when it wrote:

> The only religious connotations found in the Joint Band Program were the invocation, the performance of a piece called "Jericho Revisited" and the finale, "God Bless America." Although [the Lamb's Chapel] adduced evidence that "the Salvation Army is a church or a quasi-church," the Joint Band Program hardly can be described as any kind of a religious use of school district property. The theme of the program was not religious and any reference to religion was incidental at best. . . .
>
> The business manager [for the gospel music group] responded in the affirmative when asked if the concert could be enjoyed for the music itself. Obviously, this is so. Much of the world's greatest music has some religious connotations but can be enjoyed by people of all religious beliefs as well as people of no religious beliefs. The performance by the Southern Harmonizers was not a religious service or event but a musical or cultural one. . . .
>
> When asked whether his lecture involved matters of both a spiritual and a scientific nature, [New Age psychotherapist Jerry Huck] responded: "It was all science. . . ." Although some incidental reference to religious matters apparently was made in the lectures, Mr. Huck himself characterized such matters as "a fascinating sideline" and "not the purpose of the [lecture]."[44]

In *Lamb's Chapel v. Center Moriches Union Free School District* (1992), the appeals court held, "As is apparent from the foregoing, none of the prior uses pointed to by [the Lamb's Chapel] were for religious purposes." Thus, said the court, the school district could deny use of the school facilities to the church. The decision was a paradoxical one, since the Second Circuit had previously ruled in favor of outside groups using public high schools for religious gatherings.[45]

Because the *Lamb's Chapel* ruling conflicted with other federal court rulings prohibiting school districts that had established limited open forums from discriminating against religious groups, the United States Supreme Court accepted the case for review and in June 1993 reversed the lower courts, holding that the school could not deny use of its facilities to the church group on grounds that such use would violate the Establishment Clause. Citing *Widmar v. Vincent*, in which the Court had affirmed the right of a group of college Christians to use university facilities for religious purposes, Justice Byron White wrote for the Court:

> We have no more trouble than did the *Widmar* Court in disposing of the claimed defense on the ground that the posited fears of an Establishment Clause violation are unfounded. The showing of this film would not have been during school hours, would not have been sponsored by the school, and would have been open to the public, not just church members. The District property had repeatedly been used by a wide variety of private organizations. Under these circumstances, as in *Widmar*, there would have been no realistic danger that the community would think that the District was endorsing religion or any particular creed, and any benefit to religion or to the Church would have been no more than incidental.[46]

It is important to note that the ruling did not affirm the use of public school facilities for all religious activities. The case was limited to a specific issue: whether the school district could deny use of its facilities for the exhibition of a film series by James Dobson. Thus the court was able to avoid ruling on the films as a religious activity and limited the scope of its ruling by treating the films as addressing family issues from a religious viewpoint.

The precedent, then, appears to be that if a school district allows use of its facilities in general for activities such as concerts, magic shows, film series, lecture series that deal with neutral topics such as family issues or drug abuse, it cannot deny the use of the facilities for similar activities that integrate a religious perspective. However, the precedent does not appear to extend to pervasively religious activities such as worship services, revivals, or prayer meetings by outside groups, scenarios that may be addressed by the Supreme Court in a future case.

A Few Words for Teachers

As we have seen, with few exceptions the general principle of equal access is that students have a great deal of freedom to express their faith in public schools. Likewise, outside groups have the right to use public school facilities for religious expression if the school has established itself as a limited public forum by renting its facilities to nonreligious groups.

If you are a public school teacher, or even a teacher at a public college or university, the news is not quite as good. For better or worse, you are an agent of the state, and generally the courts have concluded that since religious activities on your part can be interpreted as representing those of the state (thus violating the Establishment Clause), you do not have the same freedom of religious expression in the context of your professional role.

Take, for example, the issue of prayer. In Warren County, Pennsylvania, a tenured fourth-grade teacher was fired after he refused to cease leading his students in prayer and reading Bible stories to them. He filed suit, and in 1983 the Pennsylvania Commonwealth Court upheld the school district's action.[47] In another case in 1991, a federal district court issued an injunction against teachers in Duncanville, Texas, who were leading students in prayer during both classes and extracurricular activities.[48]

Do these cases mean that teachers are forbidden to pray with students? That depends on the circumstances under which the prayer takes place. If the teacher is acting in his or her professional role, whether during the school day or in the context of an extracurricular activity, then any type of religious expression geared to students is unconstitutional. This includes organized prayer meetings on school facilities solely for teachers before or after school if they are prohibited by the school district.[49] However, there is nothing to prevent teachers from taking part in prayer or religious discussion with students when they are not acting in a professional role.

There may also be constitutional difficulties if teachers do not engage directly in prayer or other religious activities with their students. In *Roberts v. Madigan* (1989), for example, a fifth-grade teacher was prohibited from maintaining religious books such as *The Bible in Pictures* and *The Life of Jesus* in a bookcase in his classroom. During class reading periods, teacher Kenneth Roberts also read his own Bible, which he left on his desk during the day. A federal court held that Roberts's activities violated the Establishment Clause and had the effect of communicating an endorsement of Christianity to students at an impressionable age who might not be able to distinguish between his personal activities and state action.[50]

Another area of difficulty, especially for science teachers, is the issue of creation science versus evolution. Courts have consistently held that teachers in public schools neither have the right to teach creation science nor the right to refuse to teach evolution.[51]

At the college level, teachers have more opportunities to express their faith to students, but even here the right of free speech is not absolute during class time. In 1991, the Federal Appeals Court for the Eleventh Circuit reversed a lower court and held that Philip Bishop, an assistant professor of health and physical education at the University of Alabama, did not have the constitutional right to interject religious speech into classes. Nor, said the court, could he hold optional after-class meetings for his students, because they might feel unduly pressured and coerced into attendance.[52] Bishop might have had less of a problem had he been a religion or philosophy teacher, but clearly courts will rule against religious speech delivered in the context of secular subjects such as math or science. Hopefully, the *Bishop* case is the exception to the rule, since the Supreme Court held in *Widmar v. Vincent* that college students have the cognizant skills to differentiate between a teacher's personal opinion and state policy.

Finally, a word should be said about religious attire. In 1990, the Federal Court of Appeals for the Third Circuit decided that the Philadelphia School District's refusal to employ a female teacher who wore Muslim attire was not a violation of her civil or constitutional rights.[53] Holding that a Pennsylvania statute that prohibited religious attire worn by public school teachers was narrowly tailored to preserve an atmosphere of religious neutrality in the schools, the court's decision could limit the wearing of, among other things, a Jewish yarmulka, turban, or even jewelry such as a cross or ichthus (Christian fish symbol). If you are a teacher who wears jewelry of this type and have not been challenged, praise the Lord. However, you should realize that if you are ever challenged for wearing religious jewelry, the law may not be on your side.

Bringing Your Rights into the Schools

As in the case of shopping malls, the primary First Amendment right which applies in the public school is not freedom of religion but freedom of speech.

One of the most significant cases to come before the Supreme Court dealing with the rights of students did not address religious expression but the right to protest. In 1969, the Court held in *Tinker v. Des Moines Area School District* that public school students had the right to wear arm bands to protest the Vietnam War. Justice Abe Fortas wrote for the majority what has become one of the most widely quoted passages regarding freedom of expression in public education:

> It can hardly be argued that either students or teachers shed their constitutional rights to freedom of speech or expression at the schoolhouse gate. . . . In our system, state-operated schools may not be enclaves of totalitarianism. School officials do not possess absolute authority over their students. Students in school as well as out of school are "persons" under our Constitution. They are possessed of fundamental rights which the State must respect, just as they themselves must respect their obligations to the State.[54]

The issue in *Tinker* did not solely involve high school students but students down through the elementary school level. Legal scholar Douglas Laycock writes:

> Petitioner John Tinker, fifteen years old, and petitioner Christopher Eckhardt, sixteen years old, attended high school in Des Moines, Iowa. Petitioner Mary Beth Tinker was a thirteen-year-old student attending junior high school. Paul and Hope Tinker [who were not petitioners but who also wore the arm bands], ages eight and eleven, respectively, and brother and sister to petitioners John and Mary Beth, also wore arm bands to their schools. Paul was in the second grade and Hope in the fifth grade.[55]

Interestingly enough, one right that appears solid at this point is the wearing of T-shirts with Christian themes, a right similar to the one exercised by the *Tinker* students when they wore arm bands to protest the Vietnam War. In December 1991, Steven Redmon, an eleven-year-old student at the Green Cove Springs Elementary School in Clay County, Florida, filed a claim against his school for refusing to let him wear a T-shirt with these words: "O.K., LAST TIME . . . THIS IS YOUR BRAIN [accompanied by a picture of a brain]. THIS IS YOUR BRAIN IN HELL [accompanied by a picture of a brain in a frying pan]. ANY QUESTIONS? JOHN 3:16–18." Redmon's suit charged the school with violating his rights under the free speech clause of the First Amendment and alleged that its refusal to let him wear the shirt had the effect of denigrating and displaying hostility toward his religious beliefs, thus violating the Establishment Clause.

In January 1992, the school district settled with the Redmon family out of court and agreed to allow students to do the following:

> [W]ear any T-shirt, or other similar article of clothing, with a religious message or religious depiction illustrating a religious theme, or both, including, without limitation, any T-shirt that contains the word "Hell," when such word refers to a location in a religious context; provided, however, that the wearing of such T-shirt . . . does not materially and substantially disrupt the work and discipline of the . . . school.[56]

The T-shirt issue has not been tried in civil court, but if the *Tinker* case is any indication, the right of students to wear T-shirts with Christian words is firm. The most significant challenge thus far, the *Redmon* case, is a victory for Christian students of all ages.

In summary, three significant events have assured the rights of students to witness in public schools. In the 1981 *Widmar* case, the Supreme Court firmly established the right to religious expression for college and university students. In 1984, Congress extended that right to high school students through the Equal Access Act, affirmed by the Court in *Mergens* in 1990. The right of religious expression has not been extended below the high school level nor to public school teachers, though other free speech rights were affirmed by *Tinker* in 1969.

To determine whether students of any age should have the right to nonstate-sponsored religious expression in public schools, one need only discern the signs of the times. By the time students complete elementary school, they already know about social phenomena such as AIDS, condoms, occult video games, and rock music (and even have their own cult heroes in the Teenage Mutant Ninja Turtles). For some reason, however, the government is afraid to allow kids to be exposed to religion. Testifying before a congressional committee that held hearings on the Equal Access Act, Bonnie Bailey, a student in Lubbock, Texas, put educational priorities into perspective when she reflected, "We can picket, we can demonstrate, we can curse, we can take God's name in vain, but we cannot voluntarily get together and talk about God on any part of our campus, inside or out of the school."[57]

That, hopefully, will continue to change.

Tips on Dealing with Schools

The schools are a mission field open to Christian students more than to anyone else. If you are interested in evangelism in the public schools, here are a few hints that will help you achieve your goal:

If you want to start a Christian club or Bible study club in your high school or college, get together with a few other Christian students, pray about your idea, and formulate a plan to take to the school administration. Do your research and be prepared to cite the Equal Access Act and some of the cases that have been decided in favor of students, so the school administrator will know you have done your homework.

Prior to meeting with the school administration, make sure your own school is a limited open forum. (If the school does not have any noncurriculum-related clubs it is not subject to the Equal Access Act.) Also, be diplomatic. If you offend the administration, they have the option of discontinuing other noncurriculum-related clubs; then the school would no longer be a limited open forum.

A note to parents and teachers, included in a spirit of love: Step out of the picture (at least visibly) and let your kids do it on their own. Remember that for a club to be approved under the Equal Access Act it must be *student* initiated and *student* run. The presence of parents in anything other than an advocacy role, or of teachers in any role other than nonparticipatory supervision, would turn a student religious club into a state-sponsored activity, thus disqualifying it under the act.

Pursue all other possibilities before you consider legal action against your school. If the principal refuses to allow a religious club, approach the school district or school board. If you attempt to file suit before you have exhausted your "administrative options," the suit will most likely be dismissed before it is heard in court.

If you have had no luck, contact one of the Christian legal organizations such as the Rutherford Institute or Christian Advocates Serving Evangelism. Very often you may not have to file a suit. A letter sent to the school by an attorney has a lot of influence, and a lawsuit can often be avoided.

/ 7 /

Taking the Word to Work

If you feel you are called to proclaim the gospel, it would be nice if you were able to spend as much time as you want on the streets or at malls and schools. But there is one factor that prevents you from doing so: economic reality. Let's face it, most of us have to work for a living if we are going to be able to afford our Reeboks and Nikes, basic items such as rent or mortgage payments, food, gas to get to the streets and malls, and tracts to hand out.

That's the bad news. The good news is that working also provides another opportunity to proclaim the gospel. And as in any other environment, there are both freedoms and restrictions to witnessing on the job. Unlike witnessing in other situations, however, the job presents an unusual opportunity to express your Christianity. Usually, the primary challenge is to be able to voluntarily present your faith to those who are willing to listen. Witnessing on the job is no different, but the workplace also presents another challenge: being forced as an employee to participate in an activity to which you have a conscientious objection based on your religious convictions. American businesses have literally entered the New Age, in which they sometimes require employees to attend workshops and training seminars ranging from a new version of Erhard Seminar Training ("est") to a corporate seminar called MSIA (pronounced "Messiah"), an offshoot of the New Age consciousness-raising group Lifespring.

In this chapter we will address two issues: how to present your Christian faith in the workplace, and how to resist becoming the victim of

New Age or other religious training programs that have already been implemented by many American corporations.

Welcome to the World of Work

One thing all jobs have in common: They are a daily grind, eight hours of giving your time to an entity other than yourself to make the money you need to function in society. Past that point, jobs may have little in common. They may be blue-collar or white-collar; they may be in what are often called the manufacturing, service, or retail industries; they may be nine-to-five positions or worked during another shift; they may provide minimal contact with the public or lots of public contact. While you work, your time is not really yours. It belongs to someone else.

When you are on someone else's time, you are subject to certain regulations. Your employer can dictate, among other things, what you will wear (I have seen few stockbrokers who can get away with jeans and sneakers), when you can eat lunch or take a coffee break, and even the words you must use in dealing with customers.

Generally, there is nothing to prevent you from discussing your faith with others on your own time. Your employer, however, has some rights to restrict the content of your message to customers, clients, patients, and other consumers who patronize your place of employment. To understand when discussing your faith is permitted, it may help to look at a few situations in which that has not been permitted.

Take, for example, the case of Sharlyn Vanderlaan. Employed as a dental hygienist in Michigan, Vanderlaan regularly described to patients whose teeth she was cleaning how Jesus Christ had changed her life. Her employer, Dr. J. B. Mulder, claimed that he had lost six patients because of Vanderlaan's witnessing, and that other patients had insisted that he, rather than she, clean their teeth if he wanted to keep them as patients. Despite several warnings, she continued to witness to the patients and was fired. When she applied for unemployment compensation, her application was denied on grounds of misconduct. She requested a redetermination, stating, "I was unable to control my joy and had to share it with someone. I did not do this as an act of defiance. Jesus Christ changed my life, and I wanted to share that." Nonetheless, the denial of her unemployment application was upheld by the Michigan Employment Security Commission, a local circuit court, and the Michigan Court of Appeals.[1]

Many of the significant cases that have been heard in the courts regarding the right to witness have involved the helping professions, especially health care, counseling, and the correctional system. Following are examples:

In *In re D'Amico* (1986), a New York Appeals Court upheld the denial of unemployment benefits for Philip J. D'Amico, a respiratory therapist who resigned after he was reprimanded for discussing religion with patients while he worked. A born-again Christian, D'Amico had been asked to sign an agreement that he would not discuss religion with patients while he worked, after one patient complained about his assertion that he had cured three people through the laying on of hands. In rejecting D'Amico's suit, the court noted that his evangelism interfered with his job performance and that his employer had accommodated his free expression rights by permitting him to speak with patients during nonworking hours.[2]

Robert Spratt, a Pentecostal Christian, was fired from his job as a social worker at the Kent County Correctional Facility in Michigan, where he had conducted spiritual counseling that included Bible reading, prayer, and in at least one instance the "casting out of demons." A federal court held in *Spratt v. County of Kent* (1985) that the county did not violate Spratt's rights of free speech or free exercise of religion and, since he was an agent of the county, his counseling could violate both the Establishment Clause and the free exercise rights of the inmates he counseled.[3]

In *Goodwin v. Metropolitan Board of Health* (1983), an appeals court in Tennessee upheld the dismissal of a home health aide from her job because while acting in her official capacity she "advised clients on the use of a prayer cloth, spoke in tongues, distributed religious tapes, and precipitated heated religious discussions with clients and co-workers." The court also felt that the agency's regulations against evangelism were reasonable because clients, to be eligible for the services of home health aides, were elderly or in poor health and in no condition to take part in discussions that might be stressful.[4]

Ambrose Flynn, a guard at a Catholic hospital who was employed by a private security firm, was fired for discussing religion with patients despite several warnings that the company's policy forbade unnecessary conversations with patients. Holding that Flynn had repeatedly and admittedly violated the policy, the Maine Supreme Court upheld the denial of his application for unemployment benefits.[5]

Despite the fact that employers may prohibit personal evangelism addressed to customers, clients, or patients, there is actually a good deal of protection for employees who are subject to religious discrimination. Title VII of the Civil Rights Act of 1964 makes it unlawful for any firm with fifteen or more employees or any labor union to discriminate against a person based on his or her race, color, religion, sex, or national origin.[6] With regard to religious discrimination, the act states the following:

> The term "religion" includes all aspects of religious observance and practice, as well as belief, unless an employer demonstrates that he is unable to reasonably accommodate to an employee's or prospective employee's religious observance or practice without undue hardship on the conduct of the employer's business.[7]

If the act does not protect personal evangelism, how does it protect against religious discrimination? For the most part, cases reviewed by the courts regarding religious discrimination in employment have addressed two issues: the religious observance practices of Sabbatarians (persons who worship on Saturday rather than Sunday, such as Seventh Day Adventists or members of the Worldwide Church of God) and the payment of mandatory union dues. While the Supreme Court has not directly addressed the issue of witnessing on the job, a few cases dealing with religious discrimination provide principles on how such witnessing might be regarded legally.

In *Sherbert v. Verner* (1963), the Court addressed the case of Mrs. Adell Sherbert, a Seventh Day Adventist employed at a South Carolina textile mill who was fired because she refused to work on Saturdays. Two state courts held that she was not entitled to unemployment benefits, but the Supreme Court reversed the lower court rulings and held that the withholding of the benefits forced Sherbert to choose between following the teachings of her religion and therefore not working nor receiving benefits, and abandoning a central doctrine of her church and thereby accepting work. Justice William J. Brennan wrote for the majority of the Court, "To condition the availability of benefits upon [Sherbert's] willingness to violate a cardinal principle of her religious faith effectively penalizes the free exercise of her constitutional liberties."[8]

In a similar case thirteen years later, the Court held that Paul Cummins, a supervisor at the Parker Seal Company in Berea, Kentucky, and a member of the Worldwide Church of God, was the victim of religious discrimination because his employer had not made a sufficient effort to accommodate his Sabbatarian beliefs.[9] The following year, however, the Court held in *Trans World Airlines, Inc. v. Hardison* (1977) that another Worldwide Church of God member, Larry Hardison, was not discriminated against because of his religious beliefs since his employer would suffer undue hardship by accommodating his Sabbatarianism and would violate a collective bargaining agreement with Hardison's union that dictated seniority policies among employees.[10]

Finally, in *Thomas v. Review Board of Indiana Employment Security Division* (1981)[11] the Court held that the state could not deny unemployment benefits to a Jehovah's Witness who quit his job after he was transferred to a division of his company that manufactured military tanks. (The Jehovah's Witnesses are pacifists.) Chief Justice Warren Burger wrote for the Court, "The state may justify an inroad on religious liberty by showing that it is the least restrictive means of achieving some compelling state interest,"[12] a test that was not met in the *Thomas* case.

Based on the Court's interpretation of the law in these three cases, we can glean the following principles regarding religious discrimination in employment:

Employers have a duty to reasonably accommodate a person's religious beliefs.

An employer is exempt if such accommodation would cause an undue hardship on the company. In the *Trans World Airlines* case, for example, Larry Hardison's absence would have left an important function at the airline uncovered. The airline, therefore, was not required to accommodate Hardison, based on an undue hardship to their daily functions. Generally, the burden of proving undue hardship is on the employer.

Employers do not need to accommodate an employee's religious beliefs, at least in terms of working on the Sabbath, if the accommodation would violate a collective bargaining agreement with a union that is neutrally written and not intended to discriminate based on religion.

For a state to deny unemployment benefits to a person who leaves a job because it conflicts with his or her religious convictions, the state must demonstrate a compelling interest and prove that the denial is the least restrictive means of achieving that interest.

The same principles may be used by Christians who have a conscientious objection to working on Sundays. In one case, a federal district court held that the Greyhound Food Management company failed to reasonably accommodate John Boomsma, a member of the Christian Reformed Church who objected to working on Sundays. In *Boomsma v. Greyhound Food Management, Inc.* (1986), the court cited the *Trans World Airlines* case and held that the Civil Rights Act imposed a statutory obligation on employers to make a reasonable accommodation for the religious observances of its employees, short of incurring an undue hardship.[13] Also, in *EEOC v. Ithaca Industries* (1988), a federal appeals court held that a textile manufacturing plant in North Carolina did not adequately accommodate Daniel Dean, an employee who objected to working on Sundays based on his religious convictions. There is, however, an important distinction in the *Ithaca* case. Dean had been told at the time of his hiring that Sunday work was strictly voluntary. Had he been informed prior to his hiring that Sunday work was mandatory and taken the job nonetheless, the employer would have had the right to require him to work on Sundays.[14]

In each of these cases, employees experienced religious discrimination by refusing to do something that was required by their employers. In cases of personal evangelism, however, employees do something their employers don't want them to do, rather than that they refuse to do something their employers require them to do.

While the Supreme Court has not addressed the issue of personal evangelism on the job per se, lower court cases have indicated that employees do not have a constitutional right to witness to a firm's customers, clients, or patients. But what about employees who witness to co-workers or discuss the gospel on their own time rather than their employers' time?

There is nothing to prevent you from discussing your faith with your co-workers on your own time, such as coffee breaks or meal breaks. If you can get together with your co-workers and discuss politics, sex, or sports (all of which are generally acceptable to secular employers), to prevent you from discussing religion would amount to content-based discrimination and an infringement of your right to free speech. You may, however, be prevented from witnessing to customers, clients, and patients on your own time if your employer has a written policy against such discussions. This is especially the case in medicine, psychiatry, and psychology (including psychiatric hospitals), where religious discussions may have an impact (whether good or bad) on the patient.

This may not seem appropriate, and in many cases it is not. If Christians really believe that Jesus is who he says he is and that a person's salvation may hinge on receiving the gospel, to prevent the patient from receiving that message is hardly fair. Unfortunately, many physicians, psychiatrists, and psychologists are humanistic in their own orientation and believe that religion—especially biblical Christianity—is often a primary cause of people's problems. One study reported, for example, that only 43 percent of psychiatrists and as few as 5 percent of the members of the American Psychological Association profess a belief in God.[15] However, the survey did not indicate whether the phrase "belief in God" necessarily connotes a Christian framework.

The courts have consistently held, for better or worse, that medical professionals have the right to determine the clinical course of their patients' treatment and that employees do not have a right to preach to patients. This principle has also been applied to social service agencies. In 1980, for example, the Virginia Employment Commission upheld the dismissal of the citizen advocacy coordinator for the Northwest Virginia Association for Retarded Citizens because she refused to sign an agreement to abide by the association's policy that prohibited references to a deity or to pray during any communications with the association's clients or any "persons with whom the association has written business communications." The policy also included personal communications written on personal stationery during nonwork time.[16] That certainly constitutes religious discrimination, especially when you consider that persons who are mentally ill need Jesus as much as everyone else. Nonetheless, under the law, it is legal to engage in such discrimination.

The same situation, fortunately, does not exist with regard to witnessing to your co-workers. There is, however, one factor of which you should beware. If you are in a supervisory position, you should make sure that the person with whom you discuss the gospel does not construe that his or her employment status is dependent on accepting Christ. In one case that addressed this issue, William E. Guyer worked for Robert Temple, the surveyor for Keith County, Nebraska, over a five-year period. Guyer alleged in a lawsuit filed in a federal district court that in 1987 he started to drink heavily and did not show up for work for one week because of the "constant religious preaching of Mr. Temple and the constant playing of a religious station on the radio." He also alleged that he was rehired on the condition that he go to church and receive Christian counseling, and that he could only return to work "if he would accept the Lord Jesus Christ as his Savior, demonstrate that he had a miraculous change in his character, and showed by his actions that he is a new person."[17]

No decision was published in the case of *Guyer v. Keith County* (filed 1989), indicating that it may have been settled out of court. Nonetheless, if the scenario presented is true, there are several factors to consider. First, while there is nothing to prevent a supervisor from revealing his or her faith to an employee, to force the employee to accept Christ as a condition for employment would be a violation of Title VII of the Civil Rights Act. Second, the fact that he was a county supervisor implicates the Establishment Clause, since the supervisor was acting as an agent for the local government. Third, even if you consider that a decision to accept Christ is appropriate, the supervisor could just as easily have been a Mormon, Buddhist, or New Age adherent trying to coerce someone to accept a non-Christian belief system. (Remember, the sword cuts both ways.)

A New Age in Employee Training

Thus far, the issue in this chapter is the act of witnessing on the job. Another factor to consider is how you should deal with non-Christian evangelism that is forcibly directed toward you.

Over the past few years, several major corporations have implemented employee training and other motivational programs that have religious content, especially that favor New Age teachings with which Christians might have a problem. In one prominent case, the Pacific Bell Telephone Company (PacBell) initiated a training program called "New Age Thinking for Achieving Your Potential," for which the required readings included books ranging from *Directing the Movies of Your Mind (Visualization for Health and Insight)* to *Psychocybernetics.*[18] Later, PacBell began to require its employees to take a leadership development training program called "Kroning." The results were reported in the following excerpt from the *Wall Street Journal*:

> [PacBell] began a series of quarterly two-day training sessions for its 67,000 workers to give them a common purpose and common approach to their work.

To foster greater creativity, for example, trainers discussed different "levels" of thought, energy and behavior. (In ascending order, the six levels of energy were defined as automatic, sensitive, conscious, creative, unitive and transcendent.) That session, loosely based on the teachings of G.I. Guidjieff, an early 20th century Russian mystic, was supposed to inspire more analytical thinking among employees. In it, workers broke into groups to discuss issues like the difference between "knowledge" and "understanding."

But for many employees, that session and others inspired only anger. Shortly after the program began, workers were quoted in articles about the training in local newspapers as saying that the workshops smacked of mind control, Eastern mysticism, and coercion.[19]

Other major corporations that have integrated New Age teachings into their employee training programs include Allstate, Ford Motor Company, General Dynamics, General Motors, Hewlett-Packard, Procter and Gamble, Polaroid, Sears, TRW, and Volkswagen. According to journalist Jeremy Main, in addition to Kroning, several other cults have jumped on the corporate bandwagon in some of the following ways:

> Wernerd Erhard has abandoned his Erhard Seminars Training, or est, a program famous in the 1970s for the draconian ways it used to teach people to take charge of their lives. But in 1984, Erhard started a management consulting operation called Transformational Technologies, Inc.

> A related movement called MSIA (pronounced Messiah) offers seminars to individuals, some sent by their companies. MSIA is led by the Mystical Traveler Consciousness in the person of John-Roger (who doesn't use his last name, Hinkins).

> The Church of Scientology, a full-blown cult . . . now has two subsidiaries [WISE, a nonprofit organization, and Sterling Management, a consulting firm] that specialize in consulting to corporations.[20]

There are three problems with the implementation of New Age seminars by American employers. First and foremost, whether in the guise of religion or corporate training, New Age teachings present a false gospel. Second, many sincere, Bible-believing Christians do not know the Bible as well as they should and, because they have not "put on the full armor of God" (Eph. 6:11–13), become victims to the false religious teachings presented in these corporate seminars. Finally, and most relevant to our discussion here, is that mandatory employee training programs that invoke religious beliefs are a form of religious discrimination and a violation of Title VII of the Civil Rights Act.

Inevitably, it is not surprising that Christians who have been subjected to New Age and other cultic teachings in the guise of employee training programs have taken legal action. While so far there have been no significant court cases that set a precedent in favor of Christians subjected to New Age training techniques, the Equal Employment Opportunity Commission held in 1991 that an employer violated the Civil Rights Act by failing to provide reasonable accommodation to an employee who had religious objections to a corporate training program.[21] Several suits have been filed over the past decade, but no significant opinions have been reported (written by the courts) on the issue, perhaps because many of the cases in which religious discrimination has actually taken place have been settled out of court. In one case, an employee of the Sidha Corporation in Iowa filed a suit alleging that she was terminated because she refused to engage in mandatory Transcendental Meditation sessions twice a day which, she said, were contrary to her beliefs as a Roman Catholic.[22] While no opinion was published in this case, similar situations are generally decided in favor of the employee.

How Do You Know If the Training Is New Age?

Not all corporate seminars or training programs are necessarily New Age or religious in orientation. There is nothing intrinsically wrong in training employees to have positive self-esteem, to engage in effective sales and management techniques, and to feel good about the companies for which they work. The question to address is what techniques are used to enforce these principles. Richard Warting reports that in one survey conducted among nine thousand personnel directors regarding their exposure to New Age techniques, 45 percent of the respondents cited eleven New Age psychotechniques included in the survey: meditation, biofeedback, Silva mind control, Transcendental Meditation, visualization, hypnosis, focusing, est, Dianetics (a teaching based on Scientology), centering, and yoga. Fifteen percent of the respondents believed that these techniques were beneficial in developing human resources.[23] Warting places in perspective what should be the priority of Christians in the following:

I am usually asked certain questions as I present my arguments against the use of these techniques. Among them, "Aren't these techniques beneficial to industry? Don't they really help a company or employees in some way?" I cannot, and do not, argue against the effectiveness of many of these techniques. Meditation probably does reduce stress. Biofeedback most certainly is an effective tool for self-regulation. Hypnotic reduction can certainly be of therapeutic value when administered properly. However, I do not think that the potential benefits are worth the risks. . . .

I am often asked, "What difference does it make?" It makes a great deal of difference if you are a Christian. The underlying view of reality and the nature of human beings in the New Age movement stands in direct contrast to the primary tenets of orthodox Christianity.[24]

But let's return, for a moment, to one of the problems inherent in employee training programs. Many sincere, Bible-believing Christians may simply not recognize New Age techniques when they are utilized. Think about it. How many of the eleven techniques cited in the personnel survey are you familiar with? Would you recognize Silva mind control, visualization, focusing, est, centering, or another New Age technique if you were subjected to it?

Fortunately, there are indications of New Age teachings in employee training programs that you can be alert to. Cult expert Doug Groothuis cites the following seven signposts that, while they may not always indicate a New Age orientation, signal that you should proceed with caution:

1. Seminars that stress visualization as the key to success, emphasizing the purportedly limitless power of the imagination to "create reality." Seminar participants may be led through long and exotic "guided visualizations" for either relaxation or "empowerment," or seminar leaders may attempt to induce a hypnotic trance in which one becomes vulnerable to suggestion.

2. Seminars that strongly emphasize positive affirmations and self-talk designed to make you feel like we are "captains of our own destinies."

3. Seminars that include Eastern or occult forms of meditation or other "psychotechnologies" under the guise of stress reduction.

4. Seminars that "promise you the world" or guarantee that they will change your life.

5. Seminars that charge an exorbitant cost, which serves as a good psychological adhesive to insure that people endure the seminars

even when their better judgment would normally propel them toward the door at the first few signs of aberration.

6. Excessive secrecy about the actual content of the seminars, such as those which take the form of promoting the charisma of a particular speaker rather than divulging the content of his teaching. A typical tactic is to conceal techniques used in the seminars that would initially—and rightly—repulse many.

7. Seminars that require long hours outside of the normal work schedule and/or require a spouse's attendance may have the implicit intention of radically changing one's world view and manner of life to fit the New Age mold.[25]

In short, be discerning. If you believe you are being required to attend a corporate seminar or training program that is in conflict with your Christian beliefs, be prepared to cite both scriptural and legal principles to back up your objections. If you are not familiar with biblical research principles that will help you document your position, you should seek the advice of your pastor or a Christian counselor.

The Sword Still Cuts Both Ways

As more lawsuits are filed by Christians who are subjected to mandatory employee training that conflicts with biblical principles, it is likely that the courts will hold in favor of the Christian employees. Since there are no significant precedents, how can we make that assumption? Because, for better or worse, Christian employers have engaged in the same type of activities.

The Townley Manufacturing Company, a manufacturer of mining equipment, was founded in 1963 by Jake and Helen Townley. Born-again Christians, the Townleys had made a covenant with God that their company "would be a Christian, faith-operated business." In 1979, Louis Pelvas, an atheist, was hired by the Townleys, and when they instituted mandatory devotional services in 1984, Pelvas was forced to attend. After filing a complaint with the Equal Opportunity Employment Commission, Pelvas quit his job and launched a suit against the Townleys, charging them with religious discrimination under Title VII of the Civil Rights Act.

In 1988, the Federal Court of Appeals for the Ninth Circuit affirmed a district court ruling that the mandatory attendance at the Townleys' devotionals amounted to unlawful employment discrimination. Despite the Townleys' claim that they were running a religious corporation exempt from Title VII, the court held that only those institutions with extremely close ties to organized religions are considered to be religious corporations for the purpose of exemption from Title VII.[26]

In a 1986 case in Ohio, Sharon Wilson was subjected to religious lectures and Bible reading by her employer and filed suit against the state Bureau of Employment Services. In holding that she was not eligible for unemployment compensation, the Ohio Court of Appeals ruled that she had made no attempts to remedy the problem by notifying her employer of her displeasure. Had she done so, however, it is likely that the court would have found the employer guilty of religious harassment.[27]

In a 1992 Massachusetts case, Ruth Kolodziej, a management-level employee of Electro-Term, a Christian company, was forced to attend a training seminar which taught, based on what is perceived to be scriptural principles, that a woman's proper place in the family was subservient to the place of the man. While many evangelical Christians would not disagree with this position, it is important to realize that the seminar was religious in nature and could just as easily have been a cultic or New Age seminar. Strangely enough, in this case the Massachusetts Supreme Court held that, while the seminar used the Scriptures to support the positions it promoted, it did not constitute a devotional service. Because of the lack of precedents in this area (not to mention the unpredictability of the courts in untested areas of the law), it is difficult to speculate on whether the United States Supreme Court would reach a similar decision.[28]

The point should be made here that the courts have consistently held that religious discrimination is inappropriate in the secular workplace, whether the discrimination is in favor of or against Christianity. Religious organizations per se (including churches, religious schools, and missionary organizations) may discriminate on the basis of religion, but secular companies, even if they are owned by Christians, cannot mandate participation in pervasively religious activities by their employees. Nor, of course, can secular organizations mandate participation in New Age or other non-Christian religious activities by Christian employees or others who may object to the activities.

If you have a business that you have dedicated to the Lord, that does not mean that you are forbidden to hold religious activities such as a morning prayer session, Bible study, or devotional group. The important thing is for you to establish that attendance is voluntary, not mandatory. From an evangelistic standpoint, remember that you can still catch more flies with honey than with vinegar. Not only will this meet the requirements of the law, it may make non-Christian employees curious enough to attend—not because they have to, but because they want to.

Conscientious Objection As a Form of Witness

In this chapter, I have not even begun to treat the myriad of cases that deal generally with religious issues in the workplace. Cases that have been decided in favor of Christians include the right of Christian postal workers who are pacifists not to process Selective Service registration forms;[29] a Christian secretary who resigned from her job and was awarded unemployment compensation after she refused to copy materials from "Dungeons and Dragons" for a role-playing program in a chemical-dependency treatment center;[30] the right of a Pentecostal female school bus driver to wear a skirt rather than slacks;[31] and the right of hospital-based nurses to refuse to participate in abortion procedures.[32]

In short, there are ways to express your faith other than by direct witness. Even if you are in a position in which you cannot express your faith, your behavior can testify to the fact that you are a Christian. Jesus said, "Let your light shine before men in such a way that they may see your good works, and glorify your Father who is in heaven" (Matt. 5:16). Even your refusal to do something to which you are conscientiously opposed based on your religious convictions can allow non-Christians to see what Paul called "Christ in you, the hope of glory" (Col. 1:27).

Survival Tactics in the Workplace

There may be ramifications any time you express your Christianity on the job, whether you speak of your faith or refuse to do something that is against your convictions. Here are a few suggestions to help you in your cause.

If you are in a position in which you receive performance reviews, you have the legal right to request a copy of your appraisals. They may make good bird-cage liners, but they also serve a more important function. If you have received good appraisals, they will document the quality of your work if you are ever terminated because of your religious convictions. An employer may claim that an employee's performance was poor and that he or she was not terminated for religious reasons; good performance appraisals will serve as evidence against such a claim.

Before taking legal action against an employer, make sure you exhaust all of your administrative options. If you have a religious objection to participating in a company activity, including mandatory training sessions that are against your faith, approach your employer and explain your objections before you take legal action. If you receive no satisfaction, call the Equal Employment Opportunity Commission (EEOC), the Civil Rights Commission, or your local Department of Human Relations. They will be able to tell you if you have a case you might pursue through their agency or through the civil courts. Remember that if you file a suit without having made your objections known to your employer, it will most likely be dismissed because you have not pursued these administrative options. Some courts will not accept an employment discrimination case unless it has gone through the EEOC or a similar agency.

Remember the two standards used by the courts in the adjudication of disputes involving religion in the workplace: An employer must make reasonable accommodation for your religious beliefs, unless such accommodation would create an undue hardship for the employer. These are abstract phrases that have been interpreted in different ways by different courts, but they may help you weigh whether you are really the victim of religious discrimination.

If you believe you are being harassed because of your religious beliefs, make notes and keep them for future reference. You will more likely be able to prove religious discrimination if you have a detailed record of the discussions you have had with your employer. Include names, dates, and circumstances of any meetings, negative comments, or warnings you receive, as well as a summary of what was said by any parties present (including you). By the way, you should also assume that your employer may be making similar notes for your personnel file.

When you discuss your religion with your co-workers, try to do so only on your own time: coffee breaks, meal breaks, etc. If a company challenges your right to witness, you are more likely to be protected under the First Amendment if you do not engage in religious discussions on company time.

Remember that employers have the right to restrict religious discussions with customers, clients, and patients. If you feel called to hold such discussions, be "shrewd as serpents, and innocent as doves" (Matt. 10:16). In other words, be subtle. You will get away with it longer than if you wave a ninety-pound Bible in your hands and preach over the company's public-address system.

If you witness to a subordinate employee (an employee you directly supervise or who is in a lower-rank position than you), never imply that his or her job status is dependent upon accepting the gospel. That would make you guilty of religious discrimination.

If it is difficult to initiate a discussion with your co-workers, try to get them to ask you about your faith. If your workplace has a parking lot, a bumper sticker with a Christian message on your car may help.

If you get to the point where you feel you should take legal action against an employer or former employer, consult an attorney who specializes in employment law; he or she will probably be more knowledgeable about your rights than a general practitioner. If you feel that you have been the victim of religious discrimination in the workplace, don't rule out calling your local chapter of the American Civil Liberties Union. The ACLU often defends persons who have been discriminated against on the basis of their religion and, despite its liberal orientation, has been known to defend evangelical Christians. Even though many ACLU members will disagree with your biblical faith, they often approach these issues from a freedom of speech perspective.

/ 8 /

Taking the Word to
Stadiums and Concerts

It's Friday night, and for the next couple of days you don't have to think about work. While many of your co-workers are heading for the nearest bar to pop open a Budweiser, you are ready for some serious witnessing and want to go where there are plenty of non-Christians who might be open to receive the Word. You open the newspaper and find several events taking place in your city over the weekend that present some interesting possibilities: a rock concert or two, a football game, and even a convention of Jehovah's Witnesses.

But can you go to these events, pass out tracts, and share the gospel with people who attend? What if you are confronted by the police or ejected by security guards hired by stadium owners? Do you have as much freedom to witness at stadiums as you do on the streets? If the stadiums are not public forums, do they, like the malls, have the right to prevent expressive activities or religious speech?

Fortunately, the courts have addressed these questions, and most cases have been decided in favor of Christians. A survey of some recent stadium cases may help establish some of the principles used by the courts to adjudicate these issues.

One of the first cases over evangelistic activities at a stadium involved members of the Krishna Consciousness Movement (ISKCON) who were prevented from distributing literature and soliciting contributions at the Meadowlands Sports Complex in Hackensack, New Jersey. The New Jersey Sports and Exposition Authority, an agency created by the state legislature to manage the Meadowlands complex, had adopted a policy to prohibit anyone from soliciting money or distributing literature at the complex, and their policy was applied in a uniform and nondiscriminatory manner.

The Meadowlands complex includes a football stadium and a racetrack. The authority issued a long-term lease to the New York Giants football team and a license to the Cosmos Soccer Club, providing them with exclusive use of the stadium on designated days. The authority and the two teams share the revenues from parking charges, admission fees, and concession sales. At times the authority has also leased the stadium for events as diverse as high school and college football games, religious conventions, and commencement exercises.

The racetrack at the complex, which shares a parking lot with the stadium, is operated directly by the New Jersey Sports and Exposition Authority. The track charges an admission fee, but the chief source of revenue for the track comes from pari-mutuel betting, which takes place at nearly six hundred seller and cashier windows. The betting, rather than admission fees, carries the entire Meadowlands complex, enables the authority to meet its debts and operating expenses, and allows the authority to pay its bond holders.

ISKCON filed suit in the Federal District Court for the District of New Jersey, which, after a fifteen-day trial on ISKCON's request for a permanent injunction against the authority, concluded that neither the racetrack nor the stadium was designed or intended to be used as a public forum.[1] In 1982, the Federal Court of Appeals for the Third Circuit affirmed the district court's ruling, but noted that the scope of the ruling was directed at the specific activities in which the Krishna devotees engaged.

The problem with the case is simple. Members of ISKCON do not merely distribute literature, they also request donations. In *International Society for Krishna Consciousness, Inc., v. New Jersey Sports and Exposition Authority* (1982), the appeals court held that the act of soliciting donations conflicted with the purpose of the racetrack, which was to encourage people to bet their money on horse races. It wrote:

> The Meadowlands is a commercial venture by the state. It is designed to bring economic benefits to northern New Jersey, and is expected to generate at least enough revenue to meet its current expenses and debt service. It earns money by attracting and entertaining spectators with athletic events and horse races. . . .
>
> ISKCON proposes to intercept spectators and request donations from them. This would compete with the Authority for its patrons' money and disrupt the normal activities of the complex. . . . The Authority fears that solicitation may offend or annoy some bettors so much that they will

choose in the future to attend one of the competing, privately owned racetracks in the area where ISKCON does not pursue its activities.[2]

Would the court's ruling have been different if ISKCON merely distributed literature but did not ask for donations? The court appeared to imply that it would have ruled the same way but avoided addressing the issue directly.

> We also note that ISKCON does not wish to distribute literature without simultaneously soliciting money. Were that issue presented, the question would be whether a total ban is reasonable, taking into consideration the fact that all organizations may claim the same right.[3]

Finally, the court held that there were alternatives available to the Krishna devotees to engage in religious dialogue without distributing literature or soliciting donations.

> It is important to recognize that members of [ISKCON], like other people, are free to enter the stadium or racetrack upon payment of an admission fee. Once there, they are free to speak with anyone they choose and upon any topic, whether it be religion, politics, the merits of the Giants' and Cosmos' opponents, or a "hot tip in the fifth race." They are free to wave pennants or wear clothes that demonstrate a point of view. None of these activities is proscribed by the Authority's policy, which does not in any way touch upon the content of pure or symbolic speech.[4]

Three years later, the Federal Court of Appeals for the Ninth Circuit held in *Carreras v. City of Anaheim* (1985)[5] that ISKCON had the right to distribute literature and solicit funds at the Anaheim Stadium and the Anaheim Convention Center in California. Unlike the Meadowlands case, which was decided on the basis of the First Amendment to the Federal Constitution, the Anaheim case was decided on the basis of the California Constitution, in which the courts had previously found a wider range of free speech rights than in the First Amendment. (Remember *PruneYard Shopping Center v. Robins* in chapter 5, which dealt with shopping malls? The same principle operated in the *Carreras* case.)

Another factor operating in *Carreras* was that the Anaheim Stadium operators felt that the ISKCON members engaged in "bad conduct" that included solicitation outside agreed-upon areas, touching of stadium patrons without consent, retrieval by solicitors from patrons of "gifts" such as bumper stickers when no donation was given, and misrepresentation of the purpose of solicitation. Nonetheless, the court held that such conduct does not prove that solicitation is inherently incompatible with the intended uses of the stadium.

> A mere annoyance does not establish incompatibility. To the extent that the conduct of ISKCON solicitors is fraudulent or physically intrusive, the problem can be dealt with through narrowly tailored rules and security precautions. An occasional incident of misconduct cannot justify the absolute denial of access to ISKCON solicitors.[6]

Finally, the court held that the ordinance prohibiting solicitation was unconstitutional because it allowed impermissible discrimination, lacked adequate procedural safeguards, and permitted city officials to deny or revoke permits on the basis of unguided discretion.[7] In short, the ordinance was too vague to stand constitutional scrutiny.

So Where Are the Christians?

Thus far we have looked at two cases with rulings that were limited in scope. In the Meadowlands case, the courts ruled against ISKCON because their activities interfered with a racetrack on the premises, diverting money from the activity for which the complex was designed. In the Anaheim case, a decision in favor of ISKCON was based on the California State Constitution rather than the federal Constitution.

Fortunately, there has been a major decision in favor of the right of Christians to witness in stadiums based on the First Amendment. In 1991, the Federal Court of Appeals for the Second Circuit held in *Paulsen v. County of Nassau*[8] that members of the Christian Joy Fellowship had the constitutional right to distribute religious leaflets to persons attending a rock concert by the group Judas Priest at the Nassau County Coliseum in Uniondale, Long Island, New York.

The *Paulsen* case presents a typical scenario of evangelistic activities at rock concerts. Mitch Paulsen was detained by the Nassau County Police while he and a friend, Andrew Nesselroth, distributed tracts at the concert. Lieutenant Robert Turk informed him that if he wanted to distribute handbills he needed the permission of the coliseum's director of operations. Turk did not charge Paulsen with violating any law and returned the tracts to him following the concert. Paulsen filed suit for a preliminary injunction against enforcement of the coliseum's policy against literature distribution and presented a synopsis of the Christian Joy Fellowship's evangelistic program at trial in the Federal District Court for the Eastern District of New York.

On at least fifteen occasions, Paulsen and Nesselroth testified, they and others had circulated more than 100,000 tracts at the coliseum. On average, between six and ten individuals would stand in the mall area for approximately two hours before a scheduled event to distribute tracts to incoming patrons. The Christian Joy Fellowship, an evangelical group devoted to encouraging Bible study, often targeted heavy metal and rock concert fans because they believed that the young people who attended the concerts required spiritual guidance.

Finding a likelihood that their First and Fourteenth Amendment rights to engage in expressive activity had been violated, the trial court granted Paulsen and Nesselroth's motion for a preliminary injunction against the coliseum's management and directed the coliseum to issue them a permit allowing the distribution of noncommercial literature on the portion of the property located outside the arena, subject to reasonable regulations related to community safety and necessary expenses.[9]

As were the Meadowlands in New Jersey, the Anaheim Stadium, and the Anaheim Convention Center, the Nassau Coliseum was owned by the local government. Located on fifty-four acres of land, the coliseum was managed by the county for its first seven years of operation, after which it entered into a long-term lease with Hyatt Management in 1979. In 1988, after Hyatt Management changed its name to Facility Management of New York, it merged with Spectacor Management, a commercial firm that manages several stadium facilities. Events at the coliseum have included performances as diverse as the New York Islanders hockey team, Bruce Springsteen, Motley Crue, R.E.M., and the TNT Monster Truck Challenge, as well as parades, political rallies and speeches, religious weddings, and circuses. On five occasions over a four-year period, the coliseum had been host to rent-free charitable events, and banners were displayed by patrons on a regular basis.[10]

The trial court's granting of an injunction was affirmed by the Federal Court of Appeals for the Second Circuit, which held that the coliseum was a public forum designed to serve the interests of the county, and that the proprietary (commercial) nature of the outside coliseum managers did not render the coliseum a nonpublic forum. Additionally, the court specifically addressed the distribution of literature that, unlike the Krishna activities, was not accompanied by financial solicitation. It wrote:

> The leaflets in this case are not likely to disturb seriously the audience attending an event in the arena. Because one need not stop nor ponder the contents of a leaflet in order mechanically to take it out of someone's hand, the nature of the intrusion is minimal. And, a listener's reaction to speech does not control the permissible scope of First Amendment activities. In short, distributing handbills on the plaza and sidewalks is not likely, as [the Coliseum managers] argue, to interfere with the mood or the quality of the Coliseum arena events.[11]

Finally, in the unanimous opinion of the court of appeals, Circuit Judge Irving R. Kaufman presented an eloquent discourse on both literature distribution and the changing nature of the public forum. His words, hopefully, may provide an indication of how future cases may open other venues, such as shopping malls, to evangelistic activities. He wrote:

> From the time of the founding of our nation, the distribution of written material has been an essential weapon in the defense of liberty. Throughout the years, the leaflet has retained its vitality as an effective and inexpensive means of disseminating religious and political thought. Today, when selective access to channels of mass communication limits the expression of diverse opinion, the handbill remains important to the promise of full and free discussion of public issues. For those of moderate means, but deep conviction, freedom to circulate fliers implicates fundamental liberties. . . .
>
> In many cities and suburban environs like Long Island, the municipal stadium has replaced the town meeting hall and the public square as a gathering place for large segments of the population to engage in meaningful discourse. If free public discussion is to maintain its vitality in our national life, we must remain vigilant against unnecessary restraints on our liberty, particularly those arbitrarily imposed by government fiat.[12]

Raise the Banners High

In addition to dialogue with concert and sports fans and the distribution of literature at stadiums, another form of witnessing has become popular over the past few years. Christians who have watched football games on television cannot help but notice scriptural banners hung over balcony rails or held high by Christians.

Even a sign with a reference to the Scriptures, rather than the verses written out, can be enough to whet the curiosity of non-Christians to look up the verses in the Bibles gathering dust on their own bookshelves. One of the best examples today that God's Word never returns void (Isa. 55:11) can be seen in a stadium banner that merely reads, "John 3:16."

The bad news is that Christians have been hassled for displaying such banners at sporting events. The good news is that the courts have thus far affirmed the right to exhibit those banners.

On two occasions in 1984, Rollen Stewart and Stephen Francis posted large banners reading "John 3:16" on the railings behind the twenty-yard line at the Robert F. Kennedy Memorial Stadium in Washington, D.C., just prior to the beginning of televised games featuring the Washington Redskins. On both occasions the signs were removed by the District of Columbia Armory Board, which manages the stadium, and by representatives of CBS Sports, which televised the games. The paper banners were three feet by fifteen feet and posed neither a sight line problem nor obstructed the vision of players or spectators. On both occasions several other banners were displayed, many of which were larger than those hung by Stewart and Francis, but only the religious banner was removed.

Stewart and Francis filed suit, but their case was dismissed by the United States District Court for the District of Columbia, which held that the stadium was not a public forum. The Federal Court of Appeals for the D.C. Circuit reversed the lower court ruling,[13] after which the stadium management backed down until June 1990, when it adopted new regulations concerning RFK Stadium. The new policy permitted the exhibition of signs and banners if they met the following conditions:

1. The banner shall pertain to the event;
2. The banner shall not be commercial, vulgar or derogatory; and
3. The dimensions of the banner shall not exceed four feet by six feet.[14]

On January 4, 1992, Edwin Thate placed a Scripture sign with the reference "John 3:3" at the twenty-yard line in the stadium and another banner that said "Mark 8:36" in the end zone. By halftime, both signs had been torn down by stadium employees at the direction of the National Football League. Stephen Francis, who was watching the game at home, observed that a variety of other signs—"Hi to Kathy and Don," "Capital Punishment," "National Defense," and "2 Legit 2 Quit"—remained undisturbed throughout the game. Along with Rollen Stewart, Francis and Thate filed a new suit seeking another injunction against the stadium.

On January 10, 1992, a mere six days after the incident, the district court held in *Stewart v. District of Columbia Armory Board* that RFK Stadium is a public forum and issued both a temporary restraining order and a preliminary injunction that allowed religious banners to be displayed during another Redskins game on January 12, 1992. Noting that the stadium management had been inconsistent in the enforcement of its June 1990 regulations by removing only religious signs, the court held that the regulations were overbroad and vague:

> As illustration, the regulation prohibits "vulgar" or "derogatory" speech, but fails entirely to define those terms. In addition, the regulation prohibits speech that "does not pertain to the event," but fails to guide anyone in determining what speech pertains to an event and what speech does not.[15]

Finally, the court held that concerns about offending fans, football team owners, tenants, and the National Football League did not present a compelling state interest that would justify the prohibition of the banners based on their content, noting that "undifferentiated fear or apprehension of disturbance is not enough to overcome the right to freedom of expression."[16]

The RFK Stadium case was settled by a consent agreement in August 1992, when RFK officials agreed to draw up new regulations permitting the display of religious messages.[17]

Stadiums as Public Forums

All of the cases we have looked at in this chapter have involved stadiums that are owned by government entities. Even though such stadiums may be operated by commercial management companies, that does not change the fact that, in most cases, the exterior areas of stadiums are public forums. Likewise, if the interior section of a stadium permits expressive activities, it cannot discriminate against the exhibition of religious signs or banners based on their content.

Whether the same rights exist for Christians who carry on evangelistic activities in privately owned stadiums has not been addressed by the courts. It is likely, however, that if a stadium allows any form of First Amendment activity such as the secular signs exhibited at the RFK Stadium, it, too, could not discriminate on the basis of content.

In terms of rock concerts that are held at places other than stadiums, coliseums, or arenas, the right to witness may depend upon the location of the concert. In many cases, concert venues such as the Hard Rock Café (a popular rock club found in many cities around the nation) or other clubs often abut municipal streets, and the streets themselves are a public forum. Therefore, the right to witness at concerts appears to be in favor of Christians.

With that in mind, here are some suggestions that may help you witness at stadiums and concerts more effectively.

Work in teams, especially at rock concerts. Remember that while concerts by groups such as Judas Priest and Motley Crue present a lot of potential for evangelism, they are poor places for Christians to do "Lone Ranger" witnessing by themselves.

Remember that at most rock concerts (especially those that are sold out), police and security guards are used to people congregating outside the stadium. However, many of those who don't go into the concert are either dealing drugs or scalping (reselling concert tickets at exorbitantly high prices). Stadium police and guards are often more tolerant than you might imagine (and you can witness to them as well). However, be prepared to make it clear that you are not a drug dealer, a drug user, or a scalper.

As with the police, do not resist if you are detained or your tracts are confiscated by stadium security guards. You can always get the tracts back later, and resistance could result in criminal charges. Your best bet is to consult a lawyer. If you have been unlawfully detained by private security guards, you may have cause to bring a civil action against them.

When witnessing in a mixed group at a rock concert or a sports event, women should always be accompanied by at least two male members of the team. Both concert and sports fans tend to show up at events drunk or stoned, and they will not care if a female member of your team is Christian or not. As far as they are concerned, she is fair bait. Regardless of gender, keep a protective (and prayerful) watch on other team members.

Be careful about witnessing to people who are high on alcohol or drugs. Unless your prayers are so powerful that people who are high immediately sober up, pass by them until they come down from their high. Remember that people who are drunk or stoned are more likely to cause a confrontation.

As always, get to know the case precedents that work in your favor, whether at stadiums or at rock clubs located along a street. If you can quote case names and the year they were decided to the police or security guards, they will more likely believe that even if they don't know your rights, you do.

When witnessing at rock clubs that abut streets, use the same principles that are outlined in chapter 4. Remember not to interfere with traffic, with ingress or egress into buildings, or in a manner that creates a "clear and present danger," and that your right to witness is subject to reasonable time, place, and manner restrictions.

/ 9 /

Taking the Word to Airports

Having traveled extensively for the past few years, I have been impressed by how big, and yet how small, the United States seems to be. It is hard to imagine that some of the technologies we have today that allow fast and efficient travel were not around as recently as thirty or forty years ago. The interstate highway system, over which I have been able to travel from coast to coast in as short a time as five days, was not conceived until the 1950s. Earlier generations were limited to local highways which ran through a myriad of small towns. It still is a big country, though I have learned that wherever I go I am likely to find McDonald's and Burger King, Exxon and Mobil, and a host of other conveniences that I am used to having at home.

At the same time, this has become a small nation. We are able to travel coast to coast by jet aircraft in just over five hours; able to fly a thousand or more miles away for a quick weekend vacation; able to conduct business in two or three cities in different parts of the country on the same day. And every day, thousands of people do just that. The one thing air travelers have in common is that to board the planes that will transport them to their destinations they must go through airports.

It is not surprising, then, that airports have become another venue for personal evangelism. And, despite the stereotype many people have that only cultists like the Hare Krishna members engage in religious activities in airports, they have also become popular spots for evangelistic activities by Christians.

Airports, as any other milieu, are subject to reasonable time, place, and manner restrictions when it comes to witnessing. Nonetheless, a number of cases involving both Christians and members of the Krishna movement have affirmed the right to carry on First Amendment activities at airports around the nation. In fact, a significant 1992 case adjudi-cated by the United States Supreme Court that addressed religious rights dealt with airports. And, for better or worse, the Court has determined that airports do not constitute a traditional public forum.

That does not mean airports are totally off-limits to evangelism, but, as in other situations, it helps to know what the law has to say. Here, then, are some of the cases that have involved airport evangelism over the past few years.

The Lower Courts Speak Out

In today's Christian church one of the most active evangelistic groups is Jews for Jesus. A few years ago Moishe Rosen, chairman of Jews for Jesus, was arrested at the Portland, Oregon, airport for violating an or-dinance that required a one-day advance notice of a person's intent to distribute literature, picket, or otherwise communicate with the general public. The ordinance also required disclosure of the names, addresses, and telephone numbers of the persons who would take part in First Amendment activities. Rosen filed suit, and a federal district court up-held the ordinance as constitutional.

In *Rosen v. Port of Portland* (1981),[1] the Court of Appeals for the Ninth Circuit reversed the trial court, noting that the distribution of lit-erature is protected under the First Amendment, which had full effect in airport terminal buildings. While the regulation of activities that inter-fere with the normal function of an airport is a proper government func-tion, the court held, the challenged ordinance went too far in restricting First Amendment activities.

Regarding the submission of names and addresses to the airport au-thority by persons taking part in evangelistic activities, the court held that the advance registration requirement had a "chilling effect" that cre-ated an unjustified burden on free speech and stifled spontaneous ex-pression. Citing an early Supreme Court case that addressed the issue of mandatory registration,[2] the court ruled that the policy created a prior restraint on free speech that required an advance trip to the airport and completion of the required forms, thus discouraging political, social, and economic speech.

Also in 1981, in *Fernandes v. Limmer* the Fifth Circuit Court of Ap-peals affirmed a lower court decision that the Dallas-Fort Worth airport complex was a public forum. Susan Fernandes, a member of the Krishna Consciousness Movement, had sought an injunction against enforcement of a local ordinance that governed literature distribution and fund solicitation at the Dallas-Fort Worth airport, and a federal district court held that the ordinance violated the First Amendment. The appeals court noted that despite the fact that all of the space in the four terminal buildings was leased to private carriers, the airport constituted a public forum because of the lack of restrictions on entry by the general public and the commercial, streetlike character of the terminal concourses.[3]

A few years later, the right to conduct religious activities in airports was extended to include groups that actually rent space in airports. Since 1976, the Christian Science Reading Room had rented space at San Francisco International Airport. In 1984, it was issued an eviction notice and told that the airport had adopted a policy of not renting to religious organizations. The Christian Scientists filed suit, and a federal district court injunction was issued against the airport. In *Christian Science Reading Room Jointly Maintained v. City of San Francisco* (1986),[4] the Court of Appeals for the Ninth Circuit held that the airport's action violated the equal protection clause of the Fourteenth Amendment and that the rental of space to the Christian Scientists met the conditions of the *Lemon* test.[5] The rental of space had the secular purpose of obtaining revenue, it did not advance religion because the airport made space available to anyone who wished to rent it, and there was no ongoing entanglement between government and religion since the reading room did not tell the airport how to run its operations, nor vice versa.

Airports and the Supreme Court

In 1983, the Board of Airport Commissioners for the City of Los Angeles adopted a resolution that prohibited any First Amendment expression in the central terminal area of the Los Angeles International Airport (LAX) at all. In July 1984, Alan Howard Snyder, a member of Jews for Jesus, was stopped by an airport police officer while he distributed free religious literature on a pedestrian walkway in the central terminal area of LAX. Snyder, along with Jews for Jesus, filed suit in the District Court for the Central District of California, which held that the central terminal area was a traditional public forum under the First Amendment. The Court of Appeals for the Ninth Circuit affirmed the decision, holding that "an airport complex is a traditional public forum," and that the resolution was unconstitutional under the First Amendment. The court noted that the airport could impose reasonable time, place, and manner restrictions but could not ban all First Amendment activities without a compelling state interest, which it had not demonstrated.[6]

In *Board of Airport Commissioners of the City of Los Angeles v. Jews for Jesus, Inc.* (1987), the United States Supreme Court affirmed the unconstitutionality of the board's resolution but avoided the issue of whether the airport was a public forum.

> Because we conclude that the resolution is facially unconstitutional under the First Amendment overbreadth doctrine regardless of the proper standard, we need not decide whether LAX is indeed a public forum, or whether the *Perry* standard is applicable when access to a nonpublic forum is not restricted.[7]

Without addressing the public forum issue directly, Justice Sandra Day O'Connor wrote for the Court that the resolution prohibited First Amendment activity to the point of absurdity:

> On its face, the resolution at issue in this case reaches the universe of expressive activity, and, by prohibiting *all* protected expression, purports to create a virtual "First Amendment Free Zone" at LAX. The resolution does not merely regulate expressive activity in the Central Terminal Area that might create problems such as congestion or the disruption of the activities of those who use LAX. Instead, the resolution expansively states that LAX "is not open for First Amendment activities by any individual and/or entity" . . . The resolution therefore does not merely reach the activity of [Jews for Jesus] at LAX; it prohibits even talking or reading, or the wearing of campaign buttons or symbolic clothing. Under such a sweeping ban, virtually every individual who enters LAX may be found to violate the resolution by engaging in some "First Amendment activity." We think it obvious that such a ban cannot be justified even if LAX were a nonpublic forum because no conceivable governmental interest would justify such an absolute prohibition of speech.[8]

The Court's decision was unanimous, though Justice Byron White filed a single-paragraph concurring opinion, joined by Chief Justice William Rehnquist, chiding the Court for evading the public forum question:

I join the Court's opinion but suggest that it should not be taken as indicating that a majority of the Court considers the Los Angeles International Airport to be a traditional public forum. That issue was one of the questions on which we granted certiorari, and we should not have postponed it for another day.[9]

In their brief comment, Justice White and Chief Justice Rehnquist implied that they felt an airport was not a public forum. Five years later, the Chief Justice would write a majority opinion that confirmed this implication.

The Final Word on Airports—For Now

As we have seen in a number of other cases, members of the Krishna Consciousness Movement usually combine the distribution of literature with the solicitation of funds. For the Krishna devotees, this is more than a practice; it is a religious ritual known as Sankirtan, which "enjoins its members to go into public places to distribute or sell religious literature and to solicit donations for the support of the Krishna religion."[10] Miller and Flowers write this:

> Hare Krishnas maintain that these actions constitute a ritual (Sankirtan) essential to their religion. Because their activities have intimidated and frightened some and irritated many, practitioners have been subjected to various restrictive efforts on the part of state and local authorities. With mixed results, the constitutionality of these regulations has been challenged by ISKCON in state and federal courts.[11]

Previously, the Supreme Court had addressed ISKCON's practice in *Heffron v. International Society for Krishna Consciousness* (1981), in which it held the following:

> [ISKCON] and its ritual of Sankirtan have no special claim to First Amendment protection as compared to that of other religions who also distribute literature and solicit funds. None of our cases suggests that the inclusion of peripatetic solicitation as a part of a church ritual entitles church members to solicitation rights in a public forum superior to those of members of other religious groups that raise money but do not purport to ritualize the process.[12]

In 1992, the Court again addressed the activities of ISKCON in a case that would have broad impact on evangelism in airports.

The Port Authority of New York owns and operates three major airports in the greater New York City area: John F. Kennedy International Airport, La Guardia Airport, and Newark International Airport. Serving approximately 8 percent of the United States' domestic air travelers and over 50 percent of the trans-Atlantic market, the three airports are expected to serve at least 110 million passengers annually by the end of the 1990s.

Most of the space at the airports is leased to commercial airlines, but the port authority retains control over unleased portions that include La Guardia's Central Terminal Building, portions of Kennedy's International Arrivals Building, and Newark's North Terminal Building. All terminals are accessible to the public and have a variety of commercial establishments that include restaurants, snack stands, bars, newsstands, and stores.

The port authority instituted a regulation, applied at all three airports, forbidding literature distribution or fund solicitation in the terminal buildings, though the authority permitted both literature distribution and solicitation on the sidewalks outside the terminal buildings. The regulation stated:

> The following conduct is prohibited within the interior areas of buildings or structures at an air terminal if conducted by a person to or with passersby in a continuous or repetitive manner:
>   The sale or distribution of any merchandise, including but not limited to jewelry, food stuffs, candles, flowers, badges and clothing.
>   The sale or distribution of flyers, brochures, pamphlets, books or any other printed or written material.
>   The solicitation and receipt of funds.[13]

ISKCON filed suit against the port authority, alleging that the policy deprived them of rights guaranteed under the First Amendment. A federal district court held that the terminals were akin to public streets and declared them to be a public forum.[14] On appeal, a divided panel on the Court of Appeals for the Second Circuit held that the terminals are not a public forum and that, based on the specific case, the ban on solicitation was reasonable but the ban on literature distribution was not. The United States Supreme Court, noting that it had not resolved the public forum question regarding airport terminals in the earlier case of *Board of Airport Commissioners of Los Angeles v. Jews for Jesus* (1987), accepted the case for review.

In 1992, a divided Court affirmed the appeals decision and held in *International Society for Krishna Consciousness, Inc., v. Lee* that the port authority could not ban literature distribution but did have the right to ban solicitation. Writing for the majority, Chief Justice William Rehnquist reviewed the characteristics of a public forum:

> Traditional public forums such as streets and parks have immemorially been held in trust for the use of the public and, time out of mind, have been used for purposes of assembly, communicating thoughts between citizens, and discussing public questions.
>
> Designated public forums are those which are not created by government inaction, but by the *intentional* opening of a nontraditional forum for public discourse.[15]

Noting that airports were primarily intended to facilitate efficient air travel, the Court held the following:

> Like the Court of Appeals, we conclude that airports are nonpublic fora and that the [Port Authority] regulation reasonably limits solicitation. . . . As commercial enterprises, airports must provide services attractive to the marketplace. In light of this, it cannot fairly be said that an airport terminal has as a principal purpose "promoting the free exchange of ideas."[16]

Concluding that airports are not a public forum, Rehnquist wrote of the disruptive effect that solicitation had on airport travelers:

> Passengers who wish to avoid the solicitor may have to alter their path, slowing both themselves and those around them. The result is that the normal flow of traffic is impeded. This is especially so in an airport, where air travelers, who are often weighted down by cumbersome baggage . . . may be hurrying to catch a plane or to arrange ground transportation. Delays may be particularly costly in this setting, as a flight missed by only a few minutes can result in hours worth of subsequent inconvenience.[17]

ISKCON v. Lee, which appears to be the final word on financial solicitation at airports, at least for the moment, was a closely divided opinion. Four justices joined Chief Justice Rehnquist's majority opinion (Byron White, Sandra Day O'Connor, Antonin Scalia, and Clarence Thomas). Justice O'Connor also wrote a concurring opinion in which she observed that, despite her agreement that the airport was not a public forum, the port authority had created a "huge complex open to travelers and nontravelers alike. The airports house restaurants, cafeterias, snack bars, coffee shops, cocktail lounges, post offices, banks, telegraph offices, clothing shops, drug stores, food stores, nurseries, barber shops, currency exchanges, art exhibits, commercial advertising displays, bookstores, newsstands, dental offices and private clubs. The International Arrivals Building at JFK even has two branches of Bloomingdale's."[18]

There was, however, some notable dissent in the case. Justice Anthony Kennedy wrote a concurring opinion holding that the airports are a public forum. Charging that Rehnquist was relying too heavily on "historical pedigree," Kennedy wrote:

> Without this recognition our forum doctrine retains no relevance in times of fast-changing technology and increasing insularity. In a country where most citizens travel by automobile, and parks all too often become locales for crime rather than social intercourse, our failure to recognize the possibility that new types of government property may be appropriate forums for speech will lead to a serious curtailment of our expressive activity. . . . We have allowed flexibility in our doctrine to meet changing technologies in other areas of constitutional interpretation, and I believe we must do the same with the First Amendment.[19]

Building on the description of businesses at the airports provided by Justice O'Connor, Kennedy suggested the following:

> If the objective, physical characteristics of the property at issue and the actual public access and uses which have been permitted by the government indicate that expressive activity would be appropriate and compatible with those uses, the property is a public forum. The most important considerations in this analysis are whether the property shares physical similarities with more traditional public forums. . . . The public spaces in the airports are broad, public thoroughfares full of people and lined with stores and other commercial activities. An airport corridor is of course not a street, but that is not the proper inquiry. The question is one of phys-

ical similarities, sufficient to suggest that the airport corridor should be a public forum for the same reasons that streets and sidewalks have been treated as public forums by the people who use them.[20]

Despite classifying the airports as a public forum, Kennedy nonetheless concurred with the judgment that financial solicitation could be regulated as a reasonable time, place, and manner restriction. The opposite conclusion was reached by Justice David Souter, who wrote a dissenting opinion in which he was joined by Justices Harry Blackmun and John Paul Stevens. Not only did Souter hold that the airports are a public forum, he felt that "the [solicitation] regulation must be struck down for its failure to satisfy the requirements of a narrow tailoring to further a significant state interest and availability of ample alternative channels for communication."[21] Thus, the dissenting justices would have allowed both literature distribution and the solicitation of funds.

Nonetheless, the key issue in the opinions cited thus far is financial solicitation, not literature distribution. In a short *per curiam* (unsigned) opinion, the Court affirmed that the port authority's ban on distribution of literature is invalid under the First Amendment.[22]

Even then, however, four justices dissented on the issue of literature distribution. Chief Justice Rehnquist, joined by Justices White, Scalia, and Thomas, wrote:

> Leafletting presents risks of congestion similar to those posed by solicitation. . . . The wearied, harried, or hurried traveler may have no less desire and need to avoid the delays generated by having literature foisted upon him than he does to avoid delays from a financial solicitation. And while a busy passenger perhaps may succeed in fending off a leafletter with minimal disruption to himself by agreeing simply to take the proffered material, this does not completely ameliorate the dangers of congestion flowing from such leafletting. Others may choose not simply to accept the material but also to stop and engage the leafletter in debate, obstructing those who follow.[23]

If all of this seems a bit confusing, let's summarize this key case by looking at the scoreboard. The court of appeals had ruled that Krishna devotees could not be prevented from distributing literature at the airports, though the airports could prevent them from financial solicitation.

Both sides appealed the ruling. The Hare Krishnas appealed for the right to solicit, and the port authority appealed for the right to restrict the Krishna devotees' right to distribute literature.

The Supreme Court fully affirmed the appeals court. On the issue of solicitation, five justices held that airports are not a public forum at all; one held that they are a public forum but that the prohibition on solicitation was a reasonable time, place, and manner restriction; and three held that airports are a public forum and that solicitation should be allowed. The score: six justices favored the ban on solicitation and three were opposed.

On the issue of distribution of literature, five justices upheld the appeals court and favored the right to distribute literature, and four justices dissented and were opposed to the right to distribute literature.

At this point, then, it appears that the right to distribute religious literature in airports is firm, though the right to solicit contributions can be restricted. Whether there are unanswered questions about airport evangelism, or whether airports will attempt to skirt the issue and rely on state constitutions, remains to be seen.

A Side Note to the ISKCON Case

An interesting side observation is relevant to the issue of religious rights, including the right to engage in evangelistic activities. If you look at which opinion was signed by each justice of the Supreme Court in the case of *ISKCON v. Lee*, you might be surprised to see which justices appear to be on the side of religious rights.

I mention this because Christians tend to support the nomination of justices to the Court who are conservative, usually Republican, and preferably Christian. On some issues Christians have been pleased with their decisions; on other issues their decisions have actually hampered the right to spread the gospel.

Chief Justice Rehnquist and Justice Clarence Thomas, for example, are both known as committed Christians. (Rehnquist is a member of the Lutheran Church-Missouri Synod, and Thomas attends a charismatic Episcopal church.) Antonin Scalia, known as one of the most conservative justices on the Court, is a traditional Roman Catholic with a strong pro-life record. Nonetheless, all three voted not only to uphold the port authority's ban on solicitation but also to prohibit the distribution of religious literature at the airports.

The most liberal member of the Court is Justice Harry Blackmun, who himself admits that he will probably go down in history as the author of one of the most controversial decisions in the Court's history, *Roe v. Wade*.[24] Yet Blackmun and other liberal members of the Court have consistently voted in favor of religious rights.

We can reach a couple of conclusions by looking at the Court's voting record. First, the Court is unpredictable. We can guess at the way the justices are going to vote based on precedents, but somehow their rulings have a way of surprising us. Second, we may agree with a justice's vote on some issues (such as abortion), but he or she may not vote to our liking on other issues (such as the right to witness). About those who currently sit on the Court and the Court's religious case decisions of the past twenty years, we are left with an inescapable conclusion: Conservative justices tend to vote in favor of the unborn, but the liberal justices have often been more friendly to religious rights. It is paradoxical but one of life's realities.

/ 10 /

Taking the Word to Jails and Prisons

From Chaplain Ray to Charles Colson's Prison Fellowship, one of the most active evangelistic movements today is occurring in jails and prisons around the United States. Notwithstanding the usual puns about a captive audience, the men and women who serve time come as close to hitting bottom as anyone can, deal with the harsh realities of prison life on a day-to-day basis, and are often open to receive the gospel of Jesus Christ.

Not only does evangelism in the prison community present an opportunity for Christians, it is a ministry that was mandated by Jesus himself (Matt. 25:31–46). And, like other forms of evangelistic ministry, it can be a challenging one in which to function.

The law speaks extensively to the religious rights of prisoners. Over the past twenty years, there have been more court cases that deal with religious rights in prison than any other area in which religion and law intersect. The reason for this is simple: Most of the lawsuits that have addressed religious issues in prison have been filed by prisoners themselves, who are often more adept at legal maneuvers than are many attorneys.

How many of these lawsuits have involved the rights of Christians to witness in jails and prisons? The answer may surprise you: virtually none. To understand why, in this chapter we shall look at the prison system, discuss how you can pursue evangelistic activities in that system, and explore some of the religion cases that have been decided by the courts.

Unlike most of the other chapters in this book, this one will focus not on law but on strategy. Because the legal precedents covering your right to carry on a prison ministry are minimal, the best way to function effectively in the prison environment is to understand, from a Christian perspective, how the system works.

A Look at the Prison System

In the United States the correctional system consists of prisons, penitentiaries, and correctional facilities at the federal and state levels, as well as prisons and jails at the local level. Correctional institutions are generally segregated in three ways: by sex (with male and female prisoners being housed in different institutions or different wings of the same institution), by age (with prisoners under the age of eighteen being housed in youth facilities or detention centers), and by security level (ranging from minimum to maximum security, with prisoners on death row segregated from the general inmate population).

As of 1992, there were more than one million prison inmates in the United States, which imprisons 455 people per 100,000 in the population—more than any other nation in the world. In contrast, the rate in South Africa, the second highest in the world, is 311 people per 100,000. The incarceration rate in Great Britain is only 97 people per 100,000, and the world's lowest rate is in India, with 34 people imprisoned per 100,000.[1]

Cultural and racial factors appear to play a significant role in the American correctional system, with 3,370 black males per 100,000 in the black male population imprisoned. A 1990 report by the United States Department of Justice indicated that nearly one in four black males aged twenty to twenty-nine was either in prison, jail, on probation, or on parole.[2] This becomes relevant when one considers that one of the strongest religious movements in American prisons today is the Nation of Islam, or Black Muslims. As in the case of other cults when it comes to street ministry, there is both good news and bad news in that fact. The good news is that there have been many Black Muslim cases that have affirmed the religious rights of prisoners in general; the bad news is that many inmates are turning to the Nation of Islam instead of the cross of Christ.

Daniel Van Ness of the Justice Fellowship, the legal wing of Charles Colson's Prison Fellowship, has observed that "More people live in our prisons than live in the cities of Atlanta or Pittsburgh, in the states of Wyoming or Alaska, or in thirty-nine nations of the world."[3] In 1990, many prisons were so overcrowded that they had a higher population than the towns that surrounded them. The *Philadelphia Inquirer* listed these maximum security prisoner counts in a recent article: California State Prison at Folsom (6,564 inmates), the Louisiana State Penitentiary at Angola (5,176), Mississippi State Penitentiary at Parchman (4,641), Pennsylvania State Correctional Institution at Graterford (4,153), and the State Prison of Southern Michigan at Jackson (4,110).[4] As a result, many states have begun to implement correctional alternatives that include the privatization of prisons, house arrest (in which a person serves his or her sentence at home, wearing a tamper-proof bracelet that emits a radio frequency to a central monitoring center), intensive probation-supervision programs, and victim-offender reconciliation programs.[5]

To say that prison life is not pleasant is an understatement. The first thing that occurs when an offender is put into prison is that the offender loses his or her autonomy. Van Ness describes it in the following:

> The inmate's life is regulated to the point that his ability and need to make decisions is all but eliminated. Standard clothing is provided. Food is served at specified hours, and inmates eat what is given them. Work, if it is available, is assigned, as are educational opportunities. Hours are determined by regulation. Visiting is done at specified intervals.[6]

Van Ness notes five common elements of the prison experience: the deprivation of liberty, the deprivation of goods and services, the deprivation of heterosexual relationships, the deprivation of autonomy, and the deprivation of security.[7] Donald Smarto of the Institute for Prison Ministries at the Billy Graham Center at Wheaton College identifies factors that include the dehumanizing effects of loss of choice, the threat of violence, abuse from guards, and solitary confinement.[8]

For prisoners in solitary confinement or on death row, life is even more empty. Jack Henry Abbott, a convict, dramatically wrote:

> You sit in solitary confinement stewing in nothingness, not merely your own nothingness but the nothingness of society, others, the world. The lethargy of months that add up to years in a cell, alone, entwines itself about every "physical" activity of the living body and strangles it slowly to death, the horrible decay of truly living death. You no longer do pushups or other physical exercises in your small cell; you no longer pace the four steps back and forth across your cell. . . .
> Time descends in your cell like the lid of a coffin in which you lie and

watch as it slowly crosses over you. When you neither move nor think in your cell, you are awash in pure nothingness.

Solitary confinement in prison can alter the ontological makeup of a stone.[9]

Another trait common among prisoners is their declaration of innocence regarding the commission of the crimes for which they have been imprisoned. Bernard Adeney wrote:

Rationalizations are common among prisoners for the crimes that sent them to prison. Chaplain Harry Howard, of San Quentin, once commented to me ironically that it was hard to find a guilty man in San Quentin. One study classified typical rationalizations of prisoners into five groups: (1) denial of responsibility; (2) denial of injury; (3) denial of victim; (4) condemnation of the condemners; and (5) appeal to higher loyalties.[10]

Yet, for better or worse, the law allows inmates to proclaim their innocence and to petition for the redress of grievances by appealing to various court systems. That right has been ensured, among other methods, by the guarantee to inmates of access to an adequately equipped law library within the prison walls. In *Bounds v. Smith* (1977), the United States Supreme Court affirmed lower court decisions that require prisons to maintain law libraries for the use of inmates:

The fundamental right of access to the courts requires prison authorities to assist inmates in the preparation and filing of meaningful legal papers with adequate law libraries or adequate assistance from persons trained in the law.[11]

Thus, each prison, whether state or federal, must maintain a law library for inmates that includes, at minimum, legal reference works such as the decisions of the Supreme Court, the complete federal case reporter system, the complete regional reporter system for the region in which the prison is located, the statutes of the state in which the prison is located, the state digest, *Modern Federal Practice Digest*, and at least one set of a general reference work on criminal law.[12]

One thing a prisoner has on his or her hands is time. Combined with the precedents requiring access to legal reference materials, this has resulted in the creation of "jailhouse lawyers," inmates who have done so much research that they often end up knowing more about criminal law, constitutional law, the rules of legal procedure, and the rules of evidence than do many attorneys.

Thanks to both jailhouse lawyers and legal organizations in the prison reform movement, a number of cases have been heard by the courts that have had an impact on religious rights in prisons.

Religious Life in Prison

The court system in the United States has traditionally maintained a hands-off attitude regarding the daily operation of prisons and jails, as well as the restrictions placed upon inmates. From 1960 to 1980, however, the prison reform movement filed numerous court cases designed to increase prisoner rights, reduce overcrowding in the prison population, and expand community-based corrections. The peak period for the movement was in the early 1970s after an inmate riot at the Attica prison in New York.

Many of the cases addressed by the courts included the right of prisoners to have their religious beliefs recognized as legitimate by the correctional system, especially those that represented minority religions such as the Nation of Islam and Buddhism.[13] Other cases have addressed the establishment of indigenous religious groups founded by prisoners themselves—some borne out of serious religious commitment, some as jokes, and some as political tools to manipulate the correctional system.[14]

Religious issues that have been addressed by the courts over the past twenty years, with mixed results, include the right of prisoners to have the special dietary requirements of their religious faith accommodated by prison administrators,[15] the right of inmates to religious services in their own faiths (especially minority religions such as the Nation of Islam and the Native American Church),[16] the right of inmates to receive religious literature by mail,[17] and the right of male prisoners whose religions forbid contact with members of the opposite sex outside of marriage not to be frisked by female corrections officers.[18]

Traditionally, prisons have tended to favor the Judeo-Christian faiths, to the extent that most prison chaplains represent familiar denominations. In 1979, for example, at the height of the prison reform movement, the Federal Bureau of Prisons employed sixty-three chaplains, of whom forty-one were Protestant, twenty-one were Catholic, and one was Jewish.[19] Dale Pace of the Good News Mission, an interdenominational prison ministry, enumerates the professional qualifications for prison chaplains in the following:

> In general the government employer follows the minimum requirements recommended by the [American Correctional Association's] *Manual of Correctional Standards*. These are that a chaplain possess: (1) college and theological degrees, (2) ordination and ecclesiastical endorsement, (3) parish experience, (4) a minimum of one year of CPE [Clinical Pastoral Education], and (5) the right personality. In addition, a chaplain serving a correctional institution must have the approval of the institution's administration (sheriff, warden, superintendent, commissioner). Some penal system chaplains must also be nominated by a representative personnel committee, either local or state or National Council of Churches.[20]

While the qualifications for institutional chaplains are presumably not intended to result in religious discrimination, one result is that the overwhelming majority of chaplains tend to come from liberal and mainline denominations and do not necessarily have a personal relationship with Jesus Christ.

Generally, the mandate of institutional chaplains is to help meet the spiritual needs of persons who are unable to pursue their own religious activities outside an institutional environment. Therefore, chaplains are commonly found in jails and prisons, the military, hospitals, and other restricted settings. While the employment of chaplains by the government would appear to violate the *Lemon* test (discussed in chapter 5), the courts generally weigh any potential violation of the Establishment Clause against the Free Exercise Clause and hold that chaplains provide a reasonable accommodation of the spiritual needs of institutionalized persons.

The problem inherent in government-paid chaplaincies is that the chaplains are mandated to meet the spiritual needs of all of their constituents, regardless of whether those constituents (inmates, soldiers, hospital patients, etc.) are Christian. Hypothetically, if a prison inmate asks a chaplain to give him a copy of the Koran, two factors come into play. First, the chaplain cannot refuse the inmate's request if the prison normally provides inmates with copies of the Bible or other religious literature. Second, when the chaplain hands the Koran to the inmate, he or she (the government employs both male and female chaplains) may not say, "You know, brother, this book won't show you the way to salvation. You can only be saved through faith in Christ."

The same principle exists in other chaplaincy services such as the military. Lieutenant Commander G. M. Clifford of the Navy Surface Weapons Group at Pearl Harbor has written:

> The motto of the Navy Chaplain Corps, "Cooperation Without Compromise," implies that ministry as a chaplain is not intended to alter the chaplain's theology. Yet a likely consequence of ministering in the pluralistic setting of the sea services would seem to be a broadening of the chaplain's theology by influencing that theology to become more inclusive. For example, chaplains from Christian faith groups are responsible for facilitating pastoral care to Buddhist personnel without trying to convert the person to Christianity and without compromising the chaplain's integrity. Repeatedly engaging in this type of pluralistic ministry seems likely to impact the chaplain's own theology.[21]

Remember the cases in chapter 7 ("Taking the Word to Work") that documented how employees in government-affiliated agencies are not permitted to share the gospel on the job? Things are not quite that bad for chaplains, whose positions are, by nature, religious. But what happens when a chaplain conducts evangelistic activity? Virtually the same thing. In one case, Franklin Baz, a Veterans Administration chaplain who was an ordained minister in the Assemblies of God, was discharged, in part, because he was too evangelistic. The reasons cited by the Veterans Administration for his discharge included the following:

> [H]e failed to demonstrate ability to understand a multidisciplinary approach to patient health care; he failed to understand the need to work within established procedures to accomplish objectives; and he had difficulty in relating to other chaplains which complicated the effective coordination of their spiritual ministry.[22]

In upholding his dismissal, a federal district court acknowledged a basic difference in the concept of the chaplaincy held by Baz and the Veterans Administration. In *Baz v. Walters* (1984), Judge Harold A. Baker wrote:

> The [chaplain] saw himself as an active, evangelistic, charismatic preacher while the chaplain service saw his purpose as a quiescent, passive listener and cautious counselor. This divergence in approach is illustrated

by [Chaplain Baz's] listing "twenty-nine decisions for Christ" in his quarterly report of activities to the Veterans Administration. It was one of the matters pointed out [to Chaplain Baz by his supervisor] as unacceptable conduct on the part of a Veterans Administration chaplain.[23]

While the court acknowledged that Chaplain Baz had established a firm case of religious discrimination, it also held that the views of the chaplaincy service reflected legitimate aims and needs of the Veterans Administration in conducting its affairs.

In short, there is little room for government-paid chaplains to conduct active biblical evangelism. While the government is willing to accommodate a person's spiritual needs, chaplains are expected to subscribe to what has often been called civil religion, a faith similar to the plain label, no-name brands of foods you might find in the generic products aisle of a supermarket.[24]

The other difficulty is that members of the clergy are required to have at least one year of Clinical Pastoral Education (CPE), a psychologically based training program, to qualify for the chaplaincy. CPE is geared toward training persons in pastoral care, oriented toward a liberal perspective, and often fosters a hostility toward biblical Christianity. Dale Pace describes it in the following:

> All who go through CPE seem to be affected by the characteristic of liberalism that places the locus of authority not in theological or biblical doctrine, but vests it in the example of a religious life. . . . Thus, the CPE training process seems to cause even evangelical and fundamental chaplains to shift their emphasis and trust (at least to some degree) from God's Word and His Spirit to the influence of their presence as persons.
>
> From its inception, CPE has failed to emphasize theological content. . . . In fact, much hostility has been observed toward sound doctrine (i.e., evangelical theology) from numerous ministers with CPE training.[25]

Pace conducted extensive surveys of jail and prison chaplains and found, among other things, that CPE-trained chaplains worked fewer hours per week than those without CPE, had a smaller response by inmates to their religious and counseling programs, and spent less time with inmates in Bible and religious education classes. While non-CPE trained chaplains were less effective as program administrators, they had a greater response to their programs by inmate populations.[26]

An Opportunity for Ministry

If prisoners do not receive a biblical background from many chaplains, who is in a better position to deliver the gospel to prisoners? You are.

Many jails and prisons allow outside persons to minister to inmates, and as an outsider you have more freedom than state-paid chaplains to engage in biblical discussions that present the Christian gospel without the need to compromise the message. A chaplain cannot tell an inmate that he or she is going to hell in a proverbial handbasket if the inmate is a Muslim, Buddhist, or atheist, but you can. (I do not recommend presenting the gospel that way but use the example to illustrate that you, as a volunteer and an outsider, have more freedom to openly discuss the uncompromised message of Christ than a state-paid chaplain does.)

The ability to get your foot in the door requires some diplomacy. The fact is that no jail or prison has to allow you into the institution at all. Generally, the courts defer to prison administrators in the interest of maintaining a secure environment, and that includes the freedom of administrators to refuse admission to anyone they feel will convey a message that is not in harmony with the goals of the correctional facility.

It also includes the right of prison administrators, including chaplains, to determine who will be allowed to convey a religious message behind the institution's walls. The courts have held that as long as a prison makes a reasonable effort to accommodate inmates' religious needs, it need not even allow outside clergy into the prisons to meet specific denominational needs. Thus, if the chaplain of a prison is from any type of Protestant church, the administration can declare that all Protestant prisoners are covered. If, for example, a prison employs a Presbyterian chaplain, then a prisoner cannot demand that the prison sponsor services conducted by a Baptist. This has been an issue in several cases in which members of the Nation of Islam have sued prison authorities because of their objection to other Islamic groups.

So, let's get to the bottom line. What rights do you have under the law to go into the prisons and witness to inmates, tell the gospel, conduct Bible studies, or hold worship services? For all intent and purpose, none.

Nonetheless, outside individuals and prison ministries are granted permission to conduct such activities every day, and following are some strategic techniques with which you can pursue a prison ministry.

Be diplomatic. You and I may know there are many chaplains who are not saved, but if you expect to get your foot in the door of a prison, it's not wise to accuse a chaplain who professes to be Christian of not knowing the Lord. You may not bring him or her to the cross, but a sense of tact will allow you to reach a greater number of prisoners without having the prison door slammed in your face by a chaplain you have offended.

Despite the jaded picture I have painted of government-paid and institutional chaplains in this chapter, don't take my portrait as too wide a stereotype. There are chaplains out there who know and love the Lord, but their hands are often tied by the bureaucracy in which they work. They may see you as a vehicle for getting the gospel to inmates in a manner in which they can't. Remember, not all chaplains are the enemy.

Check out smaller, local jails located near you that don't have chaplains. Approach the warden or superintendent and ask if you can begin a Bible study at the jail for inmates. Stress that your goal is to assist in the rehabilitation of the prisoners, and that Christian prisoners have a good track record when it comes to prison behavior. If possible, avoid Christian jargon that a non-Christian administrator would not understand. If the warden perceives some benefit from an administrative perspective, he or she is more likely to grant you admission to the prison. You may also be able to serve as the volunteer chaplain for that jail, and if it does not have services already, you may be able to conduct worship for the prisoners. Remember that despite the qualifications for government-paid chaplains, you do not have to be an ordained member of the clergy to engage in this type of ministry, especially on a volunteer basis. The Lord may open a door you did not expect to be opened for you.

Even if a jail already has a chaplain, there are many opportunities to share the gospel with prisoners in the course of volunteer work. Call the chaplain and ask how you can be used to minister to prisoners. Also remember that God is sovereign. Even if the chaplain is not a born-again Christian, the Holy Spirit can still see that you are placed in a position for ministry. One helpful suggestion: Instead of approaching the chaplain and telling him or her, "Here's what I want to do," ask where there is an opportunity for you to be used. Remember that when you enter the prison, you are in someone else's domain, not your own. Believe that God will use you to his glory, and you will find the right opportunity to minister.

Even if you cannot conduct worship services or a Bible study in prison, don't rule out visiting inmates on a one-to-one basis. Even Jesus did not speak about evangelistic crusades in jails; he merely addressed visiting prisoners (Matt. 25:31–46). Your personal visitation can be more of a blessing to a prisoner, not to mention a Christian witness, than group evangelistic activities. Some prisons require that you be placed on an individual inmate's approved visitor list to enter the facility. Check with your local prison to determine its policy.

Another way to carry on a ministry with inmates is through correspondence. Residents of your local area may benefit from this type of ministry when they are arrested on criminal charges. Two suggestions regarding correspondence with inmates: First, you should consider renting a post office box so your address does not become known to prisoners. Generally, correspondence ministry is safe, but you don't want the wrong person showing up at your doorstep at three o'clock in the morning. A post office box provides an added measure of security for yourself. Second, you should be aware that some prisoners write sexually graphic letters (especially male inmates writing to women). You should discern whether you wish to correspond with a prisoner who does this type of writing (after all, he may still come to know the Lord) or whether you should terminate the correspondence relationship.

If you have foreign-language skills, especially Spanish, prisons present a special opportunity for ministry. Some prisons have significant Hispanic inmate populations, and they are often incarcerated in areas where there is not a large Hispanic population on the outside. Your skills in this area may be a real blessing to them. Other special-needs prison populations include women and Asian inmates, who are often neglected in rural prison environments.

Learn and follow jail or prison rules about the admission of visitors and other outsiders. Make sure you take identification with you, and be prepared to empty your pockets or be searched for weapons prior to entering an inmate area. Especially, be sure that you cooperate with correctional officers and guards and that you don't exhibit a poor attitude. Security measures are part of the cost of being able to enter a jail or prison to visit or minister. If you resist or act offended, the guards simply won't let you in.

When you enter a prison or jail, you may be asked to sign a waiver releasing the prison authorities from any liability if you are injured or taken hostage. The chance of anything bad happening to you is very slight; nonetheless, you should be aware of the waiver process before you go into the jails.

When you present the gospel, don't feel that you have to water down the message. However, use tact. If you preach to a group of Muslims and put too much stress on their being "damned to an eternal lake of fire and brimstone" (or emphasize other negative sermon lines), don't expect to be invited back into the prison.

When working with non-Christian inmates in a small group situation, be subtle. If the prison you visit has a large Muslim population, remember that a prisoner who accepts Jesus may be harassed by fellow inmates. A prisoner's religious affiliation is often dictated by the extent to which he or she may be hassled by other prisoners. That should not prevent you from witnessing, but keep the social factors inherent in prison life in mind and be prepared to discuss the ramifications of Christianity with inmates from their perspective.

As in other situations that may place you in a potentially dangerous situation, use a team approach when working with prisoners. If you have never taken part in prison ministry, contact a local or national prison ministry or read some books on witnessing to inmates. As always, be especially protective of any female members of your team. Women should never be left alone with male prisoners, either one-on-one or in a group situation. Remember that in a jail or prison, there is an added possibility of rape or a hostage crisis. You don't have to be paranoid, but use discernment and street smarts.

Prison inmates are often adept at psychological manipulation. Therefore, learn to know the difference between a prisoner who is making a sincere inquiry or commitment to Christ and one who, for lack of a better term, is engaging in "jive." Be wary of inmates who seek personal favors from you, especially when they write to you, and make sure you do not give anything to an inmate that is considered contraband by the prison administration. (A list of contraband items is generally available at the prison.)

The need for ministry to prisoners does not end when they are released from prison. Another opportunity to consider is to volunteer to work with released inmates in a halfway house as they make the transition back into society. There are both Christian and non-Christian halfway houses, and both types present an opportunity to spend quality time with men and women who have been released from prison and to share the gospel with them on both an individual and group basis. There is a high recidivism rate among released prisoners (the rate at which persons who have been convicted of a crime are likely to commit another crime). In addition to presenting the gospel to released inmates, your ministry in an aftercare environment can help lower the rate of recidivism.

Above all, go in prayer and come out in prayer. I have never seen a riot start as a result of prison evangelism, but it helps to remember that the early evangelists did inadvertently trigger a few riots in the name of Jesus (Acts 17:6–8). When it comes to people responding to the gospel, God has been known to perform a few miracles in jails and prisons. Strategy and technique are important, but prayer will always be your best weapon.

Jails and prisons are not pleasant places, but despite their flaws, inmates have a keen sense of reality. Many of them have been down so long that the only way they can go is up, and they are often one of the most receptive audiences for hearing and responding to the Word of God. Those who do make a commitment to Christ have had their lives changed, and from an evangelistic perspective there are great blessings to be gained from conducting a prison ministry.

/ II /

Taking the Word Home

So far we have taken the Word to streets, malls, school, work, stadiums, and a host of other places. Now let's bring it home. Literally.

Two areas may be labeled a home setting for evangelism: door-to-door and inside your own home (for such things as Bible study groups).

Taking the Word Door-to-Door

When people think of door-to-door evangelism, Christians are not the group that usually comes to mind. Going from house to house to spread one's faith is usually identified with Jehovah's Witnesses (accompanied by the ever-present briefcase filled with copies of *The Watchtower* and *Awake!*) and Mormons (young men going two-by-two, wearing white shirts and ties, and often traveling on bicycles). In many communities, however, evangelical Christians engage in door-to-door evangelism, often using an approach such as the *Evangelism Explosion* program.

D. James Kennedy, author of *Evangelism Explosion*, writes that a common technique is to use the weekly, biweekly, or monthly realtor newspaper listing of people who have bought new homes in an area.

> We begin by sending a friendly letter to these people, welcoming them into the community and offering our services in any way possible. We conclude the letter by stating that someone from the church will drop by in the near future and welcome them personally to our area and to our church. A card is then made out for the visitation team showing the date the letter was mailed and indicating that the people are new residents in the area. They are then processed in the visitation program.[1]

Under the law, door-to-door evangelism generally comes under the heading of solicitation, whether or not an actual request for money is made. Solicitation can include everything from raising funds to soliciting signatures on a political petition to, for all intent and purpose, soliciting for souls by a religious organization.

Traditionally, the Supreme Court has upheld the right of persons to engage in door-to-door evangelistic activities.[2] At the same time, according to attorney Richard Hammar, there are restrictions such as the following:

> The Court has noted that a city may protect its citizens from fraud, as by requiring strangers in the community to establish their identity and demonstrate their authority to represent the cause they espouse. Cities also may limit door-to-door proselytizing and solicitation where necessary to preserve public safety, health, order, and convenience. Strict safeguards, however, must attend any such limitations.[3]

To prevent fraud, for example, a municipality may impose a neutral ordinance that requires registration by individuals or groups who solicit on a door-to-door basis. However, such an ordinance may not impose a fee, restrict the nature of the solicitation, or place arbitrary conditions on door-to-door activities. For example, ordinances that impose a condition on a person's exercise of free speech rights—the payment of a tax to obtain a permit—were found unconstitutional in *Murdock v. Pennsylvania* (a Jehovah's Witnesses case decided in 1943), in which the Supreme Court struck down a Jeannette, Pennsylvania, ordinance that required a person to purchase a license to go door-to-door. Affirming the "honorable" nature of going door-to-door, the Court held the following:

> Those who can tax the privilege of engaging in this form of missionary evangelism can close its doors to all those who do not have a full purse. Spreading religious beliefs in this ancient and honorable manner would thus be denied the needy. Those who can deprive religious groups of their colporteurs can take from them a vital power of the press which has survived from the reformation.[4]

For solicitation ordinances to be found constitutional, they must be written in a content-neutral manner, must not impose prior restraints, and must not be arbitrarily applied at the discretion of an individual. Examples of ordinances that have been found unconstitutional include the following:

In *Village of Schaumberg v. Citizens for a Better Environment* (1980), the Supreme Court held that an ordinance prohibiting door-to-door solicitation by a charitable organization that did not use at least 75 percent of its income for charitable purposes was unconstitutional. By regulating the use of donated funds, the Court held, the ordinance burdened the freedom of speech without a compelling state interest.[5]

In *Troyer v. Town of Babylon* (1980), the Court held that to require the consent of householders before someone approaches their homes constitutes an indirect unconstitutional imposition akin to a licensing fee.[6]

In *Martin v. City of Struthers* (1943), the Court invalidated an ordinance that prohibited persons who distributed literature from summoning the occupants of a home to the door.[7]

In *Jamison v. Texas* (1943), the Court invalidated an ordinance that totally prohibited the distribution of handbills and resulted in the prosecution of a Jehovah's Witness who sold religious books and solicited funds for religious purposes. In this case, the Court held that the ordinance contravened the First Amendment freedom of the press.[8]

In *Holy Spirit Association for the Unification of World Christianity v. Hodge* (1984), a federal district court held that an ordinance as applied to Sun Myung Moon's Unification Church was invalid. The ordinance required those planning to solicit funds in Amarillo, Texas, to obtain a permit, submit detailed information about past activities and finances of the group, and pay a fee. City officials had thus authorized themselves to deny a permit based on discretionary reasons.[9]

In *Taylor v. City of Knoxville* (1983), a federal court held invalid an ordinance that required religious-group solicitors to obtain a permit unless the group solicited only from its own members, to disclose the amount sought and the purpose for which contributions would be used, to provide a statement showing the need for contributions, and to follow strict accounting procedures. The court granted an injunction in favor of the Unification Church, holding that they had

a substantial likelihood of demonstrating that the ordinance granted city officials overly broad discretion in denying permits.[10]

On the other hand, in *International Society for Krishna Consciousness of Houston, Inc., v. City of Houston* (1982), a federal appeals court
held that a similar ordinance that required information showing how
moneys were used but that did not give the city discretionary authority
to deny a permit was constitutional because the city had a compelling
interest in protecting its citizens from fraud and harassment.[11] In another case finding a compelling interest, a federal district court upheld the
constitutionality of a solicitation ordinance on grounds that restrictions
directed toward unwilling listeners after dark did not violate the First
Amendment.[12]

Remember that ordinances are generally constitutional if they are neutrally written and do not discriminate against religious activities, either
in their words or the way they are enforced. The registration of solicitors
is a reasonable requirement which, if neutrally applied, acts as a consumer protection measure against unscrupulous entities ranging from
fraudulent solicitors to fly-by-night roofing contractors. Ordinances that
have time, place, and manner restrictions that are neutrally applied may
also be reasonable. For example, it would hardly be appropriate for you
to show up unannounced at someone's home to present the gospel at three
o'clock in the morning.

Ordinances designed to regulate door-to-door solicitation are generally written not at the federal or state level but at the local level—county, city, township, town, or borough. If you wish to do door-to-door
evangelism, your best course of action is to check into any local laws
which exist and, perhaps, call a local attorney to ensure that your rights
are protected.

A Man's Home Is His Castle—Sometimes

Now that we have looked at evangelistic activities directed at other people's homes, let's turn the tables and explore religious expression in our
own homes.

The right to conduct worship, prayer, and Bible study at home is firmly established. If you own a home, you may conduct any of these activities, including Bible study groups, which others may attend. There

are, however, some neutral restrictions that have been applied to home situations.

Ordinances that affect how a house is used come under the general heading of zoning law and are usually determined on a local (rather than state or federal) level. As with other laws, they must be neutrally applied, not intended to discriminate against religious activities, and not be so vague in their content as to vest discretionary power in an individual.

In general, you have the same right to conduct a Bible study in your home as you have to throw a party or invite friends over to play cards. In other words, if you have the right to invite a dozen friends over to quaff beer and watch a football game, you have the same right to invite a dozen people to your house to quaff some prayer (for lack of a better phrase) and read the Word of God.

Any restrictions on that right must be narrowly drawn to meet a compelling state interest such as the safety of your guests or the safe passage of traffic down your street. For example, if your living room is only ten feet by ten feet, it would be reasonable for the local authorities to prohibit a hundred people from gathering in that room at the same time. If you live on a narrow residential street, it would be reasonable for the authorities to specify that you cannot have a hundred cars parked outside your house at one time. To be constitutional, however, the authorities must enforce such a restriction neutrally; that is, whether your guests have come to your house for the football and beer or the prayer and Bible study should not be a consideration.

Most home Bible study groups, of course, are a lot smaller than a hundred people. (If not, they should be, but that's a value judgment on my part rather than a legal observation.) If your own Bible study group is reasonable in size, does not cause an overt disturbance of the neighborhood (for example, twenty people praying in tongues louder than the beat of a rock band and shaking down the walls of your house), and does not rob the neighbors of their own parking spaces, your activities are absolutely protected by law.

Legal difficulties may ensue, however, if it can be construed that you are using your residence for more than a home-based Bible study or fellowship. For example, if you hold worship services on a regular basis, and, instead of home furniture you have outfitted your living room with a large number of folding chairs, a podium, piano or organ, and other accoutrements that would normally be found in a church, it may be construed that you are, in fact, operating a church.

In *City of Colorado Springs v. Blanche* (1988), for example, Ralph Blanche and the Faith Bible Fellowship had purchased a four-bedroom residential property in Colorado Springs after their church building was sold. The house was located in a residentially zoned area of the neighborhood. In the family room, Blanche had set up fifty folding chairs in rows facing a podium and a piano, and there he conducted religious services and other congregational activities four times a week. Typically attended by sixty to seventy-five people, the activities included praying, singing, studying the Bible, and teaching Sunday school. In June 1985, Blanche was charged with operating a religious institution in a residential district in violation of the Colorado Springs city code. Shortly thereafter, a local court issued an injunction enjoining Blanche and Faith Bible Fellowship's use of the home as a religious institution.

Ignoring the court order, Blanche and the church were found in contempt of court and after continued violations were slapped with twenty thousand dollars in fines. Blanche had never applied for an exemption from the neutral zoning restrictions, and in 1988 the Supreme Court of Colorado affirmed both the local court's permanent injunction and the imposition of penalties and fines.[13]

In *Grosz v. City of Miami Beach, Florida* (1983), a federal appeals court upheld a citation issued by the city against a rabbi who was holding daily religious services in his home. Naftali Grosz, a rabbi and leader of an orthodox Jewish sect, led a daily minyan in his home that was normally attended by ten to twenty men. (A minyan is an orthodox prayer group that meets twice daily for services and must consist of at least ten adult males.) However, during the winter months the congregation often consisted of as many as fifty persons, some of whom were neither friends, family members, nor neighbors.

Grosz's property included a separate building that had been used as a garage and recreation room. After applying for a permit for internal modifications to the building in which he stated it would be "for playroom use," Grosz stocked the building with benches to seat over thirty persons, Torahs, arks, a Menorah, skull caps, an eternal light, prayer books, shawls, and other religious accoutrements. Ultimately, the building was outfitted as a shul, or small synagogue.

Normally, the daily services did not cause a substantial disturbance to the neighborhood, but the larger services disturbed the neighbors as a result of large congregations of worshipers at the property, loud chanting and singing during the services, and persons seeking directions to "the Grosz shul." At trial, the city noted that it would not prosecute

Grosz for praying in his home with ten friends, neighbors, and relatives, even on a regular basis, but for the specific conduct and larger groups that turned the house into a religious institution.

Concluding that the religious ceremonies conducted on the property occasionally constituted organized, publicly attended religious services, that the home was functionally operating as a synagogue, and that the city had enforced the single-family residential limitation in the area in a neutral manner after it received numerous complaints from neighbors, the court upheld the city's actions as constitutional.[14]

On the other hand, in *Harrison Orthodox Minyan, Inc., v. Town Board of Harrison* (1990), a New York court held that the town board had abused its discretion in denying an orthodox minyan a special exception use permit for a home. The court stated that reasonable restrictions such as parking, hours, and number of people were acceptable, but the unqualified denial of the minyan's right to meet was "arbitrary, capricious, and an abuse of discretion."[15]

In *State v. Cameron* (1985), the New Jersey Supreme Court held that a municipal ordinance was unconstitutionally vague as applied to a minister who temporarily used his home to hold a one-hour service each week for his congregation. Robert J. Cameron had been convening the Mount Carmel Reformed Episcopal Church at a local school building, but a rent increase forced the group to relocate. They decided to meet in Cameron's home until a permanent location could be found, and the services were attended by about twenty-five persons each week. Neighbors complained that the services could be heard eighty feet from Cameron's home and that cars parked on the street by those attending the services hindered the passage of traffic. Nonetheless, the court held that the ordinance was too vaguely written to be interpreted fairly.[16]

If you hold a Bible study or contemplate other religious activities in your home, the key question to ask is whether the activities will change the nature of the property to anything other than a residence. If the activities consist of a reasonable number of friends, family members, or neighbors gathering for prayer, Bible study, or even worship, you have the same right to conduct the activity as other people who invite guests into their homes. If, on the other hand, you outfit your living room as a fully furnished sanctuary and invite large numbers of people, including members of the public, it could be construed that you are operating your home as a church per se.

One issue not addressed here is the establishment of a "house church," common in the Mennonite, Quaker, and some other denominations. A biblical illustration of this phenomenon can be found in the days following Pentecost when "day by day continuing with one mind in the temple, and breaking bread from house to house, [the people at Jerusalem] were taking their meals together with gladness and sincerity of heart, praising God, and having favor with all the people. And the Lord was adding to their number day by day those who were being saved" (Acts 2:46–47). The degree to which house churches will be acceptable in residentially zoned districts will most likely depend on the number of people that attend. Using the Christian community model in Acts chapter 2, you can invite people into your house for dinner every night of the week. Any legal action taken against you, however, must be based on neutral, nondiscriminatory principles in the law.

In plain words, use common sense. If you are going to have a Bible study or prayer service, or conduct other religious activities in your home to which others will be invited, don't take up all of the neighbors' parking spaces. Remember, also, that while the Lord says to proclaim the gospel upon the housetops (Luke 12:3), he also says to do all things "properly and in an orderly manner" (1 Cor. 14:40).

If a Bible study or home fellowship group is getting too big for your own living room, it's probably time to divide into two or more groups or to move to a larger home. The important thing to remember is that if you are hassled by your neighbors or by local authorities, you should be able to prove in court that you are engaging in a reasonable use of your residence and that the nature of your group does not change the residential character of your home.

/ 12 /

And to the Uttermost Parts of the Nation

We have already examined several, but not all, areas in which the right to engage in First Amendment activities has been tested in the courts. There are additional situations in which there have been no court cases, but we can discern how the courts would be likely to act in them and how firm our legal rights are in terms of evangelism.

In this final survey chapter we shall look at some of these scenarios and discuss how the law treats witnessing in some other environments. These include abortion clinics, bus and train stations, libraries, military bases, parks, and post offices.

Before we explore these areas, however, we should examine one case that currently has a significant impact on religious rights across the board. The decision is recent enough that its ramifications have not yet been fully discerned, but as a precedent it will very likely affect future cases dealing with evangelistic issues.

The Trashing of Sherbert?

In chapter 7 ("Taking the Word to Work"), we looked at the case of *Sherbert v. Verner* (1963), in which the Supreme Court affirmed the right of a Seventh Day Adventist to collect unemployment benefits because she refused to work on her sabbath and lost her job as a result. The *Sherbert* test held that for the government to restrict a person's First Amendment religious freedoms, two conditions had to exist: (1) the government must have a compelling interest in restricting free exercise, and (2) it must do so by the least restrictive means possible.[1]

The *Sherbert* test was extended to a number of other areas and was later articulated in more complete terms in a case called *Wisconsin v. Yoder* (1972), which dealt with the right of Amish parents to remove their children from public schools after the eighth grade. In *Yoder* the Supreme Court held that Wisconsin's compulsory school-attendance laws were unconstitutional as they were applied to members of the Old Order Amish religion. In discerning whether the state acted appropriately, the Court addressed the following three questions that expanded on the earlier *Sherbert* test:

Was the activity with which the state interfered motivated and rooted in a sincerely held religious belief?

Was the right to free exercise of religion unduly burdened by the state regulation, and if so, what was the extent of its impact on religious practice?

Did the state have a sufficiently compelling interest in the regulation to justify the burden on the free exercise of religion?[2]

Under the *Yoder* test, the Court held, "A regulation neutral on its face may, in its application, nonetheless offend the constitutional requirement for government neutrality if it unduly burdens the free exercise of religion."[3]

The combined *Sherbert* and *Yoder* tests formed the basis for adjudicating cases dealing with the free exercise of religion until 1990, when the Court issued an opinion that sent shock waves through the religious rights movement and has been decried by churches, synagogues, and both liberal and conservative scholars of church-state issues.

In *Employment Division, Department of Human Resources of Oregon v. Smith* (1990), the Court held that Alfred Smith and Galen Black, members of the Native American Church, were not entitled to unemployment benefits after they were fired from their jobs as counselors at a drug rehabilitation clinic because they had used peyote in the course of an outside religious ceremony.

Peyote use is a central tenet of the Native American Church, which tightly controls distribution of the drug and restricts its use to religious rites. Twenty-three states have legislated an exemption to drug abuse laws that allows ritual peyote use by Native American Church members, but Oregon is not one of those states.

The *Smith* case was one of several heard by the Court in the same year that dealt with religious issues. However, because it did not address an issue that was considered to have an impact on Christians, organizations such as the Baptist Joint Committee, the National Association of Evangelicals, and the National Council of Churches, which normally file *amicus curae* (friend-of-the-court briefs) with the Court in religion-related cases, did not do so.

Under the *Sherbert* and *Yoder* tests the normal judicial procedure would be to examine whether Smith and Black's peyote use was vital to their religious beliefs and whether the state had a compelling interest in proscribing the sacramental use of peyote. In a concurring opinion in *Smith*, Justice Sandra Day O'Connor applied this standard and found that the state did have such a compelling interest—the enforcement of laws that regulate the possession and use of controlled substances.[4] The standard was also applied, with the opposite result, in a dissenting opinion by Justice Harry Blackmun (joined by Justices William J. Brennan and Thurgood Marshall). While Blackmun agreed that a compelling interest would allow the state to proscribe Smith and Black's conduct, he felt that the state had not demonstrated such an interest.

Justice O'Connor and the dissenting justices were in the minority, however. The majority, in an opinion written by Justice Antonin Scalia, held the following:

The *Sherbert* test was not valid because the *Smith* case involved an exemption from a generally applicable criminal law.

The only decisions in which the Court has previously held that the First Amendment bars application of a neutral, generally applicable law to religiously motivated action have involved not the Free Exercise Clause alone but the clause in conjunction with other constitutional protections such as freedom of speech and of the press. [In her concurring opinion, Justice O'Connor disputed this contention.]

The right of free exercise itself does not relieve an individual of the obligation to comply with a "valid and neutral law of general applicability on the ground that the law proscribes (or prescribes) conduct that his religion proscribes (or prescribes)."

Accommodation of a person's religious rights should be left to the political process, despite the fact that this will place at a relative disadvantage those religious practices that are not widely engaged in. This, according to Scalia, is merely "an unavoidable consequence of democratic government."[5]

Prior to *Smith*, the exercise of one's religious beliefs was considered a preferred freedom by the Court. Preferring to affirm the *Sherbert* and *Yoder* precedents, Justice O'Connor wrote, "In my view, [Justice Scalia's] holding dramatically departs from well-settled First Amendment jurisprudence, appears unnecessary to resolve the questions presented, and is incompatible with our Nation's fundamental commitment to individual religious liberty."[6]

Reaction was even stronger from First Amendment scholars. Greg Ivers, assistant professor of government at The American University, wrote:

> *Smith* contains staggering implications for what religious minorities can expect in the future. The message cannot be clearer: protecting the free exercise rights of religious minorities is no longer the presumptive obligation of the courts, but of the political process. . . . In other words, the Court does not view statutes, regardless of their oppressive case, that burden religious conduct, no matter how central such behavior is to the tenets of one's faith, as deserving more than a deferential review.[7]

The *Smith* decision was more than a negative action against religious rights. According to many scholars it was an example of poor jurisprudence. Justice Scalia had disregarded the compelling state interest test of *Sherbert* in favor of the political action test used in *Minersville School District v. Gobitis* (1940),[8] an early flag-salute case involving the Jehovah's Witnesses. Unfortunately, Scalia neglected to mention in the *Smith* opinion that *Gobitis* was overturned only a few years later by *West Virginia State Board of Education v. Barnette* (1943),[9] leading one writer to comment, "Every first year law student learns that to cite as precedent a decision subsequently overturned without noting that fact will merit his teachers' wrath and his peers' scorn. Apparently Supreme Court justices aren't bound by that rule."[10]

Negative reaction to the *Smith* decision has been universal, with opposition coming from such diverse quarters as the American Civil Liberties Union, the Christian Legal Society, and the Rutherford Institute. A bill titled the *Religious Freedom Restoration Act,* designed to legislatively restore the compelling state interest test in *Sherbert* and *Yoder,* was passed by the United States Congress in October 1993, but how the courts will interpret the Act remains to be seen.[11]

One important fact is to be considered here. When one thinks of minority religions, groups that usually come to mind include the Krishna sect, the Unification Church, the Nation of Islam, Jehovah's Witnesses and Mormons, and other cults that have been involved in the cases we have looked at in this book. But from a legal perspective, born-again Christians are in the same boat. Keep in mind that most people who profess to be Christian sit comfortably in their pews on Sunday mornings and are not involved in personal evangelism or witnessing. And, as we saw in chapter 3 ("Equal Rights for Those Who Are Wrong"), even though Christians may subscribe to the majority faith, most of the population does not identify with evangelistic activities of any kind. For better or worse, cases that negatively affect what Ivers calls minority religions will ultimately have a similar effect on Christians.

One thing is certain: The *Smith* case has certainly upset the cart that carries the apples of free exercise of religion. It may be several years until we see the full ramifications of the decision, but in the meantime, all of the other precedents cited in this book remain in place.

Discerning the Law in Other Milieus

Based on the number of principles of personal evangelism and the law we have examined thus far, you probably know more than most lawyers about the law's impact on your right to publicly proclaim your faith. Summarizing some of the principles we have looked at, you can see a pattern develop that will help you discern what the law says about witnessing in other situations. For example, we know the following:

The courts have discussed three types of forums that determine how much freedom you have to engage in First Amendment expressive activities: the traditional public forum, the designated public forum, and the nonpublic forum. Additionally, the courts have discussed the existence of limited open forums, a term usually used in regard to religious activities in the public schools.

Your right to perform evangelistic activities in traditional public and designated public forums is firm but subject to reasonable time, place, and manner restrictions.

You do not have a constitutional right to perform evangelistic activities in a nonpublic, government-owned forum or a privately owned forum unless the owner of that forum has allowed such activities to take place.

The nature of a forum is largely determined by its location and geographic characteristics. For example, the inside of a rock music club is a private forum (even if it is open to the public), but the sidewalk outside the club is a public forum.

With these principles in mind, let's explore your right to witness in a few other environments.

Taking the Word to Abortion Clinics

With the growth of pro-life groups and pro-life sentiment, Christians increasingly take part in both evangelistic and protest activities at abortion clinics. Their right to do so depends, as in other situations, on the geographic characteristics of the clinic.

In large cities, for example, abortion clinics are usually located along city streets that are traditional public forums. This means that your right to witness in these areas is absolute, subject to the usual time, place, and manner restrictions.

Manner is often the key factor at abortion clinics. Keeping in mind the catch-more-flies-with-honey-than-vinegar principle, you will be harassed less by law enforcement authorities if you engage in quiet protest or simply hand out literature than if you loudly shout "Baby killers!" at persons going into the clinic. (I do not presume to make an editorial judgment here regarding different protest tactics used at abortion clinics; my purpose is simply to make a factual observation or two regarding how the law works.)

Likewise, if you intentionally block ingress into and egress from an abortion clinic, you will be found guilty of violating the law. This, of course, is often the goal of some pro-life groups' actions, which are intended to be construed as acts of civil disobedience.

In the case of suburban and rural abortion clinics that do not directly abut a city street, the law is different. Sidewalks abutting clinics that are separated from the street by a parking lot, for example, are not a public forum. In numerous cases, courts have ruled that abortion protests at such facilities constitute trespassing.[12]

Therefore, if you want to witness or demonstrate at an abortion clinic, consider the location of the clinic. If it is located directly on a city street, then the sidewalk outside the clinic is a public forum. If the clinic is located in a suburban area such as a shopping center, office campus, or other area which does not directly abut a public street, it is a non-public forum. You may choose, nonetheless, to engage in evangelistic or protest activities at such clinics, but you will be in violation of the law. This is a conscious decision you must make, however, and the debate is beyond the scope of this book.

There is, incidentally, a notable exception to the principle of public versus nonpublic forums. It has become common for some prolife groups to hold protest marches or prayer vigils outside the homes of physicians who perform abortions. Assuming a physician lives on a public street, one would think that such an action, providing it is conducted within the boundaries of the law, is a constitutional right under the freedom of assembly clause of the First Amendment. However, the Supreme Court has held that protests outside the homes of physicians who perform abortions are not constitutionally protected. In *Frisby v. Schultz* (1988), the Court ruled by a six-to-three margin that the First Amendment rights of free speech and freedom of assembly were secondary, in the specific case, to the protection of residential privacy. Justice O'Connor wrote for the majority:

> The state's interest in protecting the well-being, tranquillity, and privacy of the home is certainly of the highest order in a free and civilized society. . . . One important aspect of residential privacy is protection of the unwilling listener.[13]

The Court was careful to note that in the case of protests geared to a physician who performs abortions, the residential picketing was focused on one house rather than generally directed. Thus, rather than disseminate a message to the general public the protesters' goal was to intrude upon a specifically targeted resident. "In this case," O'Connor observed, "the [activists] subjected the doctor and his family to the presence of a relatively large group of protesters in an attempt to force the doctor to cease performing abortions. But the actual size of the group is irrelevant; even a solitary picket can invade residential privacy."[14]

Surprisingly, even though the case dealt with antiabortion picketing, even liberal justices William Brennan, Thurgood Marshall, and John Paul Stevens dissented in the case, holding that the ordinance was too restrictive on First Amendment rights because it forbade all residential picketing.[15] Nonetheless, they appeared to agree with the judgment in the specific case for the following reason:

Before the ordinance took effect up to 40 sign-carrying, slogan-shouting protesters regularly converged on [the physician's] home and, in addition to protesting, warned young children not to go near the house because [the physician] was a "baby killer." Further, the throng repeatedly trespassed onto the property and at least once blocked the exits to their home.[16]

If the picketers were peacefully protesting an issue directed at the neighborhood in general, or if abortions were actually being performed in the physician's home, it is likely the Court would have reached a different conclusion. Because of the specific circumstances of the case, however, the Court held that site-specific residential picketing legally can be prohibited by a narrowly written, neutrally applied ordinance.

Taking the Word to Libraries

For all intent and purpose, the law regarding religious expression at public libraries is similar to the equal access principles applied to public high schools. The strongest precedent to date is *Concerned Women for America, Inc., v. Lafayette County* (1989), in which a federal appeals court upheld the right of a women's prayer group to use the auditorium of a public library in Lafayette County, Mississippi, for the discussion of family and political issues and prayer about those issues. The library had a written auditorium policy which stated the following:

> The Auditorium . . . is open for use of groups or organizations of a civic, cultural or educational character, but not for social gatherings, entertaining, dramatic productions, money-raising, or commercial purposes. It is also not available for meetings for social, political, partisan or religious purposes, or when in the judgment of the Director or Branch Librarian any disorder is likely to occur.[17]

The library had allowed other groups to use the auditorium, including the American Association of University Women, the National Association of Retired Federal Workers, the American Legion, the Adult Program on AIDS, and the Oxford Swim Club.[18] Affirming a lower court decision, the court held that the library's policy had been arbitrarily interpreted by the librarian in a discretionary manner and that the use of the auditorium by a diversity of other groups had rendered it a public forum. The court also upheld the constitutionality of allowing religious groups to use the library facilities and noted the following:

> In the absence of empirical evidence that religious groups will dominate use of the library's auditorium, causing advancement of religion to become the forum's "primary effect," an equal access policy will not offend the Establishment Clause.[19]

One other issue to be explored here is the distribution of religious literature in a public library. Over the years I have seen cases in which libraries have distributed cult literature such as *The Plain Truth* (a magazine published by the Worldwide Church of God) in magazine racks within the library. I do not know of any situation where this problem has been taken into court, but I can tell you that I have had good experiences in requesting the libraries to remove evangelistic literature that cults had placed in them, based on the Establishment Clause.

If you run into cultic literature being distributed on a library counter, magazine rack, or newspaper dispenser placed outside but on library property, you have two options to take action. One is to request the librarian to distribute Christian literature as well, noting that under the *Lemon* test (see chapter 5) the library cannot favor one religion over another (which it does by allowing the distribution of magazines such as *The Plain Truth* or religious literature from other cults).

Based on normal First Amendment principles, however, this is not the preferred course of action. Very often a librarian may not be aware that *The Plain Truth* is a religious publication. It is a slick magazine that addresses social and political issues, and the fact that it is religious in nature is usually downplayed on the cover. Even if you make the librarian aware of the magazine's nature and suggest that the library include tracts or other Christian literature, you are likely to meet with some resistance.

Therefore, it is usually more effective to make the librarian aware of the nature of *The Plain Truth* and ask that it be removed. The bad news is that this does not give you a chance to spread the gospel through the library's counter or literature rack. The good news is that neither will the Worldwide Church of God or another cult.

If the librarian resists removing the literature (one never knows if he or she may be a member of the Worldwide Church of God), be prepared to document how the *Lemon* test makes the distribution of the magazine a violation of the Establishment Clause: (1) the magazine has a religious, not secular, purpose; (2) it has the primary effect of advancing religion in general, and the Worldwide Church of God in particular; and (3) by virtue of its distribution inside a public library, it fosters an excessive government entanglement with religion. You should be prepared to imply that you will take legal action if the publication is not removed. However, I have never had to go that far, as the *Lemon* argument always seems to work.

Taking the Word to Military Bases

In *Greer v. Spock* (1968), the Supreme Court held that though certain parts of a military base might be open to the public, they did not constitute a public forum in light of "the historically unquestioned power of [a] commanding officer summarily to exclude civilians from the area of his command."[20] Thus, the Court upheld a regulation banning the distribution of literature without the prior approval of the base commander.

The *Greer* case dealt with literature distribution by antiwar protester Benjamin Spock on an open sidewalk just inside the compound at Fort Dix, New Jersey, and was adjudicated during the Vietnam conflict. Even then, the Court held that the leafletting regulation did not authorize Fort Dix authorities to prohibit the distribution of conventional political campaign literature. Rather, "The only publications that a military commander may disapprove are those that he finds a clear danger to [military] loyalty, discipline, or morale," and that "there is nothing in the Constitution that disables a military commander from acting to avert what he perceives to be a clear danger to the loyalty, discipline, or morale of troops on the base under his command."[21]

It is important to keep in mind that *Greer* dealt with handbills distributed by antiwar activists—literature that, by its very nature, would undermine military discipline. One could hardly say that distributing religious tracts would have the same effect (except, perhaps, tracts distributed by pacifist denominations such as the Brethren, Mennonites, or Quakers), but the issue has not been tested at court.

The most significant recent case dealing with religious rights in the military was decided by the Supreme Court in 1986, and provides an indication of how the court might rule in an evangelism-oriented case. In *Goldman v. Weinberger*, the Court held that the military's refusal to allow Captain Simcha Goldman, an orthodox rabbi serving as an Air Force psychologist, to wear a yarmulke with his uniform is not a constitutional violation. Justice William Rehnquist (who had not yet been appointed Chief Justice) wrote for the majority:

> Our review of military regulations challenged on First Amendment grounds is far more deferential than constitutional review of similar laws or regulations designed for civilian society. The military need not encourage debate or tolerate protest to the extent that such tolerance is required of the civilian state by the First Amendment; to accomplish its mission the military must foster instinctive obedience, unity, commitment, and esprit de corps. The essence of military service is the subordination of the desires and interests of the individual to the needs of the service.[22]

As do prisons, which have unlimited authority to refuse the admission of outsiders in the interest of institutional security, military bases apparently have the right to restrict evangelistic activities (at least by outsiders).

Taking the Word to Parks

As we saw in chapter 4 ("Taking the Word to the Streets"), public parks are a traditional public forum often mentioned in conjunction with streets in those cases that have addressed free speech issues. Reviewing the primary precedent in this area the Supreme Court has written:

> Wherever the title of streets and parks may rest, they have immemorially been held in trust for the use of the public and, time out of mind, have been used for purposes of assembly, communicating thoughts between citizens, and discussing public questions. Such use of the streets and public places has, from ancient times, been a part of the privileges, immunities, rights, and liberties of citizens. The privilege of a citizen of the United States to use the streets and parks for communication of views on national questions may be regulated in the interest of all; it is not absolute, but relative, and must be exercised in subordination to the general comfort and convenience, and in consonance with peace and good order; but it must not, in the guise of regulation, be abridged or denied.[23]

Two recent cases have specifically addressed evangelistic activities in parks, both of which have been decided in favor of Christians. In January 1992, a federal district court held in *Paulsen v. Gotbaum* that it was unconstitutional for the New York City Department of Parks and Recreation to require persons to submit, for prior approval, literature they intend to distribute in the parks and to obtain liability insurance when park officials deem it necessary.

Mitch Paulsen (discussed in the Nassau County Coliseum case in chapter 8, "Taking the Word to Stadiums and Concerts") wanted to use the New York City public parks for evangelistic meetings. The parks department applies several rules for those who want to hold "special events" in the parks where more than twenty people are reasonably expected to attend. The requirements include a permit application to be filed at least twenty-one days before the requested event, payment of a nonrefundable application processing fee of twenty-five dollars, a prohibition on soliciting donations or handing out literature except from preauthorized stationary tables, and the posting of a cleanup bond. The rules are more restrictive than those for individual witnessing on the streets and in parks, but they are specifically geared to organized group events.

The parks department permitted Paulsen to solicit donations from a stationary receptacle and to distribute literature in the bandshell area, but it waived the cleanup requirement. In return, Paulsen agreed to clean the area after his special event, leaving it free and clear of any literature distributed during the event.

Paulsen alleged that the regulations were facially invalid as they applied to him. The court held that the rule on distributing pamphlets and soliciting, the application deadline, and fee requirement were valid since they were applied in a content-neutral manner, that the government had compelling interests (the safe, orderly use of public facilities and the minimization of park visitors being fraudulently solicited), and that Paulsen had ample alternative channels available. Nonetheless, the court struck down the regulations requiring the submission of literature for prior approval and the obtaining of liability insurance, holding that unlimited discretion would allow park officials to make arbitrary decisions on the insurance and content-based restrictions on literature with which an official might disagree.[24] (Note that Paulsen geared his activities toward organized evangelistic meetings rather than one-on-one or small-group evangelism, so the court was able to apply a different standard regarding solicitation and litter from what would be normal for traditional evangelistic activities in a public forum.)

Also in 1992, a federal appeals court upheld the right of a Christian evangelist to distribute religious literature in public places, including the sidewalk within the Vietnam Veterans Memorial. The National Park Service, which maintains the memorial, had a regulation against the distribution of literature, the purpose of which was to maintain an atmosphere of calm, tranquillity, and reverence at the memorial. A federal district court held that the regulation was not narrowly tailored enough to serve its asserted purpose of maintaining a tranquil atmosphere and issued an injunction against its enforcement. The appeals court affirmed, holding that the sidewalk in the park is a traditional public forum and that Henderson's peaceful leafletting activities are clearly protected by the First Amendment. Finding the restriction overly broad, the court held that the interest of the park in maintaining a tranquil atmosphere did not justify prohibiting the distribution of free literature. Noting that free distribution is far less disruptive than solicitation, however, the court indicated that it would uphold a restriction on solicitation.[25]

The right to engage in First Amendment activities in parks, then, is as firm as it is on public streets. Any regulations that restrict evangelistic activities in public parks must be narrowly tailored to meet reasonable time, place, and manner restrictions.

Taking the Word to Post Offices

Christians normally don't engage in evangelism at post offices, though traditionally there has been much First Amendment activity at post offices over the past two decades.

Since the law requires eighteen-year-old males to register for the Selective Service by filling out a form at a post office, some Christian pacifist groups such as Mennonites and Quakers have engaged in peace witness at post office locations. More commonly, however, the post offices have been used for evangelism of a political nature, specifically by the National Democratic Policy Committee (NDPC).

That sounds like a liberal group representing the Democratic Party, doesn't it? Actually, however, the NDPC is the group that represents Lyndon LaRouche, a renegade conservative political activist who has run for the office of President of the United States several times and is currently serving a federal prison term for tax evasion. It is not uncommon for NDPC members to set up a card table on the sidewalk outside a post office, where they solicit contributions, sell books and subscriptions to their publications, and distribute emotionalistic literature addressing a variety of political issues ranging from taxation to AIDS.

Marsha Kokinda and Kevin Pearl, members of NDPC, set up such a table on the sidewalk near the entrance of the post office in Bowie, Maryland, and conducted political activities for several hours, during which time postal employees received over forty complaints about their presence. The Bowie post office, a freestanding building with its own parking lot, is located along a major highway. A sidewalk runs along the edge of the property, with another sidewalk running adjacent to the building next to the parking lot. To get to the building sidewalk, cars must turn into a driveway and enter a parking lot that fully surrounds the building.

The United States Postal Service has the following regulation which prohibits solicitation on postal property:

> Soliciting alms and contributions, campaigning for election to any public office, collecting private debts, commercial soliciting and vending, and displaying or distributing commercial advertising on postal premises are prohibited.[26]

Kokinda and Pearl refused to leave the sidewalk when asked to do so by the Bowie postmaster and were soon arrested by postal inspectors. They were tried before a United States Magistrate and convicted of violating the solicitation regulation; Kokinda was fined fifty dollars and sentenced to ten days' imprisonment, and Pearl was fined one hundred dollars and received a thirty-day suspended sentence. They appealed their sentences, and a federal district court affirmed their convictions, holding that the postal sidewalk was not a public forum and that the Postal Service's ban on solicitation was reasonable.

The Court of Appeals for the Fourth Circuit reversed the district court, held that the postal sidewalk is a traditional public forum, determined that the government had no significant interest in banning solicitation, and found that the regulation was not narrowly tailored enough to accomplish government interests.[27]

There had been two previous cases at the federal appeals level in which the courts had determined that post offices do not constitute a public forum.[28] Since the Kokinda decision conflicted with the other cases, the Supreme Court accepted the case for review.

In *United States v. Kokinda* (1990), the Court held that dedicated sidewalks on post office property (that is, sidewalks that do not directly abut a city street) are, in fact, not a public forum. Noting that the Postal Service did, however, normally allow leafletting that did not constitute solicitation, Justice Sandra Day O'Connor wrote for the majority:

> The Postal Service has not expressly dedicated its sidewalks to any expressive activity. Indeed, postal property is expressly dedicated to only one means of communication: the posting of public notices on designated bulletin boards. . . . To be sure, individuals or groups have been permitted to leaflet, speak, and picket on postal premises, but a regulation prohibiting disruption and a practice of allowing some speech activities on postal property do not add up to the dedication of postal property for speech activities.[29]

In 1992, the *Kokinda* decision would be the precedent used by the Supreme Court to justify upholding a ban on solicitation at airports by the New York Port Authority in *International Society for Krishna Consciousness, Inc. v. Lee* (see chapter 9, "Taking the Word to Airports"). In language that would be adapted to airports by Chief Justice Rehnquist, Justice O'Connor wrote in *Kokinda* of the negative effects of solicitation at post offices:

> The Government asserts that it is reasonable to restrict access of postal premises to solicitation, because solicitation is inherently disruptive of the postal service's business. We agree. Since the act of soliciting alms or contributions usually has as its objective an immediate act of charity, it has the potentiality of evoking highly personal and subjective reactions. Reflection usually is not encouraged, and the person solicited often must make a hasty decision whether to share his resources with an unfamiliar organization while under the eager gaze of the solicitor. . . . As residents of metropolitan areas know from daily experience, confrontation by a person asking for money disrupts passage and is more intrusive and intimidating than an encounter with a person giving out information. One need not ponder the contents of a leaflet or pamphlet in order mechanically to take it out of someone's hand, but one must listen, comprehend, decide and act in order to respond to a solicitation.[30]

At this point, then, it appears while solicitation can be totally prohibited by the Postal Service, literature distribution will generally be permitted outside post offices, including on Postal Service-owned sidewalks.

Concluding Our Tour

Well, campers, we've hit the streets, parks, schools, malls, and a host of other places in our efforts to share the gospel with non-Christians. We've seen that the law is generally on our side, though there are exceptions to the rule.

Believe it or not, you really do know more about these issues than most attorneys do. But what happens if you follow the law, conduct reasonable activities in a public forum, but are still harassed by neighbors, the police, or others who don't want you to engage in evangelism?

In the final chapter we shall talk about some options and resources that are available to help you deal with such resistance.

/ 13 /

Getting Help When You're Hassled

Time for a reality check. You have decided to go out and do some street witnessing. You have chosen a location on a public street and have begun handing out tracts and engaging in dialogue with passersby who express an interest in learning more about the gospel. You do not block the sidewalk, you stand away from any building entrances where an intrusive crowd could gather around you and interfere with the flow of traffic, and miracle of all miracles, no one throws away your tracts! You are not creating a disturbance nor interfering with nearby business activities, and the people who pass by really seem interested in what you have to offer.

Legally, you have done everything right. The law is clearly on your side, and God is blessing your work. Nonetheless, nearby merchants do not like what you do, and you have been asked to move more than once by police officers patrolling the street.

Reality check number two: You are a high school student who wants to form a Bible study club that will meet during the extracurricular activity period after school. You have done your research and found that, among other activities, your school has a photography club, a scuba club, Future Businesspersons of America, Young Democrat and Republican clubs, and even an astrology club. A few other students are eager to participate in your Bible study, and you have approached the school administration for permission to meet on campus. You have done your legal research and are prepared to refer to your rights under the Equal Access Act and *Board of Education v. Mergens*. Nonetheless, the principal turns down your request to form an after-school club for Christian fellowship. Putting on your best clothes to make a good impression, you then take your request to the local school board meeting, and even the board refuses to allow a Bible study club to meet on campus.

If you have done everything you can to follow the law as you engage in evangelistic activities and still meet resistance, it's time to call in the big guns.

The Ramifications of Litigation

Later in this chapter we shall explore some of your legal options in fighting for your cause. Before we do that, however, it is important you understand the ramifications of taking legal action to ensure your rights.

First, let's look at the time factor. Few cases end up being accepted by the United States Supreme Court for review. We have looked at several of them in this book, but they represent a minority of the cases that are submitted to the Court each year. By the time they get to that stage, they have gone through an evolution that has taken them through the lower federal or state courts, and it's often over a period of several years that a case may be tossed around the legal system before the Supreme Court has a chance to grant or deny review.

Take, for example, the case of Bridget Mergens, whose efforts resulted in the Supreme Court upholding the Equal Access Act, which allows students to gather for religious activities in public high schools. After the Equal Access Act became law in 1984, Mergens and other students approached James Findley, the principal of the Westside High School in Omaha, in January 1985. Dr. Findley denied their request, and the following month the students presented another request to Dr. Findley and James Tangdall, the associate superintendent of schools. The administrators discussed the request with Kenneth Hansen, superintendent of schools for the Westside Community School District, and the three officials once again denied the students' request in the belief that such a club would violate the Establishment Clause. On March 4, 1985, the students petitioned the school board to approve their request, and once again permission was denied.

In April 1985, the students brought suit in federal district court, alleging that their freedoms of speech, assembly and association, and free exercise of religion had been infringed by the school board in violation of the First and Fourteenth Amendments, the Nebraska Constitution, and the Equal Access Act. On February 2, 1988, three years later, the district court entered judgment in favor of the school board, holding that the Westside High School was a closed forum.

The students appealed, and on February 8, 1989, one year later, the Federal Court of Appeals for the Eighth Circuit reversed the lower court and found in favor of the students. This time, however, the school board appealed the case to the Supreme Court, which granted *certiorari* on July 3, 1989. Arguments were presented by the attorneys for the students and the school board on January 9, 1990, and the Court issued its decision in favor of the students on June 4, 1990.

The time from the students' initial request to the principal and the decision of the Supreme Court? Almost five and one-half years.

Some religious rights cases cover a shorter time, since cases that present a significant First Amendment question sometimes go directly from the trial court level to the Supreme Court. Other cases may be longer, since they tend to go up and down the various lower court levels until they present a question the Supreme Court decides to address. But for the moment let's assume that the *Mergens* case represents a typical time frame.

Before you decide to take legal action, the first question you should ask yourself is, "Is it worth it?" Knowing that you are presenting an issue that may be tied up in the court system for several years, how important is it to you to pursue your case legally?

There are several factors to consider. First, not all cases are appealed to a higher court. The school board did not know whether Bridget Mergens would appeal the trial court's decision in their favor, nor did she know whether the board would take the appeals court decision in her favor to the Supreme Court. There was just as good a chance that either side would have accepted the lower court ruling, and the case would have been concluded.

Second, from an evangelistic viewpoint, you have to decide what is more important to you and, ultimately, God's will for you. If the Lord is calling you to reach a maximum number of people in your evangelistic activities, you can probably do so just as easily at another time, at another location, or in another manner. The time you will be tied up in legal proceedings could, perhaps, be spent more productively reaching more people with the gospel.

On the other hand, how much freedom would Christians have to meet in public schools today without Bridget Mergens? Would Christians be able to witness at the Nassau Coliseum if it weren't for Mitch Paulsen? Could you pass out tracts at the Los Angeles International Airport if

Alan Snyder hadn't brought his case to court? Will the Supreme Court ever get the chance to change the law regarding witnessing at shopping malls if no Christians pursue their legal rights? I believe that there is room for both roles.

> For just as we have many members in one body and all the members do not have the same function, so we, who are many, are one body in Christ, and individually members one of another. And since we have gifts that differ according to the grace given to us, let each exercise them accordingly (Rom. 12:4–6).

In short, God has ordained some Christians to lead the battle against the infringement of the right to proclaim the gospel of Jesus Christ in a free and open society, and he has ordained other Christians to witness directly without taking legal cases into courts of law. There is a necessity and there is room for both roles. Ultimately, prayer is the best way for you to discern your role in the big picture we call evangelism.

Finally, remember that a majority of legal cases never make it into a court of law. Very often, persons who resist your right to witness will respond in a positive manner if they receive a letter from an attorney that implies the possibility of a lawsuit. In other cases, even if a suit is filed it may be settled in your favor before it goes to trial. Most important is that you have competent legal representation so you will know your full range of options.

The Next Legal Step

Meanwhile, assume that you have retained an attorney and that he or she has contacted the parties who have interfered with your witnessing, all to no avail. Many options are available to you, ranging from a lawsuit seeking injunctive relief (the right to conduct evangelistic activities) to a suit seeking financial damages.

Most likely, your next step will be to seek a preliminary injunction or temporary restraining order from a court of law that will allow you to continue evangelistic activities while the issue is in dispute. For a preliminary injunction to be granted, you must be able to demonstrate the following four elements to the court:

1. That, if the issue goes to trial, you are likely to win the case or, in legal terms, "succeed on the merits" of your claim that your rights have been infringed;

2. That you will suffer irreparable harm *pendite lite* (pending the litigation), meaning that the continued infringement of your activities prior to the full adjudication of your claim in a court of law will cause you significant harm;

3. That neither the defendants (those infringing your rights) nor any other parties will suffer substantial harm if an injunction is granted; and

4. That the public interest favors the granting of a preliminary injunction or temporary restraining order.[1]

The principles outlined in this book become even more important if you seek an injunction or restraining order. In determining whether the court should grant you this "injunctive relief," a judge will look at your specific activities, your behavior, whether you have comported with any laws governing your activities, and whether you have pursued any administrative options available to you before you bring your case to court. If you have acted within the law and there is a likelihood that you would win your case at trial, the court will issue an injunction.

Unfortunately, in many cases Christians have not comported with the law, and when they file a suit to protect their right to engage in evangelism they are defeated by their own conduct.

A typical scenario is presented in the case of *Lickteig v. Landauer* (1991),[2] which involved the right of Christians to evangelize on South Street, a popular nighttime gathering place in Philadelphia, and at the Roosevelt Mall, an outdoor shopping center.

Plaintiffs Daniel Lickteig, Tyrone Malone, George Krail, and Kevin Liebner brought suit against the Philadelphia Police Department for interfering with their evangelism rights. Their motion for a preliminary injunction cited the following five incidents in which they claimed that their rights to conduct First Amendment activities were unconstitutionally restricted:

1. On September 22, 1990, Daniel Lickteig was playing a guitar and singing on a sidewalk outside a South Street arcade with four or five other people arranged in a semicircle. They were approached by police officer Richard Crawford, who observed that they were blocking pedestrian traffic and told them they could play music and hand out literature if they continued moving or, if they wished to remain stationary, moved to a side

street. After the group continually refused to move, Lickteig was arrested by Officer Crawford and charged with disorderly conduct and obstructing a highway. While Lickteig was being questioned by Crawford and an assisting officer, Elmer Landauer, Tyrone Malone stepped between Landauer and Lickteig. After repeated warnings not to come between Officer Crawford and Lickteig, Malone was also arrested for disorderly conduct and obstructing the highway. The Philadelphia District Attorney's Office withdrew the charges, and the court found that Crawford and Landauer's actions had prevented the situation from escalating.

2. On October 6, 1990, Officer Dennis Jones found Lickteig, Malone, and a small group on a congested corner at Sixth and South Streets during a period when over fifteen thousand people were in the South Street district. When he asked them to move on, Lickteig told Jones he was violating his rights and refused to leave the area. Jones did not arrest Lickteig or Malone but instead wrote a "pedestrian investigation" citation.

3. On October 13, 1990, Lickteig and a group were singing and distributing tracts outside the Cheers to You bar when they were asked to move on because they posed an obstruction to the door of the bar. Again, the group refused to move. A police sergeant summoned to the location told Lickteig that the sidewalk was too narrow for them to remain in that location but that they could continue their activities around the corner or on another block. Lickteig told the sergeant that "he would see him in federal court," then moved on.

4. On April 20, 1991, back at the intersection of Sixth and South Streets, Lickteig and five other Christians were singing and distributing tracts. A police officer asked them to move across the street so they would not interfere with the flow of traffic. Lickteig refused the request several times, and was arrested for disorderly conduct.

5. In October 1990, Lickteig and Malone were asked by a Philadelphia police officer to move on while they were distributing tracts and talking with young people at the Champions Arcade at the Roosevelt Mall. No arrest was reported, but the incident was cited in their lawsuit against the police department.

A hearing was held for the granting of a preliminary injunction against the police, and in an unpublished opinion the Federal District Court for the Eastern District of Pennsylvania denied the plaintiffs' motion for an injunction.

Why were Lickteig, Malone, and the other plaintiffs unsuccessful in obtaining an injunction? Because, for better or worse, their conduct did not comport with the law. Keep in mind that I do not judge their motivation. Clearly they were a group of committed Christians zealously bringing the gospel of Jesus Christ to people who did not know the Lord. Nonetheless, the following elements in their activities contributed to their failure to secure an injunction against the police department:

The South Street corridor, which covers approximately seven city blocks, regularly accommodates crowds that number up to twenty-five thousand people at peak times on Friday and Saturday evenings from mid-April to late October or early November. The crowds are heaviest after 10:00 P.M., with as many as three thousand pedestrians per block. The sidewalks vary in size from twelve to twenty feet wide but contain numerous obstacles such as sidewalk cafes, trees, plants, parking meters, trash receptacles, and telephone booths. During the incidents involving Lickteig and Malone, as many as fifteen thousand pedestrians were in the South Street corridor, and Lickteig and Malone interfered with pedestrian traffic.

On every occasion in which the group carried on evangelistic activities in a crowded location, Lickteig continuously refused to move on when the police asked him to.

In the incident outside the Cheers to You bar, Lickteig and the other Christians interfered with the ingress into and egress from the bar.

When Lickteig was arrested in the first incident, Malone stepped between Lickteig and Officer Landauer, thus interfering with an arrest.

The Roosevelt Mall had a policy requiring that individuals and organizations desiring to use the facility as a forum for distributing literature must obtain a permit from the management. The mall had previously issued such permits and had accommodated both religious and nonreligious activities. However, neither Lickteig nor Malone had applied for a permit before they conducted their activities. Thus, they had not exhausted their administrative options.

Remember the list of guidelines for street ministry in chapter 4 ("Taking the Word to the Streets")? The Lickteig case is a textbook example of how not to follow those guidelines. If Lickteig, Malone, and the other plaintiffs were, in fact, blocking pedestrian traffic, blocking ingress and egress at a building entrance, and attracting a crowd in a congested area but had moved along when the police asked them to, they could have continued their activities without interference.

Apparently, however, that was not their intent. Lickteig's statement to a police officer that "he would see him in federal court" implies that those Christians intended to bring suit and that the issue of evangelistic activities on South Street would become a test case. Lickteig was represented by an attorney from the Rutherford Institute of Pennsylvania, an organization that defends the rights of Christians, and a successful test case would have had a positive impact on many other Christians who do street ministry.

Having spent an extensive amount of time observing evangelism on South Street, interviewing persons who do street ministry, and talking with members of the Philadelphia Police Department's South Street Detail, I have found that when Christians follow the guide-lines for street ministry listed in this book, they are generally not challenged.

The bottom line is that before you take your case to court, you must ask yourself whether your activities and your conduct are such "that you may prove yourselves blameless and innocent, children of God above reproach in the midst of a crooked and perverse generation, among whom you appear as lights in the world" (Phil. 2:15). When you go out as sheep in the midst of wolves, Jesus says, be "shrewd as serpents, and innocent as doves" (Matt. 10:16). You should boldly assert your spiritual rights as Christians and your constitutional rights as citizens in a free and open society. At the same time, you should ensure that if you take your case to court you will not be defeated by questionable conduct. Had Lickteig, Malone, and the other Christians who sought an injunction not resisted the police, chances are that their activities would not have met resistance, or if the police had interfered without just cause, an injunction would have been granted.

If you feel that you have a strong case, the first thing you should do is seek a lawyer to advise you on the best course of action, to determine an appropriate venue for your case (such as a local court or federal court), and to represent you in your cause. Which brings up a logical question: How do you find legal representation?

Functioning within the Legal System

In the last chapter, I wrote that you now know more than most attorneys about the law and your right to witness. That is a pretty bold statement which, believe it or not, is not an exaggeration.

To understand how I can make such a contention, it may help you to know something of the process of legal education. In his or her three years at law school, the average student takes a certain number of core courses that include civil procedure, criminal law, property law, estate law, legal research and writing, and professional ethics. Most students take one or two semesters of constitutional law, and during those semesters most students spend three hours (clock hours, not semester hours) discussing the First Amendment religion clauses. Even though at least half of the three-year law school curriculum is elective in nature, most law schools do not offer courses in First Amendment religious issues at all.

Let's face it, even among Christian students at most law schools, there is not much interest in defending your right to engage in personal evangelism. Why? Because it does not pay as well as more profitable areas of the law such as corporate practice, litigation, environmental law, personal injury, and estate law. Even Christian students who matriculate into law school with the goal of defending religious rights usually change their focus by the time they graduate. It's a matter of human nature. Given the choice of making thirty thousand dollars a year as a religious rights attorney or ninety thousand dollars a year as a corporate or environmental attorney, which would you choose?

You could file a lawsuit yourself, but I wouldn't advise it. The old expression that an attorney who represents himself or herself in a court of law has a fool for a client is apt. That principle is even more true for persons who are not attorneys.

For better or worse, even though most lawyers do not know much about defending First Amendment issues, their role is necessary. In the five years that the *Mergens* case was in the court system, for example, attorneys did much more than present an eloquent argument or two. They filed cases, wrote legal briefs, took depositions, gathered evidence, and conducted research into the precedents that ultimately won the case. They did what you or I as nonattorneys do not have the ability to do: They navigated the maze we call the legal system.

A favorite Scripture text of Christian attorneys is 1 John 2:1: "If anyone sins, we have an Advocate with the Father, Jesus Christ the righteous." Just as Jesus is our advocate with the Father in matters of our personal lives, lawyers serve an important role as our advocates in the court system. Even if you know more about the intersection of religion and law than does the average attorney, he or she knows more about the legal maze you may have to go through to secure your rights. Remember, the practice of law is more than knowing statutes, cases, and legal principles; it also includes knowing how to work your way through the system. And for that purpose you will be most successful when you are represented by an attorney who knows that system.

Legal Resources at the Local Level

If you are committed to securing rights that have been denied to you under the law, there are two ways you might find an attorney. The first is to engage a private attorney or law firm directly. There are, however, a few factors you should consider.

First, be sure your attorney is familiar with First Amendment law. If the attorney is not, give him or her a copy of this book. (It's not that I'm trying to push my own book; but if your attorney has to do extensive research to find case precedents that work in your favor, you will receive a hefty bill for his or her legal research.)

Second, be sure your attorney is willing to discuss your case with you fully. There are two types of lawyers in the world: those who believe the law is, in the words of Abraham Lincoln's Gettysburg Address, "of the people, by the people, and for the people," and those who believe that the law is an intellectual pursuit that should be kept high on a pedestal because no layperson could possibly understand it. You want the first type of attorney, one who will respect your intelligence and allow you to play a role in your case.

Third, if your case is local in nature, your best course of action may be to engage a local attorney. Attorneys who are located in the jurisdiction in which a case is likely to go to court know both the community and the court system better than outside attorneys. Legal matters are often like business matters in which it's not what you know but whom you know that counts.

Finally, remember that you get what you pay for. Christians are often among the worst offenders when it comes to expecting free legal services, especially from Christian lawyers. Law professor John Eidsmoe writes:

> This attitude is wrong. Most of these people would not even dream of asking a Christian grocer for free groceries, or a Christian retailer for free clothing. They forget that Lincoln said, "A lawyer's time and advice are his only stock in trade." The lawyer has gone through four years of col-

lege and three years of law school to acquire his knowledge of the law, and he spends much time and money expanding and updating his knowledge. The lawyer sells his time, advice and services, just like the grocer sells groceries.[3]

Attorneys generally charge an hourly fee. Be prepared to ask about that fee up front and to decide what your priorities are, financial as well as spiritual, in terms of pursuing your case. Remember that very often, if your attorney simply writes a letter or makes a phone call to help ensure your rights, it may not be necessary to take your case into court at all.

The Ministry of Law

In addition to local attorneys, there are several legal organizations, usually referred to as public-interest law firms, that may be willing to accept your case at no charge. These include the American Center for Law and Justice, Christian Advocates Serving Evangelism (C.A.S.E.), the National Legal Foundation, the Rutherford Institute, and the Western Center for Law and Religious Freedom. Even the American Civil Liberties Union, liberal as it is, has been known to defend the right of Christians to present their beliefs in the public square.

There are three factors of which you should be aware. First, a Christian legal organization is more likely to take your case through to the trial level if it has potential precedent-setting value. Second, even if you are fighting a losing cause, a Christian organization may accept your case because it has potential appeal for fund-raising.

Neither goal is necessarily spiritual, but let's face it—we live in a fallen world. It's expensive to pursue cases in court, and the fund-raising dollar is an important consideration for the survival of any nonprofit organization. Lest I sound too jaded, let me give you an illustration of this. Shortly after the *Mergens* case was decided by the Supreme Court in 1990, several Christian legal organizations mailed fund-raising appeals in which they took credit for winning the case. These included Christian Advocates Serving Evangelism, the Christian Legal Society, National Legal Foundation, and the Rutherford Institute. The case was actually argued by Jay Sekulow of Christian Advocates Serving Evangelism, but Sekulow worked through the National Legal Foundation, which had taken the case before the federal district and appeals courts. The Christian

Legal Society and Rutherford Institute filed *amicus* briefs in the case but did not argue it before the Court.

Finally, you should know that, as with local attorneys, you may not have to take your case to court at all. If the persons or organizations who hassle you about your right to evangelize receive a letter from a national legal organization implying the possibility of a lawsuit, that may be enough to cause them to back down.

Following are some of the resources organized to help you in your legal efforts:

American Center for Law and Justice
P.O. Box 64429
Virginia Beach, VA 23467
(804) 523-7570

The American Center is closely affiliated with Pat Robertson, whose other ministries include Regent University (one of the few Christian law schools in the nation) and the Family Channel (formerly the Christian Broadcasting Network). One of the key ministries of the center is to defend the rights of Christians to engage in religious expression in public schools.

American Civil Liberties Union
(Check your local phone directory, or
call directory assistance for the ACLU
office in the major city closest to you.)

I generally do not endorse the ACLU because of its liberal stand on most social issues, but it has been known to defend the right of Christians to conduct public religious expression. In a survey of thirty-seven cases in which both the Christian Legal Society (CLS) and the ACLU filed *amicus* briefs with the Supreme Court, the ACLU agreed with CLS in seventeen cases and disagreed in twenty cases.[4] That ratio is better than most Christians give it credit for. Even though it does not operate from a Christian perspective, the ACLU is very sympathetic toward First Amendment issues such as free speech, freedom of the press, and freedom of assembly—issues on which many religious cases are won. It generally will not defend cases involving religious expression in the public schools but will usually take a position that supports evangelistic activities in traditional public forums.

Christian Advocates Serving Evangelism (C.A.S.E.)
P.O. Box 450349
Atlanta, GA 30345
(404) 633-2444

One of the most active legal organizations defending the right to witness, C.A.S.E. has represented Christians on a number of issues dealing with school Bible studies, literature distribution, and public evangelism. Its director, Jay Sekulow, argued several religion cases before the Supreme Court, including the *Mergens* case, *Lamb's Chapel*, and *Board of Airport Commissioners v. Jews for Jesus*. Even though it was not a Christian case, Sekulow even argued *United States v. Kokinda* before the Court because of the impact the case had on evangelistic rights.

Christian Law Association
P.O. Box 30
Conneaut, OH 44030
(216) 593-3933

CLA is a nonprofit ministry affiliated with a law firm in Ohio and primarily deals with cases involving the freedom of churches and Christian schools to operate without intrusive government regulation. However, it has also handled cases regarding the right to witness in public places.

Christian Legal Society
4208 Evergreen Lane, Suite 222
Annandale, VA 22003
(703) 642-1070

CLS does not litigate cases directly, but its Center for Law and Religious Freedom has filed a number of *amicus* briefs in significant Supreme Court cases dealing with religion. It maintains a referral service with an extensive listing of Christian attorneys and may be able to refer to you an attorney with First Amendment experience in your area.

The National Legal Foundation
Post Office Box D
Chesapeake, VA 23328
(804) 424-4242

NLF specializes in First Amendment cases, especially those involving religious expression in public schools, and also has a referral network for local attorneys with First Amendment experience.

The Rutherford Institute
P.O. Box 8482
Charlottesville, VA 22906-7482
(804) 424-4242

The Rutherford Institute handles all types of constitutional cases including those dealing with school prayer, equal access, and the right to evangelize in public places.

Western Center for Law and Religious Freedom
West 1402 Broadway Avenue
Spokane, WA 99201
(509) 325-5850

The only major public-interest firm dealing with Christian legal issues on the Pacific coast, the center focuses on fundamental constitutional and legal issues throughout the western states.

Where to Go from Here

The best time to become aware of how the law affects your activities is before you need to resort to legal recourse. In addition to reading this book, there are a few other ways you can pursue this.

First, read the case opinions themselves, especially the religion opinions issued by the Supreme Court. More than any book, the judicial opinions issued in cases will give you an indication of how the courts work and, for lack of a better term, why things are the way they are. Many law school and municipal law libraries admit members of the public who are not attorneys, and almost all of the decisions cited in this book are published in the myriad of legal reporters (case books) available today.[5]

Second, you may wish to get on the mailing lists of some of the Christian legal organizations listed in this chapter before you need their legal services. Many of them send out newsletters on a regular basis, and these can help keep you informed of any changes in the law.

Third, you might wish to read some other books on legal issues and Christian witness that are designed to be understood by laypersons. Two books I would especially recommend for Christians interested in evangelism are Jay Sekulow's *From Intimidation to Victory* (Lake Mary, Fla: Creation House, 1990) and John Eidsmoe's *The Christian Legal Advisor*, rev. ed. (Grand Rapids: Baker Book House, 1987). Sekulow addresses some of the legal struggles and the victories he has had in defending the right to do evangelism, and Eidsmoe's book presents a comprehensive overview of how the law affects Christians in a number of areas.

Finally, if you are a student, you might consider a legal career for yourself. Despite the skeptical picture I sometimes paint of lawyers in general, God raises up committed Christian attorneys who are dedicated to preserving the right of churches and individuals to make an impact on the world. The existence of Christian legal organizations such as those listed in this chapter testifies to the fact that some attorneys have the courage to follow their convictions and practice law as a ministry that glorifies God.

A Closing Word

The legal principles in this book will, hopefully, help you err on the side of safety and maximize your witnessing potential in both street ministry and evangelism in many other situations.

On the optimistic side, if you are like the majority of Christians who do personal evangelism, you will encounter no legal resistance to your activities. If you do encounter resistance, however, you will have to choose whether to move on to an environment where you will meet less resistance or to meet the challenge head-on and pursue your rights under the law. Neither alternative is necessarily correct or incorrect, but your decision should be based on prayer as well as discussions with your pastor or a lawyer.

From a Christian perspective, there is good news on the horizon. I am reminded of the old expression, "I read the end of the book, and we win." Regardless of the legal hurdles we may have to traverse to spread the gospel, we have the assurance that God is in control. We may lose an occasional battle in the world, but ultimately we shall win the war.

/ *Notes* /

Preface

1. Justice Fischer and Dorothy H. Lachmann, *Unauthorized Practice Handbook* (Chicago: American Bar Foundation, 1972; reprinted, Buffalo: William S. Hein & Co., 1990), 15.
2. Ibid., 22–30.

Chapter 1 The Challenge in Personal Evangelism

1. Everson v. Board of Education, 300 U.S. 1, 18 (1947).
2. Thomas Jefferson, Letter to the Danbury Baptist Association, 1 January 1802, reprinted in Daniel Dreisbach, *Real Threat and Mere Shadow: Religious Liberty and the First Amendment* (Westchester, Ill: Crossway Books, 1987), 169–170.
3. John Eidsmoe, *Christianity and the Constitution* (Grand Rapids: Baker Book House, 1987), 244–245.
4. Walz v. Tax Commission of the City of New York, 397 U.S. 664, 669 (1970).
5. Steve Levicoff, An Analysis of State-Sponsored versus Student-Initiated Religious Expression in Public Education (Master's thesis, Vermont College of Norwich University, 1989).

Chapter 2 Some Law for the Nonlawyer

1. United States Constitution, Amend. I (1791).
2. Robert L. Cord, *Separation of Church and State: Historical Fact and Current Fiction* (Grand Rapids: Baker Book House, 1988), 4.
3. John Warwick Montgomery, *The Shaping of America* (Minneapolis: Bethany House, 1976), 153–154.
4. United States Constitution, Amend. XIV (1868).
5. Barron v. The Mayor and City Council of Baltimore, 7 Peters 243 (1833).
6. Gitlow v. New York, 268 U.S. 652 (1925).
7. Everson v. Board of Education, 300 U.S. 1 at 5–6.
8. Robert P. Davidow, "Secular Humanism as an Established Religion: A Response to Whitehead and Conlan," *Texas Tech Law Review* 11 (1979): 56.

9. Richard C. McMillan, *Religion in the Public Schools: An Introduction* (Macon, Ga: Mercer University Press, 1984), 39.

10. See Frank S. Mead, *Handbook of Denominations in the United States*, 9th ed., rev. by Samuel S. Hill (Nashville: Abingdon Press, 1990), and Constant H. Jacquet, Jr., ed., *Yearbook of American & Canadian Churches* (Nashville: Abingdon Press, issued annually).

11. Everson v. Board of Education, 300 U.S. at 5–6.

12. United States v. Ballard, 322 U.S. 78, 86–87 (1944).

13. Reynolds v. United States, 98 U.S. 145, 166 (1879).

14. Ibid. at 167.

15. For more on Mormonism as a belief system, see Walter Martin, *The Kingdom of the Cults*, rev. ed. (Grand Rapids: Baker Book House, 1985), 166–226, and Ruth A. Tucker, *Another Gospel: Alternative Religions and the New Age Movement* (Grand Rapids: Academie Books, 1989), 49–91.

16. Bunn v. North Carolina, 336 U.S. 942 (1949). This is the best-known case dealing with practices such as the handling of snakes or drinking of strychnine, fairly common practices among rural white churches in pockets of the South that continue today. These churches base their activities on Jesus' statement, "And these signs will accompany those who have believed: in My name they will cast out demons, they will speak with new tongues; they will pick up serpents, and if they drink any deadly poison it shall not hurt them; they will lay hands on the sick, and they will recover" (Mark 16:17–18). Somehow, I don't think that snake handling and the drinking of poisons are intended for contemporary Christians. So, kids, don't try this at home.

17. United States Constitution, Art. III, sec. 2 (1787).

18. Marbury v. Madison, 1 Cranch 137 (1803).

19. United States Constitution, Art. I, sec. 3 (1787).

20. Roe v. Wade, 410 U.S. 113 (1973).

21. Garnett v. Renton School District No. 403, 865 F.2d 1121 (9th Cir. 1989).

22. Mergens v. Board of Education of the Westside Community Schools (Dist. 66), 867 F.2d 1076 (8th Cir. 1989), aff'd., 496 U.S. 226 (1990).

23. Board of Education of the Westside Community Schools v. Mergens, 496 U.S. 226 (1990).

24. Garnett v. Renton School District, 772 F.Supp. 531 (W.D.Wash. 1991), rev'd., 987 F. 2d 641 (9th Cir. 1993).

Chapter 3 Equal Rights for Those Who Are Wrong

1. Watson v. Jones, 13 Wallace 679, 728 (1872).

2. United States v. Ballard, 322 U.S. at 86–87.

3. For more information on the I Am Movement, see Tucker, *Another Gospel*, 369–370.

4. U.S. v. Ballard, 322 U.S. at 86.

5. Presbyterian Church in the United States v. Mary Elizabeth Blue Hull Memorial Presbyterian Church, 393 U.S. 440, 443–444 (1969).

6. Ibid. at 449.

7. Ibid. at 450.

8. Jones v. Wolf, 443 U.S. 595, 603 (1979).

9. Ibid. at 604.

10. For a survey of these and other cultic groups, see Martin, *The Kingdom of the Cults*, and Tucker, *Another Gospel.*

11. Cantwell v. Connecticut, 310 U.S. 296 (1940).

12. Ibid. at 303.

13. Murdock v. Pennsylvania, 319 U.S. 105, 108–109 (1943).

14. Marc Galanter, *Cults: Faith, Healing, and Coercion* (New York: Oxford University Press, 1989), 79.

15. Stuart A. Wright, *Leaving Cults: The Dynamics of Defection* (Washington, D.C.: Society for the Scientific Study of Religion, 1987), 2.

16. One of the most profound examples of this phenomenon is that Christian denominations and evangelical legal organizations universally supported the right of the Santeria religion, a predominantly Cuban cult which integrates Catholicism and voodoo, to practice animal sacrifice in the United States as part of their religious rites. See Church of the Lukum: Babula Aye Inc. v. City of Hialeah, 113 S.Ct. 2217 (1993).

Chapter 4 Taking the Word to the Streets

1. Hague v. CIO, 307 U.S. 496, 515–516 (1939).

2. John F. Walvoord and Roy B. Zuck, *The Bible Knowledge Commentary— New Testament* (Wheaton: Victor Books, 1983), 402.

3. Charles F. Pfeiffer and Everett F. Harrison, eds., *The Wycliffe Bible Commentary* (Chicago: Moody Press, 1962), 1156.

4. Hague v. CIO, 307 U.S. at 516.

5. Grayned v. Rockford, 408 U.S. 104 (1972).

6. Eanes v. State, 569 A.2d 604 (Md., 1990).

7. City of Lakewood v. Elsass, No. 56480–56482, 1989 WL 62236, (Oh.App. 1989).

8. Ohio v. Livingston, No. CA 9641, 1986 WL 11112 (Oh.App. 1986).

9. Heffron v. International Society for Krishna Consciousness, 452 U.S. 640 (1981).

10. Chaplinsky v. New Hampshire, 315 U.S. 568 (1942).

11. Schneider v. State, 308 U.S. 147, 162 (1939).

12. Kunz v. City of New York, 340 U.S. 290 (1951).

13. Furr v. Town of Swansea, 594 F.Supp. 1543 (D.S.C. 1984).

14. Cox v. New Hampshire, 312 U.S. 569, 574 (1941).

15. Philadelphia Police Department Directive 94A (references omitted), reprinted in Lickteig v. Landauer, Civ. A. No. 91–1843 (E.D.Pa. 1991).

16. International Society for Krishna Consciousness v. City of Baton Rouge, 876 F.2d 494 (5th Cir. 1989).

17. Gaudiya Vaishnava Society v. City and County of San Francisco, 952 F.2d 1059, No. 88–1904 (9th Cir. 1990).

18. City of Angeles Mission Church v. City of Houston, Texas, 716 F.Supp. 982 (S.D.Tex. 1989).

19. International Society of Krishna Consciousness of Houston, Inc. v. City of Houston, 689 F.2d 541 (5th Cir. 1982).

20. Jimmy Swaggart Ministries v. Board of Equalization of the State of California, 493 U.S. 378 (1990).

Chapter 5 Taking the Word to the Malls

1. NBC Nightly News report, 10 August 1992.

2. Hague v. CIO, 307 U.S. at 515.

3. Perry Education Association v. Perry Local Educators' Association, 460 U.S. 37, 45 (1983).

4. Ibid. at 46.

5. Ibid.

6. United States Constitution, Amend. V (1791), emphasis added.

7. Marsh v. Alabama, 326 U.S. 501, 502–503 (1946).

8. Ibid. at 508.

9. Amalgamated Food Employees Union v. Logan Valley Plaza, 391 U.S. 308, 320 (1968).

10. Ibid. at 320, n. 9 (emphasis added).

11. Tanner v. Lloyd Corporation, Ltd., 308 F.Supp. 128 (D.Or. 1970), aff'd., 446 F.2d 545 (9th Cir. 1971), rev'd., 407 U.S. 551 (1972).

12. Lloyd Corporation v. Tanner, 407 U.S. at 554.

13. Ibid. at 555–556.

14. Ibid. at 555.

15. Ibid. at 565, quoting Amalgamated Food Employees Union v. Logan Valley Plaza, 391 U.S. at 338.

16. Ibid. at 564–565.

17. Ibid. at 569.

18. Ibid. at 566–567.

19. Ibid. at 564.

20. Robins v. PruneYard Shopping Center, 592 P.2d 341, 347 (1979), rev'd., 447 U.S. 74 (1980).

21. Ibid. at 347–348.

22. PruneYard Shopping Center v. Robins, 447 U.S. 74 at 81.

23. Ibid. at 87.

24. Savage v. Trammell Crow Company, Inc., 273 Cal. Rptr. 302, 305 (Cal. App. 1990).

25. Ibid. at 308.

26. Ibid.

27. Ibid. at 310.

28. Ibid. at 304.

29. Ibid. at 312, quoting Cal. Code of Civ. Proc. sec. 170.2.

30. Ibid. at 312.

31. Shad Alliance v. Smith Haven Mall, 488 N.E. 2d 1211, 1215 (N.Y. Ct. App. 1985). The Court of Appeals is the highest court in the state, similar to the supreme court in other states.

32. Amalgamated Food Employees Union v. Logan Valley Plaza, 391 U.S. at 315.

33. Lloyd Corporation v. Tanner, 407 U.S. at 576, 578–579.

34. Ibid. at 586, quoting Marsh v. Alabama, 326 U.S. at 506.

35. David Rudovsky, "You Can Get a Soapbox on Main St., But They Won't Let You Do It on Mall St.," *The Philadelphia Inquirer*, 16 August 1992, p. C7.

36. D. James Kennedy, *Evangelism Explosion*, rev. ed. (Wheaton: Tyndale House, 1977).

37. *How to Experience and Share Abundant Life in Christ* (San Bernardino, Calif.: Lay Institute for Evangelism, Campus Crusade for Christ, 1971).

Chapter 6 Taking the Word to School

1. McCollum v. Board of Education, 333 U.S. 203, 212 (1948).

2. Zorach v. Clauson, 343 U.S. 306 (1952).

3. Robert T. Miller and Ronald B. Flowers, *Toward Benevolent Neutrality: Church, State, and the Supreme Court*, 3d ed. (Waco: Baylor University Press, 1987), 379.

4. Engel v. Vitale, 370 U.S. 421, 422 (1962).

5. Ibid. at 424–425.

6. Miller and Flowers, *Toward Benevolent Neutrality*, 380.

7. Abington Township School District v. Schempp, 374 U.S. 203, 226 (1963).

8. Stone v. Graham, 449 U.S. 39 (1980).

9. Wallace v. Jaffree, 472 U.S. 38 (1985).

10. Edwards v. Aguilar, 482 U.S. 578 (1987).

11. Miller and Flowers, *Toward Benevolent Neutrality*, 199.

12. Chess v. Widmar, 480 F.Supp. 907 (W.D.Mo. 1979), rev'd., 635 F.2d 1310 (8th Cir. 1980), aff'd., 454 U.S. 263 (1981).

13. Widmar v. Vincent, 454 U.S. 263 (1981).

14. Lemon v. Kurtzman, 403 U.S. 602, 613–614 (1971).

15. Widmar v. Vincent, 454 U.S. at 274.

16. Ibid. at 277.

17. Gay Rights Coalition v. Georgetown University, 536 A.2d 1 (D.C. 1987).

18. Clark v. United States, 705 F.Supp. 605 (D.D.C. 1988), aff'd., 886 F.2d 404 (D.C. Cir. 1989).

19. Gay and Lesbian Students Association v. Gohn, 820 F.2d 361 (8th Cir. 1988).

20. Brandon v. Board of Education of Guilderland, 635 F.2d 971 (1981), cert. denied, 454 U.S. 1123 (1981); Lubbock Civil Liberties Union v. Lubbock Independent School District, 669 F.2d 1038 (5th Cir. 1982), cert. denied, 459 U.S. 1155 (1983).

21. Equal Access Act, 20 U.S.C 4071(a) 4071(c) (1984).

22. Quoted in James E. Wood, Jr., "Equal Access: A New Direction in American Public Education," *Journal of Church and State* 27 (Winter 1985): 10–11.

23. Quoted in Ibid., 5–6.

24. Equal Access Act, 20 U.S.C. at 4071(d)(5), 4071(f).

25. Bender v. Williamsport Area School District, 475 U.S. 534, 536 (1986).

26. Bender v. Williamsport, 563 F.Supp. 697 (M.D.Pa. 1983), rev'd., 741 F.2d 538 (3d Cir. 1984), rev'd., 475 U.S. 534 (1986).

27. Garnett v. Renton School District No. 403, 865 F.2d 1121 (9th Cir. 1989).

28. Mergens v. Board of Education of the Westside Community Schools (Dist. 66), 867 F.2d 1076 (8th Cir. 1989), aff'd, 496 U.S. 226 (1990).

29. Board of Education of the Westside Community Schools v. Mergens, 496 U.S. 226 (1990).

30. Ibid. at 248.

31. Garnett v. Renton School District, 772 F.Supp. 531 (W.D.Wash. 1991) rev'd., 987 F. 2d 641 (9th cir. 1993).

32. Hoppock v. Twin Falls School District No. 11, 772 F.Supp. 1160 (D.Idaho 1991). The Supremacy Clause of the United States Constitution appears in Article VI, sec. 2 (1787), and says, "This Constitution, and the Laws of the United States which shall be made in Pursuance thereof; and all Treaties made, or which shall be made, under the Authority of the United States, shall be the supreme Law of the Land; and the Judges in every State shall be bound thereby, any Thing in the Constitution or Laws of any State to the Contrary notwithstanding."

33. Garnet v. Renton School District, 987 F. 2d 641.

34. Hazelwood School District v. Kuhlmeier, 484 U.S. 260 (1988).

35. Burch v. Barker, 861 F.2d 1149 (9th Cir. 1988).

36. Thompson v. Waynesboro Area School District, 673 F.Supp. 1379 (M.D.Pa. 1987).

37. Rivera v. East Otero School District, 721 F.Supp. 1189 (D.Colo. 1989); Hemry v. School Board of Colorado Springs, 760 F.Supp. 856 (D.Colo. 1991); Hedges v. Wayconda Community Unit School District No. 118, No. 90–C–6604, 1991 Wl 222163 (N.D.Ill. 1991).

38. Country Hills Christian Church v. Unified School District, 560 F.Supp. 1207 (D.Kan. 1983).

39. Gregoire v. Centennial School District, 907 F.2d 1366 (3d Cir. 1990).

40. Travis v. Owego-Appalachian School District, No. 90–CV–90, 1990 WL 94196 (N.D.N.Y. 1990), aff'd., 941 F.2d 668 (2d Cir. 1991).

41. Grace Bible Fellowship v. Maine School Administrative District No. 5, 941 F.2d 45 (1st Cir. 1991).

42. Lamb's Chapel v. Center Moriches Union Free School District, 736 F. Supp. 1247, aff'd. on reargument, 770 F. Supp. 91 (E.D.N.Y. 1991), aff'd 959 F.2d 381 (2d Cir. 1992), rev'd., 113 S.Ct. 2141 (1993).

43. N.Y. Educ. Law sec. 414 (1) (d), (1988).

44. Lamb's Chapel v. Center Moriches Union Free School District, 959 F.2d at 387–388.

45. Deeper Life Christian Fellowship v. Sobol, 949 F. 2d 79 (2d Cir. 1991); Travis v. Owego-Appalachian School District, 941 F.2d 668 (2d Cir. 1991).

46. Lamb's Chapel v. Center Moriches School District, 113 S.Ct. at 2148.

47. Fink v. Board of Education of Warren County Schools, 442 A.2d 837 (Pa. Commonw. 1982), cert. denied, 460 U.S. 1048 (1983).

48. Doe v. Duncanville Independent School District, No. CA 3–91–0291–T (N.D.Tex. 1991).

49. May v. Evansville-Vanderburgh School Corp., 787 F.2d 1105 (7th Cir. 1986).

50. Roberts v. Madigan, 702 F.Supp. 1505 (D.Colo. 1989), aff'd., 921 F.2d 1047 (10th Cir. 1990), cert. denied, 112 S.Ct. 3025 (1992).

51. Dale v. Board of Education, 316 N.W.2d 108 (S.Dak. 1982); Webster v. New Lenox School District No. 122, 917 F.2d 1004 (7th Cir. 1990); Peloza v. Capistrano Unified School District, 782 F.Supp. 1412 (C.D.Cal. 1992).

52. Bishop v. Aronov, 732 F.Supp. 1562 (N.D.Ala. 1990), rev'd., 926 F.2d 1066 (11th Cir. 1991).

53. United States v. Board of Education for the School District of Philadelphia, 911 F.2d 882 (3d Cir. 1990).

54. Tinker v. Des Moines Area School District, 393 U.S. 503 at 506, 511 (1969).

55. Douglas Laycock, "Equal Access and Moments of Silence: The Equal Status of Religious Speech by Private Speakers," *Northwestern University Law Review* 81 (Fall 1986): 17.

56. Redmon v. Clay County School Board, No. 91–1080–CIVJ12 (M.D.Fla. 1992), reported in *The Religious Freedom Reporter* 12 (March 1992): 90.

57. Quoted in Robert L. Crewdson, "The Equal Access Act of 1984: Congressional and the Free Speech Limits of the Establishment Clause in Public High Schools," *Journal of Law and Religion* 16 (Spring 1987): 171–172.

Chapter 7 Taking the Word to Work

1. Vanderlaan v. Mulder, 443 N.W.2d 491, 178 Mich. App. 172 (Mich.App. 1989).

2. In re D'Amico, No. 51581 (N.Y.App. 1986).

3. Spratt v. County of Kent, 621 F.Supp. 594 (W.D.Mich. 1985), aff'd., 810 F.2d 203 (6th Cir. 1986), cert. denied, 480 U.S. 934 (1987).

4. Goodwin v. Metropolitan Board of Health, 656 S.W.2d 383 (Tenn.App. 1983).

5. Flynn v. Maine Employment Security Commission, 448 A.2d 905 (Maine 1982), cert. denied, 459 U.S. 1114 (1983).

6. Civil Rights Act of 1964, 42 U.S.C. 2000e (as amended).

7. Ibid. at 42 U.S.C. 2000e(J), as amended in 1972.

8. Sherbert v. Verner, 374 U.S. 398, 406 (1963).

9. Parker Seal Company v. Cummins, 433 U.S. 903 (1976).

10. Trans World Airlines, Inc. v. Hardison, 432 U.S. 63 (1977).

11. Thomas v. Review Board of Indiana Employment Security Division, 450 U.S. 707 (1981).

12. Ibid. at 718.

13. Boomsma v. Greyhound Food Management, Inc., 639 F.Supp. 1448 (W.D.Mich. 1986).

14. EEOC v. Ithaca Industries, Inc., 849 F.2d 116 (4th Cir. 1988).

15. David B. Larson, et al., "Systematic Analysis of Research on Religious Variables in Four Major Psychiatric Journals, 1978–1982," *American Journal of Psychiatry* 143 (March 1986): 329.

16. Collins v. Virginia Employment Commission, No. 68142 (Cir. Ct. Fairfax Co., Virginia, 1980), reported in *Religious Freedom Reporter* 1 (March 1981): 49–50.

17. Guyer v. Keith County, No. CV–89–L–178, filed 1989, reported in *Religious Freedom Reporter* 9 (1989): 124.

18. Tom Fontanes, "New Age Profits," *Passport*, October–November 1987, p. 10–11.

19. Peter Waldman, "Motivate or Alienate? Firms Hire Gurus to Change Their 'Cultures,'" *The Wall Street Journal*, 24 July 1987, p. 19.

20. Jeremy Main, "Trying to Bend Managers' Minds," *Fortune*, 23 November 1987, p. 95.

21. EEOC Decision 91–1, DLR No. 81, D–1 (1991), reported in *Religious Freedom Reporter* 11 (1991): 348–349.

22. Wedmore v. Sidha Corporation International, No. 35–801–E (S.D.Iowa, filed October 2, 1985), reported in *Religious Freedom Reporter* 5 (1985): 180.

23. Richard Watring, "New Age Training in Business: Mind Control in Upper Management?" *Eternity*, February 1988, p. 32.

24. Ibid.

25. Doug Groothuis, "Identifying the New Age Seminar," *SCP Journal* 9 (1989): 6–7.

26. EEOC v. Townley Engineering & Manufacturing Company, 859 F.2d 610 (9th Cir. 1988).

27. Wilson v. Ohio Bureau of Employment Services, No. 12651, 1986 WL 13852 (Oh.Ct.App. 1986).

28. Kolodziej v. Smith, 588 N.E.2d 634, 412 Mass. 215 (Mass. 1992).

29. American Postal Workers Union v. Postmaster General, 781 F.2d 772 (9th Cir. 1986).

30. Auzins v. Granville House, No. 10697–2548–UC–83 (Minn. Dept. of Econ. Security 1984).

31. EEOC Decision 81–20. 2 Empl. Prac. Guide (CCH) 6769 (1991), reported in *Religious Freedom Reporter* 1 (1981): 253.

32. Kenny v. Ambulatory Centre of Miami, 400 So.2d 1262 (Fla. 1981).

Chapter 8 Taking the Word to Stadiums and Concerts

1. International Society for Krishna Consciousness, Inc., v. New Jersey Sports and Exposition Authority, 532 F.Supp. 1088 (D.N.J. 1981), aff'd., 691 F.2d (3d Cir. 1982).

2. International Society for Krishna Consciousness, Inc., v. New Jersey Sports and Exposition Authority, 691 F.2d at 161–162.

3. Ibid. at 161, n. 3.

4. Ibid. at 159.

5. Carreras v. City of Anaheim, 768 F.2d 1039 (9th Cir. 1985).

6. Ibid. at 1046.

7. Ibid. at 1040.

8. Paulsen v. County of Nassau, 925 F.2d 68 (2d Cir. 1992).

9. Ibid. at 67–68.

10. Ibid. at 70–71.

11. Ibid. at 71.

12. Ibid. at 66, 71.

13. Stewart v. District of Columbia Armory Board, 863 F.2d 1013 (D.C. Cir. 1988). Rollen Stewart was known to millions as the "Rainbow Man" because he wore multicolored wigs as he flashed Scripture references at televised sporting events. Stewart professed Christianity, but in July 1993 he was sentenced to three life sentences for kidnapping staff members at a Los Angeles hotel and holding them hostage for nine hours in a room at the hotel, in which he had posted large signs with scriptural citations in the window. Stewart claimed that he engaged in the hostage drama to "explain the love of God and how it plays out," leading a deputy district attorney to describe him as "a David Koresh waiting to happen." During his sentencing hearing, Stewart engaged in a rambling eschatological discourse and, upon being wrestled to the floor by deputies, shouted, "Forgive them, Lord, for they know not what they're doing." See, e.g., Andrea Ford, "Rainbow Man Sentenced to 3 Life Terms," *Los Angeles Times,* 14 July 1993, p. B3; Eric Malnic, "Rainbow Man Guilty in Airport Hotel Siege," *Los Angeles Times,* 12 June

1993, p. B3; "Rainbow Man Sentenced to Three Life Prison Terms," *Daily News of Los Angeles,* 14 July 1993, p. S7; Robert Fachet, "In L.A., 'Rainbow Man' is Given 3 Life Terms," *The Washington Post,* 14 July 1993, p. B2. Clearly, Stewart is psychologically disturbed, and his actions should not be endorsed by Christians. Nonetheless, the cases he spawned that are discussed in this book about evangelism at stadiums are too important not to cite here.

14. Stewart v. District of Columbia Armory Board, 789 F.Supp. 402, 403 (D.D.C. 1992).

15. Ibid. at 406.

16. Ibid. at 405.

17. "John 3:16 Scores Touchdown at D.C. Stadium," *Church & State*, October 1992, p. 3.

Chapter 9 Taking the Word to Airports

1. Rosen v. Port of Portland, 641 F.2d 1243 (9th Cir. 1981).

2. Thomas v. Collins, 323 U.S. 516 (1944).

3. Fernandes v. Limmer, 663 F.2d 619 (5th Cir. 1981).

4. Christian Science Reading Room Jointly Maintained v. City of San Francisco, 784 F.2d 1010, amended 792 F.2d 124 (9th Cir. 1986).

5. See text accompanying chapter 6, note 14, for a summary of the *Lemon* test.

6. Jews for Jesus v. Board of Airport Commissioners for the City of Los Angeles, 785 F.2d 791, 795 (9th Cir. 1986), aff'd. on other grounds, 482 U.S. 569 (1987).

7. Board of Airport Commissioners of the City of Los Angeles v. Jews for Jesus, Inc., 482 U.S. at 573–574. The Perry citation refers to the 1983 case of Perry Education Association v. Perry Local Educators' Association, in which the Court discussed types of forums. See text accompanying chapter 5, notes 3–5.

8. Ibid. at 574–575.

9. Ibid. at 577.

10. Heffron v. International Society for Krishna Consciousness, 452 U.S. at 644.

11. Miller and Flowers, *Toward Benevolent Neutrality*, 233.

12. Heffron v. International Society for Krishna Consciousness, 452 U.S. at 652.

13. International Society for Krishna Consciousness, Inc., v. Lee, 925 F.2d 576, 578–579, (2d Cir. 1991).

14. International Society for Krishna Consciousness, Inc., v. Lee, 721 F.Supp. 572 (S.D.N.Y. 1989), aff'd. in part and reversed in part, 925 F.2d 576 (2d Cir. 1991), aff'd., 112 S.Ct. 2701 (1992).

15. International Society for Krishna Consciousness, Inc., v. Lee, 112 S.Ct. at 2706.

16. Ibid. at 2706–2707.

17. Ibid. at 2708, quoting 925 F.2d at 582.
18. Ibid. at 2712, O'Connor, J., concurring.
19. Ibid. at 2717–2718, Kennedy, J., concurring.
20. Ibid. at 2718–2719, Kennedy, J., concurring.
21. Ibid. at 2725, Souter, J., dissenting.
22. Lee v. International Society for Krishna Consciousness (companion case to ISKCON v. Lee), 112 S.Ct. 2709, 2710 (1992).
23. Ibid. at 2710, Rehnquist, C.J., dissenting.
24. Roe v. Wade, 410 U.S. 113 (1973).

Chapter 10 Taking the Word to Jails and Prisons

1. Howard Goodman, "U.S. Jail Rate Still Tops World," *The Philadelphia Inquirer*, 11 February 1992, p. A3.
2. Ibid.
3. Daniel Van Ness, *Crime and Its Victims* (Downers Grove, Ill: InterVarsity Press, 1986), 44.
4. Howard Goodman, "Prison Bursting at the Bars," *The Philadelphia Inquirer*, 12 March 1990, p. 2–A.
5. For more information on prison alternatives, see Charles Colson and Daniel Van Ness, *Convicted: New Hope for Ending America's Crime Crisis* (Westchester, Ill: Crossway Books, 1989).
6. Van Ness, *Crime and Its Victims*, 53–54.
7. Ibid., 44.
8. Donald Smarto, *Justice and Mercy* (Wheaton: Tyndale House, 1987), 22.
9. Jack Henry Abbott, *In the Belly of the Beast* (New York: Vintage Books, 1981), 53.
10. Bernard T. Adeney, "Living On the Edge: Ethics Inside San Quentin," *Journal of Law and Religion* 6 (1988): 442.
11. Bounds v. Smith, 430 U.S. 817, 828 (1977).
12. Craig v. Hocker, 405 F.Supp. 656 (D.Nev. 1975).
13. See, e.g., Cooper v. Pate, 378 U.S. 546 (1964); Cruz v. Beto, 405 U.S. 319 (1972).
14. Steve Levicoff, *The New Song of Shiloh: An Historical, Legal, and Theological Exploration of an Indigenous Prison Church* (Ph.D. Dissertation, The Union Institute, 1991).
15. For a summary of cases dealing with the religious accommodation of dietary needs, see *Religion in the Constitution: A Delicate Balance* (Washington, D.C.: United States Commission on Civil Rights, Clearinghouse Publication No. 80, September 1983), 67–72, and James J. Gobert and Neil P. Cohen, *Rights of Prisoners* (Colorado Springs: Shepherd's/McGraw-Hill, 1981), 152–154.
16. See Knuckles v. Prasse, 307 F.Supp. 1036 (E.D.Pa. 1969), aff'd., 435F.2d 1255 (3d Cir. 1970), cert. denied, 403 U.S. 936 (1977). See also: Statement of Lar-

ry Taylor, warden at the Federal Correctional Institution at Lompoc, California, in *Religious Discrimination: A Neglected Issue*, a consultation sponsored by the United States Commission on Civil Rights in Washington, D.C., in April 1979 (Washington, D.C.: United States Commission on Civil Rights, 1969), 129.

17. Lawson v. Dugger, 840 F.2d 781 (11th Cir. 1987); Walker v. Blackwell, 411 F.2d 23 (5th Cir. 1969).

18. Madyun v. Franzen, 704 F.2d 954 (7th Cir. 1983); Rivera v. Smith, 472 N.E.2d 1015 (N.Y. 1984).

19. Richard A. Houlihan, priest and administrator, Federal Prison Systems Chaplaincy Services, consultation statement in *Religious Discrimination: A Neglected Issue*, 131.

20. Dale K. Pace, *A Christian's Guide to Effective Jail & Prison Ministries* (Old Tappan, N.J.: Fleming H. Revell, 1976), 117.

21. G.M. Clifford, III, "Ministry in a Pluralistic Environment," *Military Chaplains' Review* (Summer 1992): 67.

22. Baz v. Walters, 599 F. Supp. 614, 618 (C.D.Ill. 1984).

23. Ibid. at 617.

24. See Gail Gehrig, *American Civil Religion: An Assessment*, SSSR Monograph Series No. 3, (Washington, D.C.: Society for the Scientific Study of Religion, 1979). See also: Richard V. Pierard and Robert D. Linder, *Civil Religion and the Presidency* (Grand Rapids: Academie Books, 1988).

25. Pace, *Jail & Prison Ministries*, 100–101, 144. See also: Jenny Yates Hammett, "A Second Drink at the Well: Theological and Philosophical Content of CPE Origins," Journal of Pastoral Care 29 (June 1975): 86–89.

26. Ibid., 98–100.

Chapter 11 Taking the Word Home

1. Kennedy, Evangelism Explosion, 11.

2. Cantwell v. Connecticut, 310 U.S. 296 (1940); Jamison v. Texas, 318 U.S. 413 (1943); Largent v. Texas, 318 U.S. 418 (1943); Murdock v. Pennsylvania, 319 U.S. 105 (1943).

3. Richard R. Hammar, *Pastor, Church and Law,* 2d ed. (Springfield, Mo.: Gospel Publishing House, 1991), 872.

4. Murdock v. Pennsylvania, 319 U.S. at 112. The term *colporteurs* is defined in *Webster's Ninth Collegiate New Dictionary* as "peddlers of religious books."

5. Village of Schaumberg v. Citizens for a Better Environment, 444 U.S. 620 (1980).

6. Troyer v. Town of Babylon, 449 U.S. 988 (1980).

7. Martin v. City of Struthers, 319 U.S. 141 (1939).

8. Jamison v. Texas, 318 U.S. 413 (1943).

9. Holy Spirit Association for the Unification of World Christianity v. Hodge, 582 F.Supp. 592 (N.D.Tex. 1984).

10. Taylor v. City of Knoxville, 566 F.Supp. 925 (E.D.Tenn. 1983).

11. International Society for Krishna Consciousness of Houston, Inc., v. City of Houston, 482 F.Supp. 852 (S.D.Tex. 1979), rev'd., 689 F.2d 541 (5th Cir. 1982).

12. Poe v. City of Humble, 554 F.Supp. 233 (S.D.Tex. 1983).

13. City of Colorado Springs v. Blanche, 761 P.2d 212 (Colo. 1988).

14. Grosz v. City of Miami Beach, Florida, 721 F.2d 729 (11th Cir. 1983).

15. Harrison Orthodox Minyan, Inc., v. Town Board of Harrison, 525 N.Y.S.2d 434, 435 (N.Y.App. 1990).

16. State v. Cameron, 498 A.2d 1217 (N.J. 1985).

Chapter 12 And to the Uttermost Parts of the Nation

1. Sherbert v. Verner, 374 U.S. 398 (1963).

2. Wisconsin v. Yoder, 406 U.S. 205 (1972).

3. Ibid. at 220.

4. Employment Division, Department of Human Resources of Oregon, v. Smith, 494 U.S. 872, 905–906 (1990), O'Connor, J., concurring.

5. Ibid. at 890, Scalia, J., for majority.

6. Ibid. at 891, O'Connor, J., concurring.

7. Greg Ivers, *Redefining the First Freedom: The Supreme Court and the Consolidation of State Power* (New Brunswick, N.J.: Transaction Publishers, 1993), 140.

8. Minersville School District v. Gobitis, 310 U.S. 586 (1940).

9. West Virginia State Board of Education v. Barnette, 319 U.S. 624 (1943).

10. Michael A. Tyner, "In a Disastrous Decision, Justice Scalia Calls into Question Decades of Settled Law Concerning Freedom of Religion," *Liberty*, September–October 1990, p. 5.

11. *The Religious Freedom Restoration Act*, H.R. 1308, S. 578, 103d Congress, 1st session (1993).

12. See National Organization for Women v. Operation Rescue, 747 F.Supp. 760 (D.D.C. 1990); Planned Parenthood of San Diego and Riverside Counties v. Wilson, 815 P.2d 351 (Cal. App. 1991).

13. Frisby v. Schultz, 487 U.S. 474, 484 (1988).

14. Ibid. at 2503.

15. Ibid. at 2506–2510.

16. Ibid. at 2507, Brennan, J., dissenting.

17. Concerned Women for America, Inc., v. Lafayette County, 883 F.2d 32, 33 (5th Cir. 1989), aff'd. 699 F.Supp. 95 (N.D.Miss. 1988).

18. Ibid. at 34.

19. Ibid. at 35.

20. Greer v. Spock, 424 U.S. 828, 838 (1976).

21. Ibid. at 840.

22. Goldman v. Weinberger, 475 U.S. 503 (1986). The Goldman decision was reversed a year later by Congressional statute. 10 U.S.C. 774 (1987).

23. Hague v. CIO, 307 U.S. at 515–516.

24. Paulsen v. Gotbaum, No. 92 Civ. 6152 (JSM), 1992 WL 8361 (S.D.N.Y. 1992), summarized in *Religious Freedom Reporter* 12 (March 1992): 98–99.

25. Henderson v. Lujan, 768 F.Supp. 1 (D.D.C. 1991), aff'd., 964 F.Supp. 1179 (D.C. Cir. 1992).

26. 39 CFR sec. 232.1(h)(1) (1989).

27. Kokinda v. United States, 866 F.2d 699 (4th Cir. 1989), rev'd., 497 U.S. 720 (1990).

28. United States v. Belsky, 799 F.2d 1485 (11th Cir. 1986); United States v. Bjerke, 796 F.2d 643 (3d Cir. 1986).

29. United States v. Kokinda, 497 U.S. 720, 730 (1990).

30. Ibid. at 723–733, 734 quoting Postal Service regulation at 43 Fed. Reg. 38824 (1978).

Chapter 13 Getting Help When You're Hassled

1. Lickteig v. Landauer, Civ. A. No. 91–1843 (E.D.Pa. 1991). See also: Stewart v. District of Columbia Armory Board, 789 F.Supp. at 404.

2. Ibid.

3. John Eidsmoe, *The Christian Legal Advisor*, rev. ed. (Grand Rapids: Baker Book House, 1987), 408–409.

4. *Who Speaks for You in the United States Supreme Court.* Annandale, Va.: Christian Legal Society, 1990.

5. For information on how to use a law library and how to decipher the citations in the reference section of this book, both of which are easier than you might imagine, see Steve Levicoff, *Christian Counseling and the Law* (Chicago: Moody Press, 1991), 184–189, or Eidsmoe, *The Christian Legal Advisor*, 416–417.

/ *Bibliography* /

Works Cited

Abbott, Jack Henry. *In the Belly of the Beast.* New York: Vintage Books, 1981.

Adeney, Bernard T. "Living On the Edge: Ethics Inside San Quentin." *Journal of Law and Religion* 6 (1988): 435–454.

Civil Rights Act of 1964, 42 U.S.C. 2000e (as amended).

Clifford, G.M., III. "Ministry in a Pluralistic Environment." *Military Chaplains' Review* (Summer 1992): 67–80.

Colson, Charles, and Daniel Van Ness. *Convicted: New Hope for Ending America's Crime Crisis.* Westchester, Ill: Crossway Books, 1989.

Cord, Robert L. *Separation of Church and State: Historical Fact and Current Fiction.* Grand Rapids: Baker Book House, 1988.

Crewdson, Robert L. "The Equal Access Act of 1984: Congressional and the Free Speech Limits of the Establishment Clause in Public High Schools." *Journal of Law and Religion* 16 (Spring 1987): 167–185.

Davidow, Robert P. "Secular Humanism as an Established Religion: A Response to Whitehead and Conlan." *Texas Tech Law Review* 11 (1979): 51–59.

Dreisbach, Daniel. *Real Threat and Mere Shadow: Religious Liberty and the First Amendment.* Westchester, Ill: Crossway Books, 1987.

Eidsmoe, John. *The Christian Legal Advisor*, rev. ed. Grand Rapids: Baker Book House, 1987.

———. *Christianity and the Constitution.* Grand Rapids: Baker Book House, 1987.

Equal Access Act, 20 U.S.C 4071–4074 (1984).

Fachet, Robert. "In L.A., 'Rainbow Man' is Given 3 Life Terms." *The Washington Post,* 14 July 1993, p. B2.

Fischer, Justine, and Dorothy H. Lachmann. *Unauthorized Practice Handbook.* Chicago: American Bar Foundation, 1972; reprinted, Buffalo, N.Y.: William S. Hein & Co., 1990.

Fontanes, Tom. "New Age Profits." *Passport*, October–November 1987, pp. 10–11.

Ford, Andrea. "Rainbow Man Sentenced to 3 Life Terms." *Los Angeles Times,* 14 July 1993, p. B3.

Galanter, Marc. *Cults: Faith, Healing, and Coercion.* New York: Oxford University Press, 1989.

Gehrig, Gail. *American Civil Religion: An Assessment.* SSSR Monograph Series No. 3. Washington, D.C.: Society for the Scientific Study of Religion, 1979.

Gobert, James J., and Neil P. Cohen. *Rights of Prisoners.* Colorado Springs: Shepherd's/McGraw-Hill, 1981.

Goodman, Howard. "Prison Bursting at the Bars." *The Philadelphia Inquirer,* 12 March 1990, p. 2–A.

———. "U.S. Jail Rate Still Tops World." *The Philadelphia Inquirer,* 11 February 1992, p. A3.

Groothuis, Doug. "Identifying the New Age Seminar." *SCP Journal* 9 (1989): 6–7.

Hammar, Richard R. *Pastor, Church and Law,* 2d ed. Springfield, Mo.: Gospel Publishing House, 1991.

Hammett, Jenny Yates. "A Second Drink at the Well: Theological and Philosophical Content of CPE Origins." *Journal of Pastoral Care* 29 (June 1975): 86–89.

How to Experience and Share Abundant Life in Christ. San Bernardino, Calif.: Lay Institute for Evangelism, Campus Crusade for Christ, 1971.

Ivers, Greg. *Redefining the First Freedom: The Supreme Court and the Consolidation of State Power.* New Brunswick, N.J.: Transaction Publishers, 1993.

Jacquet, Constant H., Jr., ed. *Yearbook of American & Canadian Churches.* Nashville: Abingdon Press, issued annually.

"John 3:16 Scores Touchdown at D.C. Stadium." *Church & State,* October 1992, p. 3.

Kennedy, D. James. *Evangelism Explosion,* rev. ed. Wheaton: Tyndale House, 1977.

Larson, David B., et al. "Systematic Analysis of Research on Religious Variables in Four Major Psychiatric Journals, 1978–1982." *American Journal of Psychiatry* 143 (March 1986): 329–34.

Laycock, Douglas. "Equal Access and Moments of Silence: The Equal Status of Religious Speech by Private Speakers." *Northwestern University Law Review* 81 (Fall 1986): 1–67.

Levicoff, Steve. *An Analysis of State-Sponsored Versus Student-Initiated Religious Expression in Public Education.* Master's thesis, Vermont College of Norwich University, 1989.

———. *The New Song of Shiloh: An Historical, Legal, and Theological Exploration of an Indigenous Prison Church.* Ph.D. Dissertation, The Union Institute, 1991.

———. *Christian Counseling and the Law.* Chicago: Moody Press, 1991.

Main, Jeremy. "Trying to Bend Managers' Minds." *Fortune,* 23 November 1987, pp. 95–107.

Malnic, Eric. "Rainbow Man Guilty in Airport Hotel Siege." *Los Angeles Times,* 12 June 1993, p. B3.

Martin, Walter. *The Kingdom of the Cults,* rev. ed. Grand Rapids: Baker Book House, 1985.

McMillan, Richard C. *Religion in the Public Schools: An Introduction.* Macon, Ga.: Mercer University Press, 1984.

Mead, Frank S. *Handbook of Denominations in the United States*, 9th ed., rev. by Samuel S. Hill. Nashville: Abingdon Press, 1990.

Miller, Robert T., and Ronald B. Flowers. *Toward Benevolent Neutrality: Church, State, and the Supreme Court*, 3d ed. Waco: Baylor University Press, 1987.

Montgomery, John Warwick. *The Shaping of America.* Minneapolis: Bethany House, 1976.

Pace, Dale K. *A Christian's Guide to Effective Jail & Prison Ministries.* Old Tappan, N.J.: Fleming H. Revell, 1976.

Pfeiffer, Charles F., and Everett F. Harrison, eds. *The Wycliffe Bible Commentary.* Chicago: Moody Press, 1962.

Pierard, Richard V., and Robert D. Linder. *Civil Religion and the Presidency.* Grand Rapids: Academie Books, 1988.

"Rainbow Man Sentenced to Three Life Prison Terms." *Daily News of Los Angeles,* 14 July 1993, p. S7.

Religion in the Constitution: A Delicate Balance. Washington, D.C.: United States Commission on Civil Rights, Clearinghouse Publication No. 80, September 1983.

Religious Discrimination: A Neglected Issue. Washington, D.C.: United States Commission on Civil Rights, 1969.

Religious Freedom Restoration Act, H.R. 1308, S. 578, 103d Congress, 1st session (1993).

Rudovsky, David. "You Can Get a Soapbox on Main St., But They Won't Let You Do It on Mall St." *The Philadelphia Inquirer*, 16 August 1992, p. C7.

Sekulow, Jay. *From Intimidation to Victory.* Lake Mary, Fla.: Creation House, 1990.

Smarto, Donald. *Justice and Mercy.* Wheaton: Tyndale House, 1987.

Tucker, Ruth A. *Another Gospel: Alternative Religions and the New Age Movement.* Grand Rapids: Academie Books, 1989.

Tyner, Michael A. "In a Disastrous Decision, Justice Scalia Calls into Question Decades of Settled Law Concerning Freedom of Religion." *Liberty*, September–October 1990, p. 2–7.

United States Constitution (1789), as amended.

Van Ness, Daniel. *Crime and Its Victims.* Downers Grove, Ill.: InterVarsity Press, 1986.

Waldman, Peter. "Motivate or Alienate? Firms Hire Gurus to Change Their 'Cultures.'" *The Wall Street Journal*, 24 July 1987, p. 19.

Walvoord, John F., and Roy B. Zuck. *The Bible Knowledge Commentary (New Testament).* Wheaton: Victor Books, 1983.

Watring, Richard. "New Age Training in Business: Mind Control in Upper Management?" *Eternity*, February 1988, pp. 30–34.

Wood, James E., Jr. "Equal Access: A New Direction in American Public Education." *Journal of Church and State* 27 (Winter 1985): 5–17.

Wright, Stuart A. *Leaving Cults: The Dynamics of Defection.* Washington, D.C.: Society for the Scientific Study of Religion, 1987.

Cases Cited

Abington Township School District v. Schempp, 374 U.S. 203 (1963).

Amalgamated Food Employees Union v. Logan Valley Plaza, 391 U.S. 308 (1968).

American Postal Workers Union v. Postmaster General, 781 F.2d 772 (9th Cir. 1986).

Auzins v. Granville House, No. 10697–2548–UC–83 (Minn. Dept. of Econ. Security 1984).

Barron v. The Mayor and City Council of Baltimore, 7 Peters 243 (1833).

Baz v. Walters, 599 F. Supp. 614 (C.D. Ill. 1984).

Bender v. Williamsport Area School District, 563 F.Supp. 697 (M.D.Pa. 1983), *rev'd.* 741 F.2d 538 (3d Cir. 1984), *rev'd.* 475 U.S. 534 (1986).

Bishop v. Aronov, 732 F.Supp. 1562 (N.D.Ala. 1990), *rev'd.*, 926 F.2d 1066 (11th Cir. 1991).

Board of Airport Commissioners of the City of Los Angeles v. Jews for Jesus, 785 F.2d 791 (9th Cir. 1986), *aff'd. on other grounds*, 482 U.S. 569 (1987).

Board of Education of the Westside Community Schools v. Mergens, 496 U.S. 226 (1990).

Boomsma v. Greyhound Food Management, Inc., 639 F.Supp. 1448 (W.D. Mich. 1986).

Bounds v. Smith, 430 U.S. 817 (1977).

Brandon v. Board of Education of Guilderland, 635 F.2d 971 (1981), *cert. denied*, 454 U.S. 1123 (1981).

Bunn v. North Carolina, 336 U.S. 942 (1949).

Burch v. Barker, 861 F.2d 1149 (9th Cir. 1988).

Cantwell v. Connecticut, 310 U.S. 296 (1940).

Carreras v. City of Anaheim, 768 F.2d 1039 (9th Cir. 1985).

Chaplinsky v. New Hampshire, 315 U.S. 568 (1942).

Chess v. Widmar, 480 F.Supp. 907 (W.D.Mo. 1979), *rev'd*, 635 F.2d 1310 (8th Cir. 1980), *aff'd.*, 454 U.S. 263 (1981).

Christian Science Reading Room Jointly Maintained v. City of San Francisco, 784 F.2d 1010, *amended* 792 F.2d 124 (9th Cir. 1986).

Church of the Lukum: Babalu Age Inc. v. City of Hialeah, 113 S.Ct. 2217 (1993).

City of Angeles Mission Church v. City of Houston, Texas, 716 F.Supp. 982 (S.D. Tex. 1989).

City of Colorado Springs v. Blanche, 761 P.2d 212 (Colo. 1988).

City of Lakewood v. Elsass, No. 56480–56482, 1989 WL 62236, (Oh. App. 1989).

Clark v. United States, 705 F.Supp. 605 (D.D.C. 1988), *aff'd.*, 886 F.2d 404 (D.C. Cir. 1989).

Collins v. Virginia Employment Commission, No. 68142 (Cir. Ct. Fairfax Co., Virginia, 1980).

Concerned Women for America, Inc., v. Lafayette County, 699 F.Supp. 95 (N.D. Miss. 1988), *aff'd.*, 883 F.2d 32 (5th Cir. 1989).

Cooper v. Pate, 378 U.S. 546 (1964).

Country Hills Christian Church v. Unified School District, 560 F.Supp. 1207 (D.Kan. 1983).

Cox v. New Hampshire, 312 U.S. 569 (1941).

Craig v. Hocker, 405 F.Supp. 656 (D.Nev. 1975).

Cruz v. Beto, 405 U.S. 319 (1972).

Dale v. Board of Education, No. 13369, (S.Dak. 1982).

Deeper Life Christian Fellowship v. Sobol, 948 F.2d 79 (2d Cir. 1991).

Doe v. Duncanville Independent School District, No. CA 3–91–0291–T (N.D.Tex. 1991).

Eanes v. State, 569 A.2d 604 (Md. 1990).

Edwards v. Aguilar, 482 U.S. 578 (1987).

EEOC Decision 81–20. 2 Empl. Prac. Guide (CCH) 6769 (1991).

EEOC Decision 91–1, DLR No. 81, D–1 (1991).

EEOC v. Ithaca Industries, Inc., 849 F.2d 116 (4th Cir. 1988).

EEOC v. Townley Engineering & Manufacturing Company, 859 F.2d 610 (9th Cir. 1988).

Employment Division, Department of Human Resources of Oregon, v. Smith, 494 U.S. 872 (1990).

Engel v. Vitale, 370 U.S. 421 (1962).

Everson v. Board of Education, 300 U.S. 1 (1947).

Fernandes v. Limmer, 663 F.2d 619 (5th Cir. 1981).

Fink v. Board of Education of Warren County Schools, 442 A.2d 837 (Pa. Commonw. 1982), *cert. denied*, 460 U.S. 1048 (1983).

Flynn v. Maine Employment Security Commission, 448 A.2d 905 (Maine 1982), *cert. denied*, 459 U.S. 1114 (1983).

Frisby v. Schultz, 487 U.S. 474 (1988).

Furr v. Town of Swansea, 594 F.Supp. 1543 (D.S.C. 1984).

Garnett v. Renton School District No. 403, 865 F.2d 1121 (9th Cir. 1989).

Garnett v. Renton School District, 772 F.Supp. 531 (W.D. Wash. 1991), *rev'd.* 987 F.2d 641 (9th Cir. 1993).

Gaudiya Vaishnava Society v. City and County of San Francisco, 952 F.2d 1059 (9th Cir. 1990).

Gay and Lesbian Students Association v. Gohn, 820 F.2d 361 (8th Cir. 1988).

Gay Rights Coalition v. Georgetown University, 536 A.2d 1 (D.C. 1987).

Gitlow v. New York, 268 U.S. 652 (1925).

Goodwin v. Metropolitan Board of Health, 656 S.W.2d 383 (Tenn.App. 1983).

Grace Bible Fellowship v. Maine School Administrative District No. 5, 941 F.2d 45 (1st Cir. 1991).

Grayned v. Rockford, 408 U.S. 104 (1972).

Goldman v. Weinberger, 475 U.S. 503 (1986).

Greer v. Spock, 424 U.S. 828 (1976).

Gregoire v. Centennial School District, 907 F.2d 1366 (3d Cir. 1990).

Grosz v. City of Miami Beach, Florida, 721 F.2d 729 (11th Cir. 1983).

Guyer v. Keith County, No. CV–89–L–178, (D.Neb., filed 1989).

Hague v. C.I.O., 307 U.S. 496 (1939).

Harrison Orthodox Minyan, Inc., v. Town Board of Harrison, 525 N.Y.S.2d 434 (N.Y. App. 1990).

Hazelwood School District v. Kuhlmeier, 484 U.S. 260 (1988).

Hedges v. Wayconda Community Unit School District No. 118, No. 90–C–6604, 1991 Wl 222163 (N.D.Ill. 1991).

Heffron v. International Society for Krishna Consciousness, 452 U.S. 640 (1981).

Hemry v. School Board of Colorado Springs, 760 F.Supp. 856 (D.Colo. 1991).

Henderson v. Lujan, 768 F.Supp. 1 (D.D.C. 1991), *aff'd.*, 964 F.Supp. 1179 (D.C. Cir. 1992).

Holy Spirit Association for the Unification of World Christianity v. Hodge, 582 F.Supp. 592 (N.D. Tex. 1984).

Hoppock v. Twin Falls School District No. 11, 772 F.Supp. 1160 (D.Idaho 1991).

In re D'Amico, No. 51581 (N.Y.App. 1986).

International Society for Krishna Consciousness v. City of Baton Rouge, 876 F.2d 494 (5th Cir. 1989).

International Society for Krishna Consciousness, Inc., v. New Jersey Sports and Exposition Authority, 532 F.Supp. 1088 (D.N.J. 1981), *aff'd.* 691 F.2d (3d Cir. 1982).

International Society for Krishna Consciousness, Inc., v. Lee, 721 F.Supp. 572 (S.D.N.Y. 1989), *aff'd. in part and reversed in part*, 925 F.2d 576 (2d Cir. 1991), *aff'd.*, 112 S.Ct. 2701 (1992).

International Society for Krishna Consciousness of Houston, Inc., v. City of Houston, 482 F.Supp. 852 (S.D.Tex. 1979), *rev'd.*, 689 F.2d 541 (5th Cir. 1982).

Jamison v. Texas, 318 U.S. 413 (1943).

Jews for Jesus v. Board of Airport Commissioners of the City of Los Angeles, 785 F.2d 791 (9th Cir. 1986), *aff'd. on other grounds*, 482 U.S. 569 (1987).

Jimmy Swaggart Ministries v. Board of Equalization of the State of California, 493 U.S. 378 (1990).

Jones v. Wolf, 443 U.S. 595 (1979).

Kenny v. Ambulatory Centre of Miami, 400 So.2d 1262 (Fla. 1981).

Knuckles v. Prasse, 307 F.Supp. 1036 (E.D. Pa. 1969), *aff'd.*, 435F.2d 1255 (3d Cir. 1970), *cert. denied*, 403 U.S. 936 (1977).

Kolodziej v. Smith, 588 N.E.2d 634, 412 Mass. 215 (Mass. 1992).

Kunz v. City of New York, 340 U.S. 290 (1951).

Lamb's Chapel v. Center Moriches Union Free School District, 736 F.Supp. 1247, *aff'd. on reargument*, 770 F.Supp. 91 (E.D.N.Y. 1991), *aff'd.*, 959 F.2d 381 (2d Cir. 1992), *rev'd.* 113 S.Ct. 2141 (1993).

Largent v. Texas, 318 U.S. 418 (1943).

Lawson v. Dugger, 840 F.2d 781 (11th Cir. 1987).

Lee v. International Society for Krishna Consciousness (companion case to ISKCON v. Lee), 112 S.Ct. 2709 (1992).

Lemon v. Kurtzman, 403 U.S. 602 (1971).

Lickteig v. Landauer, Civ. A. No. 91–1843 (E.D. Pa. 1991).

Lubbock Civil Liberties Union v. Lubbock Independent School District, 669 F.2d 1038 (5th Cir. 1982), *cert. denied*, 459 U.S. 1155 (1983).

Madyun v. Franzen, 704 F.2d 954 (7th Cir. 1983).

Marbury v. Madison, 1 Cranch 137 (1803).

Marsh v. Alabama, 326 U.S. 501 (1946).

Martin v. City of Struthers, 319 U.S. 141 (1939).

May v. Evansville–Vanderburgh School Corp., 787 F.2d 1105 (7th Cir. 1986).

McCollum v. Board of Education, 333 U.S. 203 (1948).

Mergens v. Board of Education of the Westside Community Schools (Dist. 66), 867 F.2d 1076 (8th Cir. 1989), *aff'd.*, 496 U.S. 226 (1990).

Minersville School District v. Gobitis, 310 U.S. 586 (1940).

Murdock v. Pennsylvania, 319 U.S. 105 (1943).

National Organization for Women v. Operation Rescue, 747 F.Supp. 760 (D.D.C. 1990).

Ohio v. Livingston, No. CA 9641, 1986 WL 11112 (Oh. Ct. App. 1986).

Parker Seal Company v. Cummins, 433 U.S. 903 (1976).

Paulsen v. County of Nassau, 925 F.2d 68 (2d Cir. 1992).

Paulsen v. Gotbaum, No. 92 Civ. 6152 (JSM), 1992 WL 8361 (S.D.N.Y. 1992).

Peloza v. Capistrano Unified School District, 782 F.Supp. 1412 (C.D.Cal. 1992).

Perry Education Association v. Perry Local Educators' Association, 460 U.S. 37 (1983).

Planned Parenthood of San Diego and Riverside Counties v. Wilson, 815 P.2d 351 (Cal. App. 1991).

Poe v. City of Humble, 554 F.Supp. 233 (S.D.Tex. 1983).

Presbyterian Church in the United States v. Mary Elizabeth Blue Hull Memorial Presbyterian Church, 393 U.S. 440 (1969).

PruneYard Shopping Center v. Robins, 592 P.2d 341 (1979), *rev'd.*, 447 U.S. 74 (1980).

Redmon v. Clay County School Board, No. 91–1080–CIVJ12 (M.D.Fla. 1992).

Reynolds v. United States, 98 U.S. 145 (1879).

Rivera v. East Otero School District, 721 F.Supp. 1189 (D.Colo. 1989).

Rivera v. Smith, 472 N.E.2d 1015 (N.Y. 1984).

Roberts v. Madigan, 702 F.Supp. 1505 (D.Colo. 1989), *aff'd.*, 921 F.2d 1047 (10th Cir. 1990), *cert. denied*, 112 S.Ct. 3025 (1992).

Roe v. Wade, 410 U.S. 113 (1973).

Rosen v. Port of Portland, 641 F.2d 1243 (9th Cir. 1981).

Savage v. Trammell Crow Company, Inc., 273 Cal. Rptr. 302 (Cal. App. 1990).

Schneider v. State, 308 U.S. 147 (1939).

Shad Alliance v. Smith Haven Mall, 488 N.E. 2d 1211 (N.Y. Ct. App. 1985).

Sherbert v. Verner, 374 U.S. 398 (1963).

Spratt v. County of Kent, 621 F.Supp. 594 (W.D. Mich. 1985), *aff'd.*, 810 F.2d 203 (6th Cir. 1986), *cert. denied*, 480 U.S. 934 (1987).

State v. Cameron, 498 A.2d 1217 (N.J. 1985).

Stewart v. District of Columbia Armory Board, 863 F.2d 1013 (D.C. Cir. 1988).

Stewart v. District of Columbia Armory Board, 789 F.Supp. 402 (D.D.C. 1992).

Stone v. Graham, 449 U.S. 39 (1980).

Tanner v. Lloyd Corporation, Ltd., 308 F.Supp. 128 (D.Or. 1970), *aff'd.*, 446 F.2d 545 (9th Cir. 1971), *rev'd.*, 407 U.S. 551 (1972).

Taylor v. City of Knoxville, 566 F.Supp. 925 (E.D. Tenn. 1983).

Thomas v. Collins, 323 U.S. 516 (1944).

Thomas v. Review Board of Indiana Employment Security Division, 450 U.S. 707 (1981).

Thompson v. Waynesboro Area School District, 673 F.Supp. 1379 (M.D.Pa. 1987).

Tinker v. Des Moines Area School District, 393 U.S. 503 (1969).

Trans World Airlines, Inc. v. Hardison, 432 U.S. 63 (1977).

Travis v. Owego-Appalachian School District, No. 90–CV–90, 1990 WL 94196 (N.D.N.Y. 1990), *aff'd.*, 941 F.2d 668 (2d Cir. 1991).

Troyer v. Town of Babylon, 449 U.S. 988 (1980).

United States v. Ballard, 322 U.S. 78 (1944).

United States v. Belsky, 799 F.2d 1485 (11th Cir. 1986).

United States v. Bjerke, 796 F.2d 643 (3d Cir. 1986).

United States v. Board of Education for the School District of Philadelphia, 911 F.2d 882 (3d Cir. 1990).

United States v. Kokinda, 866 F.2d 699 (4th Cir. 1989), *rev'd.*, 497 U.S. 720 (1990).

Vanderlaan v. Mulder, 443 N.W.2d 491, 178 Mich. App. 172 (Mich.App. 1989).

Village of Schaumberg v. Citizens for a Better Environment, 444 U.S. 620 (1980).

Walker v. Blackwell, 411 F.2d 23 (5th Cir. 1969).

Wallace v. Jaffree, 472 U.S. 38 (1985).

Walz v. Tax Commission of the City of New York, 397 U.S. 664 (1970).

Watson v. Jones, 13 Wallace 679 (1872).

Webster v. New Lenox School District No. 122, 917 F.2d 1004 (7th Cir. 1990).

Wedmore v. Sidha Corporation International, No. 35–801–E (S.D. Iowa, filed October 2, 1985).

West Virginia State Board of Education v. Barnette, 319 U.S. 624 (1943).

Widmar v. Vincent, 480 F.Supp. 907 (W.D.Mo. 1979), *rev'd.*, 635 F.2d 1310 (8th Cir. 1980), *aff'd.*, 454 U.S. 263 (1981).

Wilson v. Ohio Bureau of Employment Services, No. 12651, 1986 WL 13852 (Oh.Ct.App. 1986).

Zorach v. Clauson, 343 U.S. 306 (1952).

/ *Index* /